Laying Down
the
Sword

LAYING DOWN THE SWORD

Why We Can't Ignore
the Bible's Violent Verses

PHILIP JENKINS

HarperOne
An Imprint of HarperCollinsPublishers

HarperOne

HarperCollins books may be purchased for educational, business, or sales promotional use. For information, please e-mail the Special Markets Department at SPsales@harpercollins.com.

HarperCollins website: http://www.harpercollins.com

HarperCollins®, 📖 ®, and HarperOne™ are trademarks of Harper-Collins Publishers

FIRST HARPERCOLLINS PAPERBACK EDITION PUBLISHED IN 2012

Library of Congress Cataloging-in-Publication Data is available upon request.

ISBN 978–0–06–199072–4

12 13 14 15 16   RRD(H)   10 9 8 7 6 5 4 3 2 1

Contents

PART THREE
Truth and Reconciliation

DEFINITIONS

Most of this book concerns the scriptures that Jews know as the *Tanakh,* or simply as "the Bible." Christians acknowledge these books as only a portion of the whole Bible, under the name "the Old Testament," which is for many a controversial term because it implies that these scriptures are somehow obsolete or outmoded. Many writers prefer the neutral term "Hebrew Bible," but this is itself problematic. If the Old Testament is the Hebrew Bible, then the New Testament presumably becomes the Greek Bible or Greek Testament, with no recognition that Christians accept *both* portions of the scripture as authoritative. I will sometimes use the term "Old Testament," partly because so much of my own work concerns specifically Christian responses to the scripture. Whenever I use that phrase, however, the implied quote marks should be understood.

The Bible, and specifically the Old Testament, developed over a long period of time, with many authors and editors. Few scholars today believe, for instance, that Moses personally was the author of any or all parts of the books that bear the names Exodus and Deuteronomy. However, many of the writers I will discuss in these chapters knew no such caveats, so that when discussing Deuteronomy, they had to deal with the issue of how Moses himself could have said such things. Because my main interest in this book is how the texts are understood and remembered, I will on occasion write of a book such as Deuteronomy as if it really did represent what "Moses wrote."

The Qur'an offers similar problems of authority and authenticity. For a faithful Muslim, the text was dictated directly by God, and the Prophet Muhammad played precisely no role in forming or issuing any of the actual words. For these reasons alone, it would be quite wrong to write a sentence beginning, "As Muhammad said in the Qur'an . . ." As I am not a Muslim, I do not believe in the precise divine inspiration of the text, and my remarks on that scripture will give Muhammad at least some credit for the message. The question of authorship becomes ever more complex in light of recent theories that trace the origins of parts of the Qur'an to earlier spiritual writings, both Christian and Jewish.

Christians traditionally date history from the birth of Christ and use the abbreviations BC (before Christ) and AD (*anno Domini*). I will here use the religiously neutral terms CE (Common Era) and BCE (before the Common Era).

Except where otherwise specified in the notes, Bible translations are given in the King James Version. On occasion I give preference to a modern translation where this yields significantly better results in terms of clarity, euphony or accuracy.

INTRODUCTION

Motes and Beams

*In the practical use of our intellect, forgetting
is as important as remembering.*

—WILLIAM JAMES

WE HAVE A GOOD idea what was passing through the minds of
the September 11 hijackers as they made their way to the airports.
Their al-Qaeda handlers had instructed them to meditate on *al-
Anfal* (the Spoils) and *at-Tawba* (Repentance), two lengthy suras,
or chapters, from the Qur'an. The passages make for harrowing
reading. God promises to "cast terror into the hearts of those who
are bent on denying the truth; strike, then, their necks!" God instructs his Muslim followers to kill unbelievers, to capture them, to
ambush them:

> Then, when the sacred months have passed, slay the idolaters
> wherever ye find them, and take them captive, and besiege
> them, and prepare for them each ambush.

> O Prophet! Strive against the disbelievers and the hypocrites!
> Be harsh with them. Their ultimate abode is hell.

The word used for *striving* or *struggle* in the final verse quoted above gives rise to the term *jihad,* and later advocates of jihad ground themselves in these passages.[1]

The hijackers should not shrink from killing prisoners. As they were instructed, God told Muhammad that "no prophet should have prisoners until he has soaked the land with blood." Everything contributes to advancing the holy goal, as described in *al-Anfal*: "Strike terror into God's enemies, and your enemies."[2] Perhaps in their final moments, the hijackers took refuge in these words, in which God seemingly lauds acts of terror and massacre.

Other extremists have found inspiration in these passages. After U.S. Army Major Nidal Hasan went on a murder rampage at Ford Hood in Texas in 2009, authorities sought clues about his ideological development. They found that two years previously, Hasan had lectured his puzzled non-Muslim colleagues about the demands of the Qur'an, as he focused on one verse from *at-Tawba:* "Fight against such of those who have been given the Scripture as believe not in Allah nor the Last Day, and forbid not that which Allah hath forbidden by His messenger, and follow not the religion of truth, until they pay the tribute readily, being brought low."[3]

Parts of the Qur'an can shock. One verse warns, "Those who make war against God and his apostle . . . shall be put to death or crucified." Another begins, "When you meet the unbelievers on the battlefield, strike off their heads." When Osama bin Laden issued his declaration of war against the West in 1996, he quoted this verse, together with others from *al-Anfal* and *at-Tawba*.[4]

Violence and the Qur'an

Such texts have a special power because faithful Muslims believe that the Qur'an is the inspired word of God, delivered verbatim through the prophet Muhammad. That is one of the great differences between the Qur'an and the Bible. Even for dedicated Christian fundamentalists, inspired Bible passages come through the pen of a venerated historical individual, whether it is the prophet Isaiah or the apostle Paul, and that leaves open some chance of blaming embarrassing views on that person's own prejudices. The Qur'an gives no such option. For believers, every word in the text—however horrendous a passage may sound to modern ears—came directly from God.[5]

Western critics portray the Qur'an as the engine driving violent jihad and global terrorism. These critics might be secular conservatives, evangelical Christians, or Zionist defenders of Israel, but all agree in presenting the Qur'an as a terrorist tract loaded with hate propaganda. How, they worry, can the vast Muslim world possibly reconcile itself to modernity when the scripture on which the religion is based is so deeply flawed? One essay that appears on multiple anti-Islamic websites states simply, "All you need to see that Islam is not a religion from God but a dangerous cult that promotes hate and violence, is [to] read the Qur'an." Christian evangelist Franklin Graham believes that the Qur'an "preaches violence." Dutch politician Geert Wilders faced hate-crime charges for his film *Fitna,* in which he demanded that the Qur'an be suppressed as the modern-day equivalent to Hitler's *Mein Kampf.* American conservatives Paul Weyrich and William Lind argued that "Islam is, quite simply, a religion of war," and urged that Muslims be encouraged to leave U.S. soil. For televangelist Pat Robertson, Islam is not even a religion, but "a violent political system bent on the overthrow of governments of the world and world domination." In 2009, a survey of U.S. Protestant pastors found that 70 percent regarded Islam as a dangerous faith. Images of Qur'anic violence were much in evidence during the 2010 debate over the creation of an Islamic Center at New York's Ground Zero.[6]

Such critics condemn any attempt to separate the atrocities of a movement such as al-Qaeda from its religious roots, any claim that the terrorism committed in the name of Islam is a perversion of the faith, or that "authentic" jihad is nothing more than an inner spiritual struggle. To the contrary, say critics, violence and terrorism are the natural and inevitable outcomes of Islam and its scriptures. In 2008, for instance, the U.S. Department of Homeland Security (DHS) claimed that Islamists were twisting the true meaning of the word "jihad." Conservative critic Andrew McCarthy protested:

> The Koran . . . commands, in Sura 9:123 (to take just one of many examples), "O ye who believe, fight those of the disbelievers who are near you, and let them find harshness in you, and know that Allah is with those who keep their duty unto him." What part of that does DHS suppose needs to be "twisted" by terrorists in order to gull fellow Muslims into believing Islam commands Muslims to "fight those of the disbelievers who are near you, and let them find harshness in you"?

For many, the potent enemy threatening the West is not "radical Islam," "extremist Islam," or "fundamentalist Islam," but Islam pure and simple. As McCarthy writes, "It is not accurate to say there is 'enormous' disagreement between the mass of Muslims and the terrorists. The difference is narrow and nuanced."[7]

Even more convincing, for critics, are the attacks by former Muslims who have left the faith, and who denounce what they see as Islam's pervasive violence and intolerance. One such former insider is Ayaan Hirsi Ali, the Somali-born human rights campaigner whose activities in the Netherlands placed her in danger of assassination by Islamist extremists. Another highly visible convert from Islam is Mosab Hassan Yousef, the son of one of the founders of the Palestinian group Hamas. After some years as a double agent for Israeli intelligence, Yousef defected from the Palestinian cause and, moreover, announced his conversion to Christianity. Yousef has spoken vehemently against the whole religion of Islam and particularly its scriptures, which he sees as pervaded by violence and deceit. While he agrees that ordinary Muslims are usually peaceful, he argues that this is only because they remain ignorant of the truly dangerous core of their faith, which is epitomized by the belligerent verses of *at-Tawba*. Yousef declares that the Qur'an is "the war-manual for Islamic terrorism," that it commands the killing of innocent people, and that the whole scripture should therefore be banned within America and the free world. A fringe group called Muslims Against Sharia has ventured to create a new Qur'an that omits the most violent and confrontational verses.[8]

Some non-Muslim critics agree that the "hateful" passages in Islamic scripture are so extreme that they demand suppression. In 2008, Jewish groups at the University of Southern California protested the use by the Muslim Students Association of the Hadith, a collection of reputed sayings of the prophet Muhammad that carries authority little short of the Qur'an itself. Protesters complained that the Muslim students' website included some strongly anti-Jewish hadith, and university authorities ordered the removal of the offending texts. Americans would not usually contemplate censoring the holy texts of any religion, unless they believed their words provided a direct incitement to violence and hatred.[9]

The Bible Speaks

MANY WESTERNERS CONSIDER ISLAM to be a kind of dark shadow of their own faith, with the words of the Qur'an standing in vicious contrast to the scriptures they themselves cherish. In the minds of ordinary Christians and Jews, the Qur'an teaches warfare, while the Bible offers a message of love, forgiveness, and charity. For the prophet Micah, God's commands to his people are summarized in the words "to do justly, and to love mercy, and to walk humbly with thy God." Christians recall the words of the crucified Jesus: "Father, forgive them: they know not what they do."[10]

But in terms of ordering violence and bloodshed, any simplistic claim about the superiority of the Bible to the Qur'an would be wildly wrong: it's easy to see the mote in somebody else's eye while missing the beam in your own. In fact, the Bible has its own bloody and violent passages, which have troubled faithful readers for centuries, and have attracted still more intense attention during recent debates over the relationship between religion and violence. Among many powerful contributions, I think of John J. Collins's book *Does the Bible Justify Violence?* and Eric Seibert's *Disturbing Divine Behavior.* Yet the Bible's dark passages are still nothing like as well known as they should be. Otherwise, Christians and Jews would not be so confident in denouncing the Qur'an as a militarist manifesto, supposedly a work of archaic savagery.[11]

The Bible overflows with "texts of terror," to borrow a phrase coined by American theologian Phyllis Trible, and biblical violence is often marked by indiscriminate savagery. One cherished psalm begins with the lovely line, "By the rivers of Babylon, there we sat down, yea, we wept, when we remembered Zion"; it ends by blessing anyone who would seize Babylon's infants and smash their skulls against the rocks.[12] If the Qur'an urges believers to fight, as it undoubtedly does, it also commands that enemies be shown mercy if they surrender. Some frightful portions of the Bible, by contrast, order the total extermination of enemies, of whole families and races—of men, women, and children, and even their livestock, with no quarter granted.[13]

If Christians or Jews needed biblical texts to justify deeds of terrorism or ethnic slaughter, their main problem would be an embarrassment of riches.[14] Is someone looking for a text to justify suicide terrorism? The Qur'an offers nothing explicit, beyond general exhortations to warfare in the name of God. Some passages of the Bible, in contrast, seem expressly designed for this purpose. Think

of the hero Samson, blinded and enslaved in Gaza, but still prepared
to pull down the temple upon thousands of his persecutors:

> **And Samson said, Let me die with the Philistines. And he
> bowed himself with all his might; and the house fell upon the
> lords, and upon all the people that were therein. So the dead
> which he slew at his death were more than they which he slew
> in his life.**[15]

Could a text offer better support for a modern-day suicide attack, in
Gaza or elsewhere?

The richest harvest of gore comes from the biblical books that
tell the story of the children of Israel after their escape from Egypt,
as they take over their new land in Canaan. These events are foreshadowed in the book of Deuteronomy, in which God proclaims,
"I will make mine arrows drunk with blood, and my sword shall
devour flesh." We then turn to the full orgy of militarism, enslavement, and race war in the books of Joshua and Judges. Moses himself reputedly authorizes this campaign when he tells his followers
that, once they reach Canaan, they must annihilate all the peoples
they find in the cities especially reserved for the Hebrews.[16] They
should follow the terrifying rules of *herem* warfare, placing the city
under a ban. Under this code, every living thing found in the city,
everything that breathes, should be slaughtered in a kind of mass
human sacrifice. God commands: Show them no mercy! Joshua,
Moses's successor, proves an apt pupil. When he conquers the city of
Ai, he follows God's orders to take away the livestock and the loot,
while exterminating the twelve thousand inhabitants. When he defeats and captures five kings, he murders his prisoners of war, either
by hanging or by crucifixion.[17] If the forces of Joshua and his successor judges had committed their acts in the modern world, observers
would not hesitate to speak of war crimes, even of genocide, and

they would draw comparisons with the notorious guerrilla armies of Uganda and the Congo.[18]

The Bible's God, moreover, shows no patience for those who resist commands to slay. According to the first book of Samuel, God orders King Saul to strike at the Amalekite people, killing every man, woman, child, and animal. When Saul fails to annihilate the enemy, he earns a scolding from the prophet Samuel, who himself slaughters and dismembers the Amalekite king Agag. Saul's sin was failing to be sufficiently total in acts of massacre, and his reluctance led to his own destruction and the fall of his dynasty. Later, with his regime in ruins, Saul summons the spirit of the now dead Samuel, who warns him that he is beyond saving: "Because you did not obey the LORD or carry out his fierce wrath against the Amalekites, the LORD has done this to you today."[19]

Later attempts to understand the slaughter of Canaanites and Amalekites have parallels to theological discussions of the Holocaust. Not, of course, that the two are alike in historical terms. Even if the biblical stories are literally true, the numbers involved were minuscule compared to the mass killings of Jews and others in the 1940s. In other ways, though, the Canaanite story raises issues that are even thornier than the more recent events. In contemplating the Holocaust, believers struggle to explain how God could have let such horrors take place; in the ancient context, God *commanded* the bloodshed and intervened forcefully when it was not pursued with enough vigor. This is not a case of "Why do bad things happen to good people?" but rather "Why does God drive his people on to do worse and worse things to any people whatsoever?"

Canons of Hate

OTHER BIBLICAL PASSAGES REINFORCE the picture of a divinely sanctioned hostility between the nation of Israel and its neighbors. Fun-

damental to both Old and New Testaments is the story of the calling and creation of a people, which was pledged to keep a covenant
with God. Part of that covenant involved keeping the people and,
eventually, their Promised Land free of pernicious foreign influences, and of any concession to foreign deities. Readers of the Bible,
whether Jews or Christians, are reminded of heroic instances of
prophets and ordinary believers who fought against pagan incur-
sions, leaving mighty examples for later generations, and for any
people struggling against tyranny. Elijah gathered the faithful hard
core who had not bowed the knee to Baal; Samson brought down
the temple of Dagon; the Maccabees liberated Jerusalem from its
pagan occupiers. Those who threatened to contaminate the land are
remembered as arch-villains whose names survive as insults: think
of Jezebel or the Philistines.[20]

Less remembered today are other biblical heroes whose acts fit
neatly into modern categories of racism and segregation. If we had
to choose the single biblical story that most conspicuously outrages
modern sentiment, it might be the tale of Phinehas, a story unknown to most modern readers. The story begins when the children
of Israel have intermarried with Moabite women, so that the two
peoples begin to share in worship. God furiously commands that
the chiefs of Israel be impaled in the sun as a means of quenching
his anger. Moses commands his subordinates to kill anyone who has
married a pagan, or "yoked themselves to Baal," while a plague kills
twenty-four thousand Hebrews. Fortunately, Phinehas, grandson
of Aaron, preempts the worst of the catastrophe by slaughtering a
mixed-race couple, a Hebrew man married to a Midianite woman.
Mollified, God ends the plague and blesses Phinehas and his descendants.[21]

Modern American racists love the story of Phinehas. In 1990,
Richard Kelly Hoskins used the story as the basis for his manifesto
Vigilantes of Christendom. Hoskins advocated the creation of a new
order of militant white supremacists, the Phineas [sic] Priesthood,

and since then a number of sects have assumed this title, claiming Old Testament precedent for terrorist attacks on mixed-race couples and abortion clinics. Opinions vary as to whether Oklahoma City bomber Timothy McVeigh himself was a Phineas Priest, but he was close to the movement.[22]

"Be Not Righteous Overmuch"

WHEN WE COMPARE THE Qur'an and the Bible, we might be tempted to see a critical difference between the texts. While the Bible *reports* violence in the distant past, some argue, the Qur'an *commands* violence here and now. The Bible, in this view, records ancient campaigns against forgotten peoples, which are of interest only to archaeologists, while the Qur'an commands "Fight infidels!"—an order valid in any age.

But such a contrast is false. However commentators have read it, it is not obvious that the Qur'an was commanding violence without end against unbelievers, as opposed to warfare against specific Arabian tribes or factions in the seventh century CE. On the other hand, many generations of Christian and Jewish readers have found no difficulty in applying the biblical commands in their own day. If the Bible aims its harshest words at ancient peoples who no longer exist as identifiable ethnic groups—Amalekites or Canaanites—plenty of later commentators, Christian and Jewish, have had no problem in applying those imprecations to modern races and nations.

Stories of hatred and conflict have had an influence that went far beyond crazed extremists, isolated readers who sought justification for atrocities that they would have committed in any case. Not only does the Bible contain so many unforgiving stories, but these have through the centuries influenced some of the greatest thinkers in both the Jewish and Christian traditions. While some have decried the morality suggested in these books, most mainstream theologians until quite modern times have fully justified the acts of violence and extermination.

One Talmudic account that probably comes from the third century CE tells how Saul protested God's commands to exterminate the Amalekites. Yes, said Saul, reflecting the qualms of humane-minded readers, perhaps the men deserve to die for their sins, but how have the women sinned? What is the children's sin, and what is the sin of the cow, the ox, and the donkey? But a heavenly voice ordered him not to try to be more moral than God himself: "Be not righteous overmuch."[23] Some prominent Christian theologians pursued this approach to its logical conclusion and managed, at least in their own minds, to justify the mass slaughter of enemy children. They produced an effective theology of massacre, which readily bears comparison with the apocalyptic fantasies of the most extreme modern-day Islamists.

Throughout Christian history, believers have used the stories of Moses and Joshua to formulate their theories of warfare, arguing that such biblical examples showed the legitimacy of fighting and struggling for God's cause—of a kind of Christian jihad. While mainstream thinkers constructed well-thought-out ideas of "just war," placing appropriate limitations on military conduct, extremists sought to restore the ruthless practices of *herem* and biblical holy war, war without mercy.[24]

Like the Islamists, Christians put their beliefs into practice, basing their actions explicitly on scripture. The resulting violence was at its peak in Europe during the religious wars of the sixteenth and seventeenth centuries, when each faction labeled its (Christian) opponents as Amalekites fit only for slaughter. To take just one example of many, after Scottish Protestants defeated an Irish Royalist army in 1646, their clergy advisers ordered a complete massacre of prisoners. Scots soldiers drowned eighty women and children, while "again and again were the conquerors told that the curses which befell those who spared the enemies of God would fall upon him who suffered one Amalekite [Catholic] to escape." Everyone is an Amalekite or a Canaanite to somebody.[25]

When an exhausted Christian Europe settled into an uneasy religious settlement in the late seventeenth century, new waves of colonists applied these biblical precepts overseas, to conquered peoples in the Americas and Africa. Christians have long been fascinated by the exodus myth, the vision of escaping oppression with the goal of building a holy realm in newly discovered lands. But the exodus from Egypt necessarily leads to a conquest of Canaan, and to rooting up native peoples. At the start of the twentieth century, a Bible-steeped German administration in the colony of South-West Africa devised a radical new policy for its native subjects, for which they took the biblical name of *Vernichtung,* annihilation. The language—and the practice—would return to haunt Europe. Through the Bible, Christians immersed themselves in the language of annihilation.[26]

In comparing the Bible and the Qur'an, I offer no judgment about the historical experience either of Islam, or of Christianity and Judaism. Islam has a long history of conquest and religious warfare, in which Muslim armies and regimes subjugated or slaughtered members of other faiths: armed military jihad in the name of God is no myth. From the seventh century through the seventeenth, Muslim rulers cited religious justifications for their wars of conquest and imperial expansion, just as Christian Western powers would from the Renaissance onward. Only a wide-ranging historian with a truly global vision could comment plausibly as to whether, across the centuries, more aggression and destruction has been undertaken in the name of Islam than of Christianity. But in terms of the violent and unacceptable faces of their fundamental scriptures, differences between the faiths are minimal.

To say that terrorists or extremists can find religious texts to justify their acts does not mean that their violence actually grows from those scriptural roots. Indeed, such an assumption itself is based on the crude fundamentalist formulation that everything in a given religion must somehow be authorized in scripture—or, conversely, that the mere existence of a scriptural text means that its doctrines must shape later history. Why, for instance, has the story of Samson's death not inspired a Jewish or Christian tradition of suicide terrorism? When Christians or Jews point to violent parts of the Qur'an (or the Hadith) and suggest that those elements taint the whole religion, they open themselves to the obvious question: What about their own faiths?[27] If the founding text shapes the whole religion, then Judaism and Christianity deserve the utmost condemnation as religions of savagery. Of course, they are no such thing; nor is Islam.

Holy Amnesia

ALTHOUGH THE BIBLE PORTRAYS divine savagery, today this registers little, at least in the West, with the faithful who find in that book their principal source of spiritual authority. Even if they read the relevant passages, they neither see nor comprehend them. Although the Bible is the most purchased and best known book in the world, large portions of it remain all but unread and in effect forgotten. After so many sensational attempts in recent years to rediscover various so-called Hidden Gospels and Lost Books of the Bible, many lost or forgotten books can still be found within the standard Bibles that so many people have on their shelves, in the pages they never turn to.

However faithfully and fundamentally readers claim to be following the original text, in practice they omit major sections, to the point that they practically deny their existence. Understanding the ways in which believers cope with their unpalatable texts suggests the limits of scriptural authority, as well as its changing power in the churches. It could also provide a powerful model for the development of Islam. Can a faith grow past scriptures that seem to teach primitive brutality? Christians and Jews offer proof that this is possible.

All faiths contain within them some elements that are considered disturbing or unacceptable to modern eyes; all must confront the problem of absorbing and reconciling those troubling texts or doctrines. In some cases, religions evolve to the point where the ugly texts so fade into obscurity that ordinary believers scarcely acknowledge their existence, or at least deny them the slightest authority in the modern world. Texts, like people, can live or die. This whole process of selective forgetting and remembering, of growing beyond the harsh words found in a text, is one of the critical tasks that all religions must learn to address. Far from being a compromise or betrayal of religious values, it is the culmination of a natural trend within the faith. Euro-Americans often express the hope that Islam can somehow escape its violent associations by undergoing the same kind of Enlightenment experience that has over the centuries transformed Christianity. In practice, any such change need not wait until Muslims borrow lessons from other traditions, but rather will occur when they pursue the internal logic of their own faith, as believers apply the same kind of amnesia to the most violent and aggressive texts.[28]

Believers develop various strategies of coping with texts that have become repulsive. If a text cannot be actively suppressed or removed, then it must be tamed in various ways. It must be reread, reremembered, reinterpreted, to the point that it ceases to be dangerous. In modern times, Western Christian churches have largely dropped the most frightening and troubling passages from their public readings, and generally from preaching. If not actually excluded from the biblical canon, the disturbing texts are at best coldly tolerated. Even a faithful churchgoer probably would not encounter such dilemmas as Saul's slaughter of the Amalekites, the tale of Phinehas, or God's command to show no mercy to conquered peoples.

As an illustration, we might look at the book of Esther, a romantic fiction that tells of conspiracies at the court of the Persian king Ahasuerus. The king's evil counselor Haman plots to kill all the Jews of the empire, but is prevented by the wise Jewish courtier Mordecai, together with the glamorous queen Esther. Few historians would treat the work seriously as a record of fact. But Esther is also a book of blood, one of the most brutal tracts in the Bible. After Haman is hanged, the Jews inflict on his people all the slaughter he had intended against them. In their victory, "the Jews smote all their enemies with the stroke of the sword, and slaughter, and destruction, and did what they would unto those that hated them." Many convert to Judaism because of "the fear of the Jews" who "slew of their foes seventy and five thousand." Although God did not command the act, the massacre is commended and later commemorated. It happened "on the thirteenth day of the month Adar; and on the fourteenth day of the same they rested, and made it a day of feasting and gladness" (the feast of Purim).[29] The book of Esther was duly canonized in the Hebrew scriptures and the Christian Bible.

How would modern Christians hear all this? Actually, most wouldn't. Think of a modern believer attending one of the many mainline churches that use the popular *Revised Common Lectionary*. This collection of readings organizes Bible passages over a three-year cycle, so that attending church diligently every Sunday would mean a good deal of exposure to the Old Testament texts, but on a very selective basis. Over the whole three years, the church member would hear just one brief and highly edited extract from Esther— around 6 percent of the whole text.[30] While the reading reports the hanging of Haman, it has nothing about the massacres. The text culminates with the establishment of the sacred feast, marked by joy and gift-giving, but with no hint about the reason for the merriment. In terms of the ordinary experience of Christian church life, the book of Esther has virtually ceased to exist. So has most of Joshua. Both have been subjected to an effective textual cleansing. What remains is an acceptable Bible Lite.

Learning to Forget

SUCH EDITING CONTRIBUTES TO a selective amnesia that is integral to the evolution of any scripture-based religion. The words for *memory* and *remembering* are among the most frequently used in the Bible: God *remembers* his covenants; he *remembers* his prophets; the faithful are told to *remember* his deeds and his statutes. Much of that memory work is undertaken by writing and copying, by the creation and canonization of what becomes Holy Scripture. But equally significant is the process of forgetting that allows a religion to develop to meet changing circumstances, and that means constant reinterpretation. If writing is the tool by which memory is preserved, then editing offers the means of forgetting, of selectively consigning memories to oblivion.[31]

For contemporary historians, themes of memory and forgetting are central to understanding societies, and we now have a vast literature on monuments, memorials, and collective acts of commemoration, the work of a flourishing memory industry. Cultures are defined by what they remember and choose to commemorate, and that issue of commemoration can be fiercely contentious. In 2010, for instance, the state of Virginia faced harsh criticism for supporting a Confederate History Month. Of necessity too, choosing to remember some events or persons demands forgetting and neglecting others. This issue is still more acute in Europe, given its savage record of war and genocide, but without selective amnesia, a society can never move forward. Historian Tony Judt declared that "the first postwar Europe was built upon . . . forgetting as a way of life."[32]

A biological comparison is relevant here. Scientists recognize the critical significance of memory functions as a means of understanding the human brain, but only recently have they understood the biology of forgetting. We have to remember things in order to function in everyday life, but we must also learn to forget. Could there be a worse nightmare than being forced to remember every single event in life, every trivial conversation we ever had from childhood on? Our memories would crush us. Such a medical affliction does exist, and it is a dreadful malady. But some of our neural circuits work specifically to allow us to forget, in order to move on. A key player is a neurotransmitter identified just twenty years ago, which was given the appealing (and religious-tinged) name of anandamide, using the Hindu word for pleasure or bliss, *ananda*. Without pleasure or joy, there is no forgetting, and vice versa. Forgetting lays the foundation for remembering.[33]

Religions, like people, grow by forgetting. Religions formulate scriptures, which acquire canonical status. As religions grow in scale and sophistication, they evolve to the point that they realize the failings and limitations of portions of those original scriptures, which they then come to treat in historical context. If religions are to succeed—if they are to live, and grow, and change the societies around them—then of necessity, they must outgrow at least parts of their scriptures. Meanwhile, the higher ethical and moral standards formulated by the religions themselves are disseminated in the wider society, to became standard and normal, even inevitable. As philosopher René Girard comments, "The Bible is the first text to represent victimization from the standpoint of the victim, and it is this representation which is responsible, ultimately, for our own superior sensibility to violence. . . . It is for biblical reasons, paradoxically, that we criticize the Bible."[34]

Such changes over time, ironically, drive antireligious sentiment. Not realizing that those ethical insights themselves grew from religious roots, later generations of secular critics use these standards as a means of denouncing the religions and their texts. But such a critique is grossly unfair. The uglier we come to find texts such as Joshua, the more appalled we are by the slaughter of the Canaanites and the Amalekites, the more evidence we have of the *success* of the biblically based religions, rather than of their primitivism or blood lust.

The Dangers of Forgetting

BUT FORGETFULNESS IS A mixed blessing. Initially, the ability to forget the bloodiest elements of the biblical story might seem thoroughly desirable, and Christians and Jews might optimistically think that they have achieved a state to which Islam might one day aspire— that Muslims too might similarly learn to pass over their texts of war and bloodshed. But it would be wrong to imagine that the Bible-based religions are more evolved or sophisticated than Islam, or that they have somehow moved further along a standard evolutionary scale. In reality, religions do not follow neat linear paths of evolution, and passages that seem forgotten have not vanished entirely. Rather, they have slipped back from conscious reality: they remain in the scripture as unconscious texts. The abhorrent words remain dormant, returning to life in conditions of extreme stress and conflict. As William Faulkner observed, "The past is never dead. It's not even past."

Islam too has often practiced such scriptural editing and self-censorship in its past, and will do so once again. It is absurd to imagine the world of Islam waiting passively to receive the scholarly and critical benefits of the Euro-American Enlightenment before that faith can proceed to some more exalted and peaceful stage of religious evolution. From earliest times, some readers of the Qur'an have used rationalistic and symbolic approaches, which have been popular far beyond narrow intellectual circles. Long centuries passed when peaceful Muslim societies placed little stress on warlike texts such as *al-Anfal* and *at-Tawba,* except when mystics turned to them as models of internal spiritual warfare, the "greater jihad" of the soul. That interpretation of jihad is thoroughly authentic, even if it is not the only one. Sufi Muslims especially favored allegorical and spiritual readings of the Qur'an, scorning those literalists who believed that the scripture advocated real warfare. Yet when parts of the Muslim world suffered periods of deep political humiliation and systematic cultural crisis, militants turned again to the bloody passages, and to their stark doctrines of armed conflict. For a thousand years, Sufis found their greatest areas of strength in North Africa and South Asia, regions that in recent decades have become heartlands of radicalism and military jihad, in lands like Pakistan and Algeria. Even multiple generations of spiritualizing the Qur'an did not inoculate later believers from rediscovering those fiery ancient readings.

For the Bible-based religions too, merely pretending that their troubling texts do not exist poses dangers, because extremists revive them in times of conflict. Most Jews would be baffled to learn that they are subject to an ancient commandment to hate Amalek, to exterminate that people and blot its name from the earth. And just where, today, could we find an Amalekite to persecute, even if we wanted to? In modern times, though, biblical injunctions to fight Amalekites and Canaanites drive ultra-Orthodox Jewish extremists to attack Arabs and Muslims; and, increasingly, they target liberal or moderate Jews. The Amalekite command sparked one of the worst massacres in the history of modern Israel, when a Jewish terrorist slaughtered dozens of Muslims worshipping in a Hebron mosque. Even when most scholars and clergy have reinterpreted troubling passages to prevent them inciting violence, we need only a few extremists to revive the original texts, red (and read) in tooth and claw.

Biblical memories also resonate at the government level. Asked to explain the hard-line attitude of Israeli Prime Minister Benjamin Netanyahu toward the nation of Iran, one of his advisers told a U.S. journalist, "Think Amalek." That comment went far beyond a simple soundbite; it reflected a deep-rooted worldview that framed any and all foes of the Jewish state. When in 2010 the devastating computer worm Stuxnet was directed against Iran's nuclear program, the main suspect was predictably enough the state of Israel. Confirming this interpretation, the worm's code included what looks like an arcane reference to the Book of Esther, that ancient account of how the Jews avenged themselves against their enemies. Observers of Middle Eastern affairs invoke the Bible when they discuss the Samson Option, the notion that an Israel on the verge of defeat might use its nuclear arsenal to precipitate a nuclear Armageddon. If Israel ever does launch its nuclear weapons, they will be carried on that nation's Jericho-3 ballistic missiles. That weapon's name, of course, harks back to the book of Joshua.[35]

The Bible of the South

AMONG CHRISTIANS LIKEWISE, FORGOTTEN texts are not eliminated, but await rediscovery by churches outside the current Western consensus. These may be fringe sects or cults, or new churches that grow in other parts of the world. This is a pressing issue today given the tectonic shift of Christian numbers to the Global South—to African and Asian countries still smarting from memories of colonial and imperial oppression. These new Christians appreciate the power of such ancient biblical themes as the possession and defense of the land, colonization and the expulsion of native residents.[36]

These newer Christians face agonizing dilemmas when they read biblical accounts of the Hebrews' conquest of the Canaanites and other rivals after their exodus from Egypt. They know that they must take the Bible seriously, but they find there stories in which it is easy to identify with the displaced people of the land, as opposed to the expanding invaders—with Canaanites and Moabites rather than the Hebrews. The parallels are all the more painful as European colonialists over the centuries consciously used the conquest of Canaan as a model for their own activities. Zimbabwean Dora Mbuwayesango calls the tale of Joshua "a blueprint for the colonization of southern Africa." In an article entitled "Canaanites, Cowboys and Indians," Native American scholar Robert Allen Warrior points out what a hard time his own people had seeing anything positive or liberating in these tales of ethnic dispossession. Some Third World biblical scholars claim that a pathological Joshua Syndrome underlies historic Western imperialism and ideas of Manifest Destiny.[37]

Texts like Joshua are today receiving more attention than they have done for centuries, as readers come to terms with massacres that no longer register for most Western Christians. Tongan scholar Jione Havea records the horrors of reading these passages in former European colonies in the South Pacific. Church members give "a cry of despair . . . as they hear the stories of the natives of Transjordan, a people whose land was conquered and whose cities, towns and villages were totally destroyed."[38] African readers are all too familiar with the concept of wandering militias led by self-styled prophets, who order mass slaughter and rape in the name of God. Such movements represent their own distinctive form of Joshua Syndrome.

But while some Christians struggle to understand texts that justify colonialism, other believers pursue their passionate affair with the literal text of the Bible—the whole Bible, including Deuteronomy and Joshua. Faced with the threat of jihad or persecution by hostile faiths, Nigerian or Sudanese Christians might initially turn the other cheek, but after a while some turn instead to the fearsome warrior God who is such a prominent figure in the Old Testament, the Lord God of Hosts. At least some view themselves as the victorious Israelites, destined to conquer and purge. In Rwanda in 1994, Hutu preachers invoked King Saul's memory to justify the total slaughter of their Tutsi neighbors. The last Christian who will seek to exterminate another nation on the pretense of killing Amalekites has not yet been born.

If newer believers turn to the violent passages and draw alarming lessons from them, it is currently all but impossible for mainstream Western churches to provide a corrective based on their centuries of experience in handling and debating unsettling scriptures. Not having to face the texts themselves in recent times, churches have lost that institutional memory. They have no basis for dialogue with Global South Christians and thus are laying the foundation for new global schisms.

Reopening the Bible

FOR OTHER REASONS TOO, the violent portions of the biblical text assume a more central place in religious debate. One development has been the modern Western encounter with Islam, and the need to explain terrorist acts committed in the name of that religion. The more Westerners probe the unacceptable portions of the Qur'an, the more urgent becomes the need to confront the texts of terror in their own heritage. As Muslims and Christians encounter each other more frequently around the globe, they have to find ways of interacting with each other peacefully, of finding forms of dialogue. If Western believers, either Jews or Christians, start from a wholly inaccurate and selective view of their own faith, and its violent or intolerant components, they have no basis for dialogue with Islam.

Western Christians who scarcely know the dark passages potentially face real difficulties in their own faith. Although they are not likely to come across these texts in church, they still find them through their own reading or, just as likely today, through hearing the militantly antireligious attacks of a New Atheist writer, a Sam Harris or Christopher Hitchens. Richard Dawkins, for instance, finds much to lament in the Bible: "the carnage, the smiting, the vindictive, genocidally racist jealous monster God of the Old Testament."[39] When atheist writers point out the alarming texts, contemporary Christians have little effective response, and many are unnerved to find that, yes indeed, God does apparently offer these frightful commands. Believers who ignore their own scriptural realities have no credible basis on which to debate atheists or secularists.

Unless they hear these texts read and discussed, what is an ordinary believer to make of them? The greatest menace, perhaps, is that a modern reader simply dismisses a text such as Joshua as no more than a primitive substratum of the Bible that has no possible relevance to later eras, and certainly not to Christianity. It thus becomes "just the Old Testament." Such a reading encourages a Marcionite approach, unconsciously following the ancient heretic who sought to eliminate the entire Old Testament from a wholly new religion allegedly founded by Jesus. In practice, many Christians treat the Old Testament as basically archaeological or historical material, not terribly relevant to the content of the New. At its most perilous, this approach tends to dismiss the brutality of Joshua as typical of the now-obsolete Hebrew Bible, and blames the violence on the Jewish tradition from which we have now, supposedly, been liberated.

Truth and Reconciliation

RELIGIONS NEED TO GROW past their bloody origins, but at the same time they must be able to admit those origins, come to terms with them, and understand where they fit into the broader scheme of faith. My goal in writing this book is to suggest specific ways of reading and hearing the texts—even the most difficult passages, such as Phinehas and the Canaanite massacres—and to show how they can be absorbed, comprehended, and freely discussed. Modern believers need to confront those dark passages, to acknowledge perhaps the evil committed in their name, but also to build upon them, to understand the processes that make the scripture and the religion. When we have that foundation, we can proceed to discern which texts (if any) might legitimately be rejected, and which offer an ineradicable source of teaching and inspiration. Not only can those seemingly threatening texts speak to us, but we hear their voices in all their power and richness. And at that point, we realize the mistake of attempting to suppress the dark passages. For Christians, the guiding principle should be the words of Jesus himself, to those of insufficient faith: Why are you afraid?[40]

Only through such a reading can we appreciate that individual scriptural texts are incomprehensible except in the context of the historical development and maturing of particular traditions. Again from a Christian point of view, this means wholeheartedly acknowledging the Old Testament roots of that faith. Christianity only makes sense as the culmination of the whole Hebrew Bible, including its most unsettling portions. Jesus was Yeshua, *Yesu,* whose name was the local dialect form of Joshua and thus commemorated that great and deeply flawed warrior. In the Greek text, both names appear as *Iesous:* one *Iesous* annihilated the people of Jericho; another *Iesous* died on the cross. One *Iesous* slaughtered Canaanites; another healed the daughter of a Canaanite woman. Christian scholars understood the continuity for many centuries, before Marcion scored his latest posthumous victories. Furthermore, according to the New Testament, Jesus was immersed in the Hebrew Bible and, specifically, in the book of Deuteronomy, which contains so many stumbling blocks for modern-day believers. Paul was no less fascinated. If you take Deuteronomy out of the New Testament, that later work loses much of its structure and rationale.[41]

Using such approaches to reading, modern readers can appreciate books like Joshua as so much more than vestiges of primal barbarism. When we read the Bible, many of us tend to think that the order in which books appear reflects their order of composition, so that the works we encounter first must be very ancient—much earlier and more primitive than more attractive and sophisticated texts such as the books of the prophets, of Isaiah and Jeremiah with their universalist visions. Yet this approach is very misleading. Deuteronomy and Joshua not only come from an era much later than the events they describe, but they were written exactly in the era of the great prophets, and they present the same message as those prophets, albeit in different literary forms. Although they tell their stories in the form of a history, or pseudo-history, of battles and massacres, the books have one overarching and quite revolutionary goal, which is to stress the need for radical monotheism. As for the prophets, the message is not that the God of Israel is greater than the gods of other peoples, but that he is the one Lord of all creation; and from that insight grows the whole message of universalism, of a promise extended to all.

Specific stories in Joshua (for example) might seem noxious, but the central goal and message of the text is awe-inspiring, and it lays a foundation for the whole later development of both Judaism and Christianity. We have to read such texts in context, holistically, and we have to know the history. Above all, we need to rise above individual verses or stories—to see the scripture for what it is.

CHRISTIANS CAN DEPLOY EVEN what seem like the grimmest texts to create a deeper-rooted faith. Reading the text as a whole, mature believers would be equipped anew to live in a world alongside Christians of very different traditions, and alongside followers of other faiths who likewise struggle to resolve their own scriptural issues. Ideally, the experiences of each religion would help inform the others. Rediscovering the most alarming parts of the Old Testament would remove any triumphalist sense that non-Christians, and above all Muslims, are in any way unusual in having to deal with harrowing scriptures. The process would inoculate Christians

against readings that are painfully literal and ahistorical, vapidly antireligious, or even straightforwardly anti-Old Testament (and anti-
Judaic).

What we need is a process of truth and reconciliation. Christian believers should be able to discuss or even preach on the really
hard sayings of the Bible—even a text as raw as "Show them no
mercy"—and to deal with them without compromise or apology.

PART I

Scripture as Problem

The LORD is a man of war: the LORD is his name.

—EXODUS 15:3

The Bible records the annihilation of the native peoples of Canaan. Looking at such accounts, we may find comfort in the belief that total massacres of this sort were regrettably normal practice for conflicts in this primitive age, and that however dreadful such acts might appear now, they were nothing exceptional for the time. That view would be wrong. Even by the standards of the ancient world, the reported biblical massacres were incomprehensibly savage. Nor does anything in the later biblical record condemn or question these campaigns. To the contrary, these events represent the foundations of later biblical faith.

CHAPTER ONE

Everything That Breathes

*For it is not up to me, but to Muslims themselves to
tear out the hateful verses from the Quran.*

—GEERT WILDERS, *FITNA*

EVANGELICAL CHRISTIANS OFTEN CHOOSE a life verse, a short biblical text that summarizes the teachings they want to keep before their minds. Usually, such passages teach reliance on God, or faith in his love, and they give comfort in moments of stress or conflict. But imagine meeting a Christian who wanted to share his life verse with you, and it was Deuteronomy 7:1–2:

> When the LORD your God brings you into the land you are
> entering to possess and drives out before you many nations
> . . . and when the LORD your God has delivered them over to
> you and you have defeated them, then you must destroy them
> totally. Make no treaty with them, and show them no mercy.

Or perhaps verse 16, from the same chapter of Deuteronomy:

> You shall devour all the peoples that the LORD your God is
> giving over to you, showing them no pity.[1]

Your first reaction might be to doubt strongly that such passages—such death verses—exist in the Bible at all. Surely the fact that God forbids pity or mercy for the victims is in monstrous contrast to the underlying themes of the whole book? But once you had established the bona fides of these verses, you would be horrified that any modern believer could view them with anything but loathing. Anyone who regarded these passages as guides for life would not be someone you would wish to know under any circumstances. However passionately one may believe in the inspired truth of the Bible text, parts of it seem so tainted as to be beyond redemption.

Tales of Terror

THE BIBLE CONTAINS MANY passages that to us seem bloodthirsty or upsetting—stories of casual murder, mass slaughter, rape, adultery, and treachery. In many cases, these texts are so ugly that they have dropped out of memory. How many faithful believers know the macabre story from the time of Elisha the prophet, when a woman begs the king to enforce the contract she had made with her neighbor in response to the raging famine? They had agreed to eat the son of one woman, then the son of the other, and they had already completed the first stage of the gruesome deal. Now, though, the second woman was reneging on the deal. Would the king not grant her justice, by ordering the promised second act of cannibalism? Few readers meditate profitably on the closing chapters of Judges, an incredibly violent saga of rape, mutilation, dismemberment, and military extermination. Other portions of the Bible recall instances of human sacrifice.[2]

Actually, these cases should be fairly easy for modern readers to deal with, because the acts are not described as divinely ordained. Biblical authors offer a faithful depiction of the world they knew, which was barbaric and violent. The authors were not justifying cannibalism or rape, still less crediting this behavior to divine command. Had they failed to describe such acts, the authors would be failing in their duty as historians and social commentators.[3]

But in other cases, accounts of violence lead the authors far beyond merely depicting or reporting the world around them. Instead, they state explicitly that God actively commanded such actions, including the extermination of whole races. Most of these instances occur during the period after the Hebrew escape from Egypt, in movement toward the land of Canaan, and then during the actual period of conquest, around 1200 BCE. Both under Moses and his chosen successor, Joshua, the Hebrews encounter a number of rival peoples, including other wandering tribes like themselves, but also settled city-states. According to the Bible—chiefly in the books of Numbers, Deuteronomy, and Joshua—the Hebrews waged very destructive wars against these rivals.[4]

Biblical accounts of the conquest tell two distinct stories, one east of the Jordan and one to the west. In Numbers and Deuteronomy, we hear of Moses's eastern wars in the lands of Transjordan, while Joshua describes a full-scale invasion of the land of Canaan, later Palestine.[5] Numbers recounts Moses's war against the Midianites. Under the leadership of Phinehas, Hebrew armies devastate the people of Midian, killing every man and taking all the women and children as plunder. Moses, however, is furious at their leniency. He commands, "Now kill all the boys. And kill every woman who has slept with a man, but save for yourselves every girl who has never slept with a man." These virgins—reportedly, some thirty-two thousand in number—were to become sexual slaves for Hebrew warriors.[6]

One short passage in Exodus describes the Israelites' interaction with the people of Amalek, who ambush the children of Israel as they pass through Rephidim in the desert. Under the generalship of Joshua, Israel defeats the raiders. God then commands Moses:

> Write this for a memorial in a book, and rehearse it in the ears
> of Joshua: for I will utterly put out the remembrance of Amalek
> from under heaven. . . . For [Moses] said, Because the Lord
> hath sworn that the Lord will have war with Amalek from
> generation to generation.

Not only is the Amalekite race to be utterly destroyed, but the last
verse explicitly proclaims an eternal conflict against them, a struggle
without end. The text has had an astonishing afterlife.[7]

Other massacres follow. In Deuteronomy, Moses tells how he re-
quested safe passage for the wandering Hebrew people from Sihon,
king of Heshbon, but he refused. God then commands his followers
to conquer and possess Sihon's land. As Moses reports,

> The Lord our God delivered him before us; and we smote him,
> and his sons, and all his people. And we took all his cities at
> that time, and utterly destroyed the men, and the women, and
> the little ones, of every city, we left none to remain.[8]

Lethal Sanctity

In Deuteronomy, Moses outlines the rules that the children of
Israel must pursue in their upcoming wars, presenting three options.[9] When approaching a city, the Hebrews must first offer peace,
and if the offer is accepted, then the residents become tributaries and
must perform forced labor. If the natives reject the offer, then the
city must be defeated and every male must be killed: the Hebrews
are allowed to take the women, children, and animals for their own
property. But in other select instances, the children of Israel must be
nothing like as generous or forbearing. Where God has given lands
as part of the Hebrew patrimony, all current residents must be subject to the law of *herem*—that is, of extermination. In those cities,

"thou shalt save alive nothing that breatheth: But thou shalt *utterly destroy* them; namely, the Hittites, and the Amorites, the Canaan-ites, and the Perizzites, the Hivites, and the Jebusites; as the LORD thy God hath commanded thee."[10]

Herem, usually interpreted as "utter destruction," is the single most frightening term in the whole Bible.[11] A related word is actu-ally quite familiar today in another religious setting, but one that is far less brutal. In Islam, a behavior or object that is ritually forbid-den is *haram,* as in the case of pork, as opposed to *halal,* or approved. The term *haram* also applies to a place of special sanctity, so that Jerusalem's Temple Mount is for Muslims the *Haram al-Sharif,* the Noble Sanctuary. In domestic use, a related word describes another special or forbidden place—namely, the *harem* in which wives live in seclusion.

But in the biblical context, the word has very different implica-tions. The noun *herem* represents a "ban," but translators use dif-ferent forms when describing how a city is given this status: it is "devoted" or "accursed" to God, or "set apart for YHWH under a ban." Few Bible translations accurately give the full connotations of the language, generally using a phrase such as "destroy utterly," but the meaning is clear. Every living thing in the doomed city must be destroyed wholly. Any valuables, any gold or silver, must be consecrated to God and given to the priestly caste, to be reserved for ritual use. When the text was translated into Greek, the "ban" became *anathema,* and that word provides another way of under-standing the process: cities like Jericho were placed under an anath-ema, given a lethal sanctity.[12]

Herem warfare has its origins in the common mythology of a warrior god defeating the forces of chaos. In the Hebrew tradition, though, we have the idea of holy war or YHWH war, named for the sacred and unpronounceable name of the Lord. This kind of combat had its elaborate rules and even an ideal sequence, from the initial trumpet call that proclaimed the state of war, through

the consecration of the warriors, followed by their ritual preparation, and on to the final dismissal. This was a war *for* God, which
was also at the same time a war *by* God. Earthly warriors served as
God's auxiliaries, while all treasures taken in the fight were devoted
to God. Battle itself became an act of worship. A strong sexual element ran through the mythology, with God as the king and Israel
as his chaste bride. God fought to prevent his people falling away
into seduction or adultery by other lovers. The resulting wars were
the ultimate manifestation of God's holiness, a concept inextricably
bound up with earthly notions of honor.[13]

In practical terms, this kind of warfare is unconditional, in that
defeated inhabitants have literally no chance, no way out, no option
to surrender. Once banned, once devoted to God, they cannot win
their lives by offering to convert to the faith of the conquerors, to
raise an altar to YHWH. They cannot agree to hand over all their
possessions, to abandon the land forever. They can't even voluntarily
accept the most degrading form of slavery or sexual submission.
They are pledged to death. As the story of King Saul demonstrates,
God left no room for waverers or fainthearts. Far from being marginal or incidental to the biblical tradition, this type of genocidal
warfare was associated with some of Israel's greatest heroes, including Moses, Samuel, and Joshua.[14]

Joshua's Wars

IN NUMBERS AND DEUTERONOMY, accounts of warfare and massacre punctuate longer and more systematic statements of ritual and
legal code. In Joshua, however, the massacres occupy center stage.
The fall of Jericho itself begins the bloodiest portion of the saga of
conquest. As a banned city, everything within its walls is destroyed,
except for the prostitute Rahab, who sheltered the Israelite spies,
winning salvation for herself and her family. The Israelites then

move on to Ai, where they meet unexpected defeats. The reason for this soon becomes apparent: it is revealed that a Hebrew named Achan has violated the taboos of *herem* by keeping for himself part of the loot from Jericho. The Israelites can restore cosmic order only by stoning and burning Achan together with his entire family. This brutal purgation then opens the way for the sanctified conquest of Ai. The Hebrews take the city, killing all its inhabitants: the king himself is "hung on a tree" until evening. Joshua then burns Ai, which remains desolate centuries afterward.[15]

The remaining kings of the region unite against these lethal invaders, but to no avail. Joshua's forces eliminate the rival cities one by one:

> And that day Joshua took Makkedah, and smote it with the edge of the sword, and the king thereof. He utterly destroyed [imposed *herem* on] them, and all the souls that were therein; he let none remain: and he did to the king of Makkedah as he did unto the king of Jericho[;] . . . and he smote [Libnah] with the edge of the sword, and all the souls that were therein; he let none remain in it; but did unto the king thereof as he did unto the king of Jericho.

And then Joshua's forces moved through Lachish, and Eglon, and Hebron, and Debir, in each case killing "all the souls that were therein." The book then summarizes recent accomplishments:

> So Joshua smote all the country of the hills, and of the south, and of the vale, and of the springs, and all their kings: he left none remaining, but utterly destroyed all that breathed, as the LORD God of Israel commanded.[16]

He distributed the conquered lands among the Hebrew tribes. In the final chapter of Joshua, God recalls the blessings he has given his people: "And I have given you a land for which ye did not labour, and cities which ye built not, and ye dwell in them; of the vineyards and oliveyards which ye planted not do ye eat."[17] (See Table 1: "The Most Disturbing Conquest Texts").

TABLE 1
THE MOST DISTURBING CONQUEST TEXTS

Exodus
17:8–16
Israel's struggle with Amalek: "[God] will utterly put out the remembrance of Amalek from under heaven. . . . The LORD will have war with Amalek from generation to generation."

23:23
The expulsion of Canaan's native peoples: "For mine angel shall go before thee, and bring thee in unto the Amorites, and the Hittites, and the Perizzites, and the Canaanites, the Hivites, and the Jebusites: and I will cut them off."

34:11–17
The expulsion of Canaan's peoples and the destruction of their religious practices: "ye shall destroy their altars, break their images, and cut down their groves."

Numbers
chap. 21
Herem *destruction of Canaanite cities (vv. 2–3):* "they utterly destroyed them and their cities."

The destruction of King Sihon and King Og (vv. 21–35): "So they smote [Og], and his sons, and all his people, until there was none left him alive: and they possessed his land."

25:1–18

Phinehas's murder of Zimri and his Midianite wife.

31:1–24 (NIV)

Massacre of the Midianites, in which Moses protests against leaving survivors: "Now kill all the boys. And kill every woman who has slept with a man, but save for yourselves every girl who has never slept with a man."

33:50–56 (NIV)

Expulsion of native peoples and destruction of their religious sites: "Destroy all their carved images and their cast idols, and demolish all their high places."

Deuteronomy

2:24–37

Destruction of King Sihon and his people: "And we took all his cities at that time, and utterly destroyed the men, and the women, and the little ones, of every city, we left none to remain."

3:1–7

Total destruction of King Og of Bashan and his people: "And we utterly destroyed them, as we did unto Sihon king of Heshbon, utterly destroying the men, women, and children, of every city."

7:1–2

God's command to annihilate the native peoples of Canaan: "thou shalt smite them, and utterly destroy them; thou shalt make no covenant with them, nor shew mercy unto them."

7:16 (NIV)

"You must destroy all the peoples the LORD your God gives over to you. Do not look on them with pity and do not serve their gods, for that will be a snare to you."

chap. 13

> *Moses's order to kill anyone who tries to lead Israel to worship other gods:* Even if it is your brother, your wife or your child, "neither shall thine eye pity him, neither shalt thou spare, neither shalt thou conceal him: But thou shalt surely kill him." Any Israelite town that goes astray must be annihilated.

chap. 20 (NIV)

> *God's rules of war for the conquest; the command to exterminate the native peoples:* "In the cities of the nations the LORD your God is giving you as an inheritance, do not leave alive anything that breathes."

chap. 25

> *Memory of Amalek:* When the Hebrews have settled in the new land, they must remember their war against Amalek: "Thou shalt blot out the remembrance of Amalek from under heaven; thou shalt not forget it."

Joshua

chap. 6

> *The conquest of Canaan, and destruction of Jericho:* "And they utterly destroyed all that was in the city, both man and woman, young and old, and ox, and sheep, and ass, with the edge of the sword."

chap. 8

> *Ai's destruction:* "All that fell that day, both of men and women, were twelve thousand, even all the men of Ai."

chap. 10

> Herem *destruction inflicted on Makkedah:* "he left none remaining, but utterly destroyed all that breathed, as the LORD God of Israel commanded." Similar fates befall several other cities: "He totally destroyed all who breathed, just as the LORD, the God of Israel, had commanded."

11:20

> Herem *destruction in several other cities:* God directly in-
> spires the resistance that leads to these events: "For it was
> of the LORD to harden their hearts, that they should
> come against Israel in battle, that he might destroy them
> utterly, and that they might have no favour, but that he
> might destroy them, as the LORD commanded Moses."

1 Samuel
chap. 15

> *God's instructions to Saul:* "Now go and smite Amalek,
> and utterly destroy all that they have, and spare them
> not; but slay both man and woman, infant and suckling,
> ox and sheep, camel and ass." Saul leaves the king alive,
> until Samuel intervenes: "And Samuel hewed Agag in
> pieces before the LORD in Gilgal."

The story of Joshua illustrates the themes of memory and oblivion that I suggested in the Introduction. Over the past two thousand years, Christian art has amply illustrated countless themes in
the biblical tradition, but no less significant are the vast areas of the
Bible text that have received virtually no coverage. Painters have
certainly rendered scenes from the book of Joshua—Rahab and
the spies, or Joshua crossing the Jordan—while a popular hymn
tells us of Joshua fighting the battle of Jericho ("and the walls
came tumbling down"). But little else registers from that book.
Artists depict the siege of Jericho, not the ensuing mass killing,
not the hanging or crucifixion of defeated kings.[18] Inspiring art
depicts noble subjects as victims and resisters, not as conquerors
and *génocidaires.*

Nor do later stories of Rahab generally quote the verse in which
she explains her treachery to her own people—namely, the ruthless
effectiveness of Joshua's campaign. As she says, "I know that the
LORD hath given you the land, and that your terror [*'emah*] is fallen

upon us, and that all the inhabitants of the land faint because of you."[19] Terror worked.

Ordered to Kill

LATER APOLOGISTS URGE US to treat those atrocities as less shocking than they might strike us today. However dreadful they appear to us now, we are told, they represent the standard operating practices of ancient warfare, and we have to understand them in that light. In a violent Iron Age world, people could have known no better. In support of this theory, commentators point to examples of similar divinely ordained warfare among neighboring peoples, including the Hittites and Akkadians. They quote a ninth-century inscription known as the Mesha stele, in which the king of Moab (in present-day Jordan) celebrates his triumphs in the name of his god Kemosh, as he visits *herem* upon the Israelites themselves. Commanded by Kemosh, he takes the city of Nebo and its inhabitants, "and I slew all of them: seven thousand men and boys, and women and maidens, because I had dedicated it to Ashtar Kemosh. I took the vessels of YHWH, and I dragged them before Kemosh."[20]

Actually, the argument that "everybody did it" works poorly. In fact, the more we explore comparable societies, the more distinctive and the bloodier ancient Israel appears in its ideology of warfare. Now, religious warfare was common in itself. The mighty Assyrian conquerors from the ninth through the seventh centuries BCE spoke of their forces as the army of their god Ashur, and recorded their victories as his. They were ruthless conquerors who perpetrated massacres and mass enslavement. The Assyrians hanged captured kings as a warning to anyone who might resist in the future, they impaled survivors, and they built pyramids out of the severed heads of their victims. Other peoples could be just as savage, even without invoking supernatural commands. At the height of the Athenians' much-admired democracy in 415 BCE, they destroyed the island of Melos: they slaughtered every man capable of bearing arms, and resettled Melos with a wholly new Athenian colony.[21]

But if violence and warfare abounded in ancient times, full-scale genocide was rare—not unknown, but not common. Even the records that declare that the Assyrians or Hittites destroyed city X then proceed to describe the rich haul of slaves captured in the struggle. This point emerges from the Greek *Iliad,* which describes events from the same era as Joshua's wars, although neither account was set down in writing for centuries afterward. The *Iliad's* Agamemnon foretells not just the destruction of Troy, but the total massacre of all its inhabitants: "Let us not spare a single one of them—not even the child unborn and in its mother's womb; let not a man of them be left alive, but let all in Ilius perish, unheeded and forgotten!"[22] But some works of classical Greek literature depend on the fact that this supposed extermination did not extend to the women, whom the conquerors took home as slaves. In better-recorded history, the Athenians who slaughtered the adult men of Melos also enslaved the women and children: What sensible conqueror would do otherwise? When the Romans annihilated Carthage in 146 BCE, ruining that city so totally that the victors reputedly sowed salt on the site where it had stood, they still took tens of thousands of slaves. Roman writers themselves noted with horror the extermination that northern European tribes, Germans and Scandinavians, visited upon their enemies. Yet genetic evidence shows that these peoples not only spared the conquered women, in Ireland and elsewhere, but interbred with them enthusiastically. Biologically, the medieval Icelanders who populate the great Norse sagas were largely descended from those thousands of captive Irish women.[23]

Even acts heralded as genocide usually were not. The main exceptions to this rule were acts committed by the Romans themselves, as they expanded their Mediterranean empire from the third century BCE onward. The Roman manner of fighting appalled a world numbed to violence. The Greek historian Polybius describes the massacre of the city of Cartagena in 209 BCE, when the Romans slaughtered every inhabitant, killing men, women, and children alike:

> They do this, I think, to inspire terror, so that when towns are taken by the Romans one may often see not only the corpses of human beings, but dogs cut in half, and the dismembered limbs of other animals, and on this occasion such scenes were very many owing to the numbers of those in the place.[24]

That sounds like the biblical accounts of the conquest almost a thousand years earlier. But the fact that Polybius spells out the atrocities in such detail—believe it or not, he suggests, they even killed the children—shows just how exceptional such acts were. Most of the truly genocidal acts of antiquity, in which all women and children were killed, emerged either in this exceptional Roman context, or in a deliberate reaction against Roman policies. The other commonly cited example of ancient genocide occurred in 88 BCE, when king Mithridates of Pontus slaughtered most of the Italians he could find in regions of Asia Minor subject to his control.[25]

Refraining from extermination was a matter of self-interest rather than morality. Undoubtedly, wars of extermination are known around the globe, in prehistoric communities, and in surviving primal societies. Commonly, though, societies sought to kill adult male enemies while exploiting the survivors economically or sexually. While some survivors could be killed, perhaps as human sacrifices, victims taken in war were a valuable resource, not to be squandered, and that became increasingly true as communities became larger and more organized. If the conqueror was a stable community, a kingdom or a nation-state, then victors gained a new source of tribute and taxation. Smaller groups such as nomadic tribes fought for slaves who could be traded, perhaps to more economically developed entities.[26]

It made no sense to kill women or children, who were part of the conquerors' inventory. The Song of Deborah in the book of Judges describes what contemporaries wanted from a successful battle: a girl or two as a prize for every man, and plenty of clothing and treasure to divide up. While defeat usually meant catastrophe for the losing side—the loss of independence, freedom, and dignity—life went on, in however miserable a way, and there was at least some chance of release or escape in years to come. This was the sense in which the Babylonians destroyed the Hebrew kingdom in 586 BCE, deporting the survivors—but at least there *were* plenty of survivors. Except in early Israel, even annihilation had rational limits.[27]

If not unique, *herem* warfare was abnormal, and we see just how distinctive it was when we look for comparisons. Although the Mesha stele mentions *herem,* the text comes from a culture that had a long-standing relationship with Israel, and the Moabites might well have borrowed the institution from their neighbors. That weak comparison seems to be the best that scholars can find to argue that Joshua's wars represented any kind of common Middle Eastern pattern.

The Lord's Resistance

AS A MENTAL EXERCISE, we might suggest a modern parallel for "Joshua warfare," and it is an uncomfortable one. Assuming that the accounts are historical, let us look at this story from the point of view of the Canaanite cities, contemplating the marauding bands that kill everyone they encounter, that murder children and even animals, and do so in the name of religious belief. To find anything comparable in recent times, we would look to African societies where state mechanisms have virtually collapsed, and where groups of bandits, guerrillas, and tribal militias coalesce around charismatic leaders claiming special divine revelation.

Such, for instance, is the apocalyptically oriented Lord's Resistance Army (LRA), which emerged in Uganda in 1987 under its monstrous prophetic leader Joseph Kony and is still active. Kony claims to speak directly for God. The LRA is legendary for the savage violence, mass killings, and torture by which it secures the loyalty of the areas under its control. It is notorious for its recruitment of child soldiers and for its murder of other children. Women are routinely abducted as sex slaves. Such acts leave the LRA with no defenders or sympathizers in the modern world, and the group is widely seen as a kind of ultimate evil. That ugly reputation reflects the ability of modern media to project local horrors onto a national stage. In their day, though, and in local areas, the followers of Moses and Joshua would have been regarded with just as much loathing as those of the modern-day Joseph.[28]

Scarcely less hideous in reputation is the Janjaweed, the mounted militia that the Sudanese government deployed to annihilate its tribal rivals in the Darfur region of that country. Religion plays little part in the ongoing conflict, as the two sides represent different traditions of Islam, but the group uses a mythological theme in its title, the Mounted *Djinn* (spirits or genies): Riding Angels would be a loose translation. The group has killed some three hundred thousand victims since 2003, and expelled three million, in a ruthless campaign of ethnic cleansing. In 2009, official involvement in such outrageous acts led to Sudan's president being indicted for war crimes, the first instance in which a sitting head of state was so identified. In the modern world at least, ethnic cleansing and mass murder earn the condemnation of even a complacent international community.[29]

In its account of mass enslavement too, the Bible text suggests painful analogies in later history. Although not all the native peoples of Canaan were subjected to genocide, those not actually killed were reduced to the status of subject peoples or hereditary serfs. The book of Joshua tells the story of the Gibeonite people, who deceived the Israelites into believing that they were not actually native Canaanites (who qualified for extermination). The Israelites were bound to keep the oath they had made with these tricky neighbors, and allowed them to live. But although the Gibeonites kept their heads, they survived as a servile caste, as hewers of wood and drawers of water. In later Christian societies shaped by the Bible, this passage became the charter for forms of slavery and forced labor, especially when the subject peoples belonged to another race. The book of Judges gives a list of regions and villages where the native peoples were not expelled, but rather subjected to forced labor and serfdom.[30]

Surviving subject peoples had other uses. The Bible reports that other native peoples remained intact and independent for the purpose of ensuring that the Hebrews would maintain their warlike spirit. According to Judges, God left some native peoples in place to test those Israelites who had not acquired combat experience, and to train their descendants in warfare. As long as they had Philistines to fight, together with the remnants of the Canaanites and Hivites, Israel would not grow soft.[31]

Hardening Their Hearts

WHY, ACCORDING TO THE Bible, was God so lethally furious with the peoples of Canaan? The biblical text offers different explanations, and some passages cite the extraordinary wickedness of the native peoples of Canaan. Reportedly, those peoples had raised evildoing to a level at which God simply had to intervene. When God promised the land to Abraham, he warned that his Israelite descendants would not possess it for several generations, "for the iniquity of the Amorites is not yet full."[32] When that point came, God would intervene, much as he had previously come close to wiping out the whole sinful human race in Noah's time.

But before we grapple too long with such ideas—just what could those unimaginable atrocities have been?—we must realize that such a moralistic interpretation is a late and retroactive addition to an older story. As I will explain in the next chapter, for earlier generations Israel's claim to the land had no connection with any misbehavior on the part of native peoples. The Canaanites and other peoples were not uniquely sinful; they just happened to be there, and needed to be displaced. That is, if anything, a still harder interpretation to deal with theologically, but the view is authentically earlier.

Actually, if we search the Bible for moralistic explanations of the violence, we find an unsettling paradox. Not only do many parts of the Bible fail to give any (to us) plausible explanation, but they regularly add a feature that makes the massacre tales even more difficult to stomach. Biblical authors repeatedly credit God personally with making the Israelites' enemies more wicked and threatening than they might otherwise have been. When Israel's enemies have to choose a course of action, God "hardened their hearts," deliberately making their decisions more unreasonable than they would otherwise have been, and thus inciting bloodshed.

In the tale of the exodus, the theme of God hardening Pharaoh's heart occurs like a refrain, suggesting that God repeatedly intervened to prevent any peaceful outcome. God acted similarly with King Sihon: he "hardened his spirit, and made his heart obstinate," leading to the mass slaughter of his nation. After listing the massacres perpetrated by Joshua's forces, the repeated killing of "everything that breathed," the historian reports:

> For it was of the LORD to harden their hearts, that they should come against Israel in battle, that he might destroy them utterly, and that they might have no favor, but that he might destroy them, as the LORD commanded Moses.[33]

On each occasion, a ruler has to make a decision about his response to the people of Israel. He faces multiple options, some of which would lead to a peaceful and harmonious resolution. Yet according to the text, God drives him to a course of conflict that will lead to massive bloodshed, or the extinction of his people. The only reason given for such divine malice is that YHWH wishes to demonstrate his power, to manifest the "mighty acts of God." This is not so much a tale of the battle between good and evil, but rather of God intervening to make one side evil, so that it might serve as a warning to others.

READING SUCH CLAIMS, a question presents itself. If such stories reported the works of Satan or Moloch, rather than of a good God, how would his actions have differed?

CHAPTER TWO

Truth and History

Men never do evil so completely and cheerfully as
when they do it from religious conviction.

—BLAISE PASCAL

FOR PEOPLE READING THE biblical accounts of the conquest today, the obvious question is: Did all this happen as described? Many contemporary scholars have serious doubts about reading these stories as literal, accurate history. For modern-day believers, Jews and Christians, that skeptical approach is a mixed blessing. Believers can take little comfort from boasting, "Our scriptures aren't as bad as they seem. They're really not true!" Even if these horrifying tales are myths, why do our sacred texts enshrine such Satanic verses?

Pursuing that question raises others scarcely less difficult. Assuming that we can eliminate the massacres as untrue, we still must deal with many other passages characterized by violence and racial intolerance, and these instances do not allow us the alternative of pure skepticism.

Hearing Voices

MOST OF THE DARKEST passages cluster in two closely related books of the Old Testament—namely, Deuteronomy and Joshua, which describe the conquest of Canaan in the thirteenth and twelfth centuries BCE.[1] Before we can accept these accounts as historically accurate, we need to know where they stood in the process of constructing the Bible. Were they early or late? How close were the authors or editors to the events they describe? Do scholars treat these texts as more or less authoritative than others claiming equal authority? As I'll explain, Deuteronomy and Joshua appear to have emerged relatively late, with much of their content dating from the eighth century BCE or later, sixteen generations after the actual conquest. If that's true, then the historical credibility of these books is severely limited.

To understand how we can make such statements about the dating of biblical books, we need to know the means by which scholars analyze such texts. Scholars recognize the existence of multiple stages and traditions within the scriptures, and some voices are much older than others: it is rather like excavating through an archaeological site and finding successively deeper levels, or strata. These levels are especially apparent in the Bible's first five books—namely, Genesis, Exodus, Numbers, Leviticus, and Deuteronomy—collectively known as the Pentateuch. Few now believe that these so-called Books of Moses were in fact the work of a single hand, and certainly not that of Moses himself. This point was argued convincingly as far back as 1670 by Baruch Spinoza, the founder of modern biblical criticism. One giveaway clue is the passage in Deuteronomy in which we read about Moses's death and burial. That at least demands the existence of a later author or editor, whom some have identified as Joshua himself. Spinoza thought that Moses might at best have written only small fractions of the five books (although, intriguingly, he included the Amalek story in that select category).[2]

Already in the 1750s, French scholar Jean Astruc noted that different passages in the Pentateuch used different names for God, and that these different names occurred in closely parallel passages. Some spoke of Yahweh, while others used the name Elohim. Seemingly, the first books of the Bible drew on at least two different sources, which are commonly called J, for the Yahwistic passages, and E, Elohistic. Further work uncovered two other main sources. One was a body of Priestly writings and materials, called P for convenience, while the material in the book of Deuteronomy is so independent of the other books that it seems to be a source in its own right, called D.[3]

By the nineteenth century, Bible scholars were confidently speaking of J, E, P, and D as the four strands that made up the Pentateuch, or Torah. More recent scholars have challenged the framework of this so-called Documentary Hypothesis, denying that separate strands can be so readily identified. In particular, some reject the idea of J as any kind of unified work, rather than a gradual accretion of individual stories. Others respond that J is still a valid concept for particular levels of early tradition. However we view the different components, many believe that, at some point—probably in the sixth century BCE—some brilliant editor or group of writers knitted the various fragments together to create the books that we know. In the process they "wrote the Bible," or at least a critical portion of it.[4]

These different sources emerged at different times. By common consent, J and E are the oldest. Although they drew on much older traditions, mainly oral, both were probably written down in the ninth or eighth centuries. The other sources are later: although P may have emerged over a lengthy period, it took final shape in the fifth century BCE.

The Second Law

THE FOURTH SOURCE, D, can be dated with most confidence, and it can also be most directly linked with a specific set of political and religious agendas. In particular, it is associated with a great monotheistic reform movement that began in the kingdom of Judah at the end of the eighth century BCE, under its ruler Hezekiah (c. 715–686), and that continued to shape Hebrew thought and religion until the exile to Babylon in 586. That chronology provides a context for many of the works we are discussing here, and helps explain the religious and cultural agendas of the historical texts produced in those years.

We get a hint of the chronology of the D source from a story told in the second book of Kings. Around 620 BCE, while the temple was being refurbished, the high priest reportedly found an ancient copy of the Book of the Law, which he brought to Judah's king, Josiah. Josiah was appalled by how far the Israelite nation of his time had fallen from the exalted standards laid out in this supposedly ancient text. Inspired, he launched a radical reformation to root out remnants of paganism and to restore the lost glories of Moses's era. This potent book almost certainly contained the core of what we know as Deuteronomy, which had been composed some decades earlier, probably around 710.

At many points, the language of D confirms this general historical setting, in the late eighth century. When God speaks in Deuteronomy, he uses language very similar to what the splendid Assyrian kings might have employed around 700 BCE. At the time, this would have represented the most magnificent image of monarchy and power conceivable to a priestly writer in Palestine. D sources did not suddenly emerge in Josiah's time, but this is when they were organized and codified. Later writers regarded the book as a valuable restatement of the law, a Second Law, which in Greek gives us *Deuteronomion*.[5]

Deuteronomy is integral to a much larger structure within the Bible, a sequence of books united by common themes, interests, and styles, which is commonly known as the Deuteronomistic History. This history, which would have reached final form in the sixth century, runs from Deuteronomy through Joshua, Judges, and what were traditionally called the four books of Kings (what Protestant Christians know as 1 and 2 Samuel and 1 and 2 Kings). In recent years, in fact, the whole idea of the Deuteronomists and their work has expanded and even run riot, as scholars detect related themes in many hitherto unsuspected places, including in the great Hebrew prophets. Some critics talk of pan-Deuteronomism, the scholarly tendency to see Deuteronomists lurking behind every text.[6]

This focus on the Deuteronomistic History does not mean that someone sat down in 700 or 600 BCE and wrote the whole work as an extended fiction. The various books used older sources, and in some cases much older. The Song of Deborah in Judges is ancient—possibly from the eleventh century BCE—and many scholars believe that the story of King David is based on a near-contemporaneous history, dating back to the tenth century. But when we read the various parts of the history, we must always be conscious of the hands of these much later editors. Particularly in the case of Deuteronomy and Joshua, later hands are very much in evidence.

The Missing Half-Millennium

BEARING THESE DATES IN mind, let's look again at the accounts of the conquest, assuming that most of that story occurred during the twelfth century BCE. Even by the most optimistic estimates, J would not have been written down until 900 or 850. Deuteronomy itself did not take its final form until five hundred years after the massacre of King Sihon and his subjects. That book's authors were as far removed from the conquest as we today are from the time of Martin

Luther or Christopher Columbus. Any approach to Deuteronomy or Joshua has to read it in the context of around 700 BCE, or even later, not of 1200.

That chronology is not a devastating argument against the historical truth of the conquest. Oral tradition can preserve accurate memories, while later writers used older written sources that are now lost to us. But for many reasons, we need to treat the war stories with real skepticism. Actually, some authorities go much further in critiquing the biblical accounts. Some reputable writers form the so-called minimalist school, which doubts that the Bible reports any reliable history whatever for the period before the sixth century BCE, and which denies the existence of the kingdom of David and Solomon (c. 1025–925). Other scholars feel that this hypercritical approach goes much too far, but they nonetheless doubt the credibility of the accounts of Moses and Joshua.[7]

Also telling are the serious contradictions that distinguish the stories of Deuteronomy/Joshua from other parts of the Bible, even those books within the larger Deuteronomistic framework. Joshua, for instance, tells us about the annihilation of various cities and tribes. The book of Judges, which takes off after the end of Joshua, lists many of these very groups as still in existence decades later, still unconquered and posing a threat to Israel. Both accounts cannot be true. Already in the eighteenth century, English skeptic Thomas Woolston declared that "either the story of Judges is false, or that of Joshua is, from one end to the other."[8]

No Invasion?

EVEN IF THE ACCOUNTS they offered were internally consistent, the Deuteronomistic books face real obstacles before we can accept them as straight factual history. Archaeology offers an insuperable stumbling block. Bluntly, we see no evidence of an invasion, or of invaders, at anything like the period in which Joshua should have flourished.[9]

The archaeology of Israel/Palestine is a thriving field of study, with much of the best work being done on the era known as Late Bronze/Early Iron Age, which should be the time of the conquest of Canaan and the Hebrew settlement. But these tumultuous events have left few obvious physical remains. If the mighty conflicts occurred as the Bible describes, they should have left significant traces in the landscape, particularly when biblical authors took such pains to identify exact sites. (We can look at the Canaanite stories in some detail, though the nomadic and pastoral nature of the societies involved means that material remains can teach us little about the Midianite or Amalekite stories).[10]

If we are tracking a war marked by the destruction of Canaanite cities and fortresses, then first of all, we need to find those settlements. These places should have flourished at the correct time—say, between 1500 and 1200 BCE—and then should have ceased to exist shortly after that point. Canaanite cities should reveal clear destruction layers, marked by evidence of tumbled walls and burning, together with unburied bodies. Because archaeologists are well used to finding such telltale marks of conquest and slaughter in other regions and from other eras, they know exactly what to look for. Not only should we be finding precisely such remains, but we should ideally see such catastrophes hitting several cities within a few years of each other, as a once-civilized region became a killing ground. We might also find material remains of the conquerors, perhaps in the form of new styles of pottery or architecture. It would be a useful indicator if these supposed newcomers brought with them some tokens of the Egyptian land they had supposedly left only a few decades beforehand.

A much later North American example shows us exactly how the remains of something very much like *herem* warfare is preserved in the archaeological record. (In citing this parallel, I am obviously not claiming any direct linkage between the societies involved and those of ancient Palestine.) In the American Southwest, a landscape of burned houses and ruined ritual buildings commemorates the extraordinary bloodshed of the thirteenth century CE among the so-called Anasazi people. Sacked villages and fortresses are littered with the unburied skeletons of men, women, and children, some disarticulated. Archaeologists can determine confidently not just that warriors had perpetrated indiscriminate slaughter at these places, but just how their victims had perished—how so many had been tortured, mutilated, or burned alive. Human bones regularly display wounds made by the common weapons of that era, an arsenal not too different from that of Joshua's time. Even animals were destroyed wholesale. In this Native American instance, the tale of massacre and cataclysm is unequivocal. Here at least, someone definitely did decide to show no mercy, and the material evidence is overwhelming.[11]

In the Canaanite context though, we find virtually no comparable evidence. Canaanite cities fought each other, and some communities were attacked and overcome, but we find nothing like the systematic ruin within a brief period that we would expect from the texts. Some cities supposedly conquered by Joshua did indeed exist long before the era of the conquest but had ceased to function by the appropriate time; others would not be founded for centuries afterward. In a few cases, cities that actually were destroyed around 1200 simply do not feature in the biblical conquest account, suggesting perhaps that they fell to enemies other than the Hebrews.

Many examples illustrate the disconnect between scripture and scholarship. The city of Jericho, for instance, is authentically ancient, one of the oldest known human settlements anywhere on the planet, but it went through several stages of occupation and desertion, and scholars are reasonably confident that no actual city of Jericho stood at the time of the conquest. Nor did Ai, supposedly the scene of another spectacular mass killing. Makkedah did not even come into existence until the tenth century BCE. Of all the alleged sites of massacre named in the Bible, archeologists can point to just one plausible candidate—namely, Hazor—where a city probably was conquered and burned about the right time; and even here, the dating leaves room for controversy.[12]

Putting the archaeological evidence together, Joshua's conquest is close to invisible. Archaeologist William Dever concludes that available material evidence "supports almost *nothing* of the biblical account of a large scale concerted Israelite military invasion of Canaan."[13] Probably an author in the eighth century BCE looked around the landscape of his time and singled out the most spectacular sets of ruins, but without any accurate sense of the cities that had existed on those sites. Ai, in fact, comes from the Hebrew word for "ruins." Having no sense of just when those old settlements had existed—had they fallen three hundred years before, or a thousand?—the author devised a saga of mass conquest intended to account for their destruction.

No Invaders?

ALSO MYSTERIOUS ARE THE supposed Hebrew invaders. Scholarly opinion about these matters changes over time, but at present, next to no evidence points to a mass incursion of foreign settlers from outside Canaan anywhere near the relevant dates. The closer we examine the early Hebrews, the more they look like Canaanites.[14]

The conquest was part of a general upheaval and catastrophe around the Middle East, in the era that marks the transition from the late Bronze Age to the early Iron Age. That change of name in itself may have had something to do with the traumas of the age, as new military technologies and weapon types shifted the balance of power. Some scholars believe that a planetary catastrophe drove the political turmoil—either a sudden climatic change or perhaps the effects of a gargantuan volcanic eruption in some distant corner of the globe. Whatever the cause, the consequences were devastating.[15]

Between 1600 and 1200 BCE, a series of wealthy and flourishing empires dominated the Near East and the Mediterranean world: Egypt's New Kingdom, the Hittite Empire in Asia Minor and Syria, the Mycenaean kingdoms of Greece and the Aegean. Within a few decades, though, all came under mortal threat. With the exception of Egypt, most crumbled, ushering in an age of warfare and mass migration. Powerful wandering raiders called the Sea Peoples challenged the states of the old imperial order, posing a special menace to coastal cities like those of Syria and Canaan. One of those newly arrived migrant nations was the Philistines, who so often appear as the deadly enemies of the Israelite kingdom in the time of Saul and David. Around the civilized world, great cities and palaces were destroyed or abandoned; urban life and commerce fell apart. In some areas society disintegrated to the point of losing literacy.[16]

The consequence was a first Dark Age. In fact, this period resembled the later fall of the Roman Empire; and, as in that instance, this became a legendary era that celebrated its heroes and sagas. Theoretically, one individual might have witnessed both the fall of Troy and the Hebrew conquest of Canaan.

Were it not for the various biblical texts, many contemporary archaeologists would reconstruct the story of ancient Israel something like this. Through the Bronze Age, Palestine and southern Syria were home to a flourishing culture of small city-states, whose inhabitants were the Canaanites. We know a good deal about these communities from the extensive fourteenth-century-BCE correspondence found at Amarna, in Egypt, which shows local Egyptian representatives and vassals in Syria and Palestine asking the pharaonic court for aid and protection. By the thirteenth century, Egypt dominated this region, though it faced a constant rivalry from the ambitious Hittite Empire to the north. Late in the Bronze Age, new communities emerged in the poorer hill country, roughly the West

Bank area of Palestine that was under Jordanian control prior to the 1967 Arab-Israeli war. Late in the thirteenth century, older social structures were devastated by the general unrest then afflicting the whole Middle East. As cities and trade declined, pastoral and nomadic ways of life grew in significance. The crisis forced enough Canaanites to take to the hills to cause a population boom in that area.[17]

Possibly these communities represented a conscious defection or withdrawal from the Canaanite mainstream, a rebellion against taxes, forced labor, conscription, and general oppression by wealthy elites. Among these defectors, according to William Dever, were urban dropouts, social bandits, refugees and displaced peoples from the troubled cities, and pastoral nomads. There may well have been some former slaves who had fled from Egypt. This last group brought with them the stories of exodus and liberation that the whole society would later adopt. After a period of coalescence on the margins of Canaanite society, these groups emerged in later history as the people of Israel, who first made their historical appearance in an inscription by the Egyptian pharaoh Merneptah in 1207 BCE. Even then, their numbers might not have been huge—perhaps a few hundred extended households. "Some were born Israelites; some became Israelites by choice." But something called Israel certainly did exist.[18]

In understanding this new community, we can usefully compare other upland societies around the globe, which existed tenuously on the fringes of nearby states and empires. Some of these societies became refuges for escaped slaves, who created enduring communities. Certain languages even commemorate the linkage between escape and geography. When the Spanish conquered the New World, they invented a special word for a fugitive slave, which was *cimarrón*, a person who lived on the summit (*cima*) of a mountain. (In turn, this gave rise to the English word for runaway slaves, "maroons.") But whatever their origin, these upland societies resisted the oppressive demands of established states and kingdoms, and some looked to charismatic or prophetic leaders as their founders and liberators. Israel, in this view, would not be an exceptional society in historical terms, although it was uniquely successful in creating and sustaining a mythology of its origins.[19]

What exactly this new society was, and how distinctively Israelite, is controversial. The Biblical account offers next to no hint of a relationship between Hebrews and Canaanites, to the extent that the latter seem have come from another planet. Yet the two languages were very close, to the point that an eighth century BCE passage in Isaiah 19 accurately describes Hebrew as "a language of Canaan." Their written forms were also near relatives. The earliest ancestor of Aramaic and Hebrew script was Canaanite, and the earliest known example of written Hebrew—the so-called Qeiyafa Ostracon, from the tenth century BCE—is in proto-Canaanite script. The scribes who recorded the supposed annihilation of the Canaanites thus used a script adapted from those loathed enemies. Probably, Israel became much more distinctive in the century or so following Merneptah's time, as it grew into something that we might recognize from the Biblical accounts. In the archaeological record, the emerging Israel shows its presence subtly—by new patterns of house construction, and possibly by an avoidance of pork—but the differences with the older society would not have been overwhelming. If you saw a man walking along a Palestinian road around 1150 BCE, what distinctive features might have marked him as Canaanite or Israelite? Would it have been something he wore, some ornament or hairstyling, something in his way of speech—perhaps a regional accent? No less interesting, what special features would have marked a woman? Were women faster or slower in adopting the Israelite identity, whatever that meant? However small initially, these ethnic markers came to matter immensely, and it is quite possible that over the decades, recognizably Israelite and Canaanite peoples fought each other. But the distinctions originated within Canaan itself, rather than being imported on the spears of Joshua's hordes sweeping in from the desert.[20]

We can't even be too certain how different Israelite religion might have been from that of its neighbors. Canaanites worshipped extended families of gods and goddesses, who were celebrated in seasonal rituals at shrines scattered around the country, the high places, with their altars and images. According to the Bible, Israelites practiced a rigid monotheism that set them entirely apart from the Canaanite world. They supposedly believed in one God, who was free of any competition from other gods or goddesses, and who was worshipped in only one temple, at Jerusalem. This faith was pure Yahwism, adherence to the one true God, YHWH, whose very name became so sacred that it could never be pronounced. Later biblical writers show that Yahwism coexisted with other forms of religion, and kings and prophets struggled to prevent the Israelites slipping back to ancient polytheism, paganism, and nature worship. Reading the Bible, we imagine a centuries-long conflict between two utterly distinct and warring forms of belief and practice.[21]

But those accounts are historically suspect. As they stand, the Bible's books portray those pagan practices as manifestations of the ancient peoples of the land, whom Joshua's conquistadors had unaccountably failed to expel or kill. However, that view represents a retroactive attempt by Yahwistic reformers in the eighth or seventh centuries BCE to apply their views and concerns onto much earlier eras. In earlier years, say in the twelfth or eleventh century, Israelite religion was still very much like its Canaanite counterpart, complete with goddess figures. The rural holy places, the shrines so loathed by prophets and reformers, belonged to an older kind of Hebrew religion, in which the great God YHWH was worshipped alongside other deities, male and female.[22] Even if invading Hebrews undertook a systematic conquest of Canaan, we can say nothing about its religious motives or justifications.

Why the Myth?

For the sake of argument, assume that the tale of Joshua's invasion is a mythical construct designed to show how the nation of Israel emerged within its later boundaries. Yet even if the events depicted did not happen exactly as described in the Bible, the story is troubling enough as it stands. It would have been easy enough to record or invent some kings and warlords to provide role models for the later societies, together with some inspiring battles against overwhelming odds. Why the tales of genocide? And why, far from seeking to conceal earlier horrors, did later Hebrew writers both preserve and even exaggerate ancient savagery?

This rewriting makes sense only if we understand the era in which Deuteronomy and Joshua were written. At various points during the history of Israel, from the Davidic kingdom until the exile in Babylon (roughly from 1000 through 586 BCE), the Hebrew people agonized over how distinct their religious life should be from that of surrounding nations.[23] The decisive move to absolute monotheism was a response to the existential crisis that faced the Hebrew nation from the late eighth century BCE onward. Two kingdoms existed during the eighth century: the northern realm of Israel, based in Samaria, and the southern kingdom of Judah, with its capital in Jerusalem. Both, though, existed uneasily within a wider imperial world dominated by Egypt and, increasingly, Assyria. Under its ruler Tiglath-Pileser III (reigned 745–727 BCE), the Assyrian Empire began a triumphant period of expansion, through aggressive warfare and diplomacy. In 721, the Assyrians conquered the northern kingdom of Israel and transported its peoples into distant exile: ten of the historic twelve tribes then largely vanished from history. There remained the southern kingdom of Judah, but how long would this endure? Jerusalem endured a mighty siege in 701.[24] Although Assyrian power declined over the following decades, other players emerged in the Middle Eastern imperial system. In 612, the renascent Babylonian Empire crushed a failing Assyria, and this state in turn presented a new menace. Finally, in 586, the Babylonians conquered Jerusalem and transported its people into exile.

Observing these disasters, Hebrew thinkers saw worship both as the cause and as the solution of the crisis. The nation was in danger because it had betrayed its covenant and worshipped other gods. It could be saved only by returning unconditionally to the exclusive worship of one God (whether or not such a creed had ever existed in reality) and annihilating all signs of rival faiths. This was the solution of the southern king Hezekiah in the late eighth century, when he successfully resisted the Assyrian onslaught. But it was far from obvious that such a policy could be sustained: so much depended on the attitudes and quirks of individual kings. Hezekiah was reacting against the syncretistic policies of his father, Ahaz, and Hezekiah's own son Manasseh in turn reversed the monotheist revolution and restored the pagan altars. Manasseh's grandson was that Josiah who restored the monotheist ideal. In Josiah's time, around 620, it was a wide-open question whether strict monotheism would survive indefinitely, or if it would prove to be a historical blind alley.

In light of that history, let's look again at Deuteronomy, which gave Josiah his manifesto for a sweeping religious revolution. The harder the seventh-century elite had to struggle against rival religious forms, the more bitter the confrontations they depicted in their historical accounts. The book's authors had an overwhelming political motive to present a historical picture of all-out struggle between Israel and its neighbors, and to demand the utter purging of alien influences. The single theme uniting the Deuteronomistic History is that of Israel's faithfulness to the teachings of Moses—or, more commonly, its falling away from that strictly monotheistic faith. Israel's continued occupation of the land depended on that exclusive religious purity. Reading about the destruction of the Canaanites, we are meant to understand that such extreme solutions were what awaited the Hebrew people if they compromised their covenant. The portrait of *herem* is deliberately meant to be extreme, to grab readers' attention: it's even worse than what the Assyrians do![25]

At every stage, a tougher new attitude replaces the earlier approaches in Genesis and Exodus, which stem from the J and E traditions. In Genesis, God promises Abraham a land for his descendants, but not necessarily with the elimination of earlier peoples. In fact, the intended fate of these sitting tenants is not clear, and genocide is not specified. It is in the Deuteronomistic History that God not only commands annihilation, but actively punishes those Israelites who try to weasel out of his commands.[26] Whereas earlier accounts describe the expulsion of native peoples, the Deuteronomist rewords the stories to specify extermination. In Exodus, God promises that he will spread panic among the enemies of Israel, and force them to flee; in Deuteronomy, this becomes "The LORD your God will deliver them over to you, throwing them into great confusion until they are destroyed." In Exodus, God sends hornets to drive out the Canaanites; in Deuteronomy, the hornets make the survivors reveal themselves so that they can be killed.[27]

The Iniquity of Canaan

OVER TIME, SIMILARLY, BIBLICAL writers offer new explanations for God's decision to destroy the Canaanites. Older J and E accounts do not suggest that Canaan was destroyed because it was so evil or rebellious. The one verse in Genesis that does offer this interpretation—the reference to the "iniquity of the Amorites"—is a later addition.[28] It is rather in later sources, Deuteronomistic and Priestly, that authors build their indictments of the native peoples, imagining them being annihilated as a punishment for outrageously sinful behavior.

Possibly these later writers felt a need to justify the land seizure in explicitly religious terms. But also, eighth- and seventh-century writers were using the historical sagas to pursue their far-reaching religious agendas. If, as they believed, Israel's possession of the land depended on its covenant with God, they wanted to show just what happened to a people that failed to keep its word. They were warning contemporary elites just how severe would be the consequences if they continued to dally with foreign faiths. God tells the conquering Israelites not to rest confident in their supposed moral superiority to the native peoples. They should never say, " 'For my righteousness the LORD hath brought me in to possess this land': but for the wickedness of these nations the LORD doth drive them out from before thee." The Canaanites had sinned and been removed, and if Israel were not careful, it could be next. [29]

The Priestly account in Leviticus uses the destruction of the Canaanites as a horrible warning for Israelites who failed to observe a long list of sexual "Thou shalt nots." The catalogue of sexual vices concludes, "Defile not ye yourselves in any of these things, for in all these the nations are defiled which I cast out before you: And the land is defiled: therefore I do visit the iniquity thereof upon it, and the land itself vomiteth out her inhabitants." Much later writers thus devised a moral rationale for the earlier slaughters. [30]

The clearest use of the Canaanite removal as an ultimatum to Israel occurs in the Song of Moses in Deuteronomy 32. Prior to entering the Promised Land, Moses augurs the destruction of the native peoples, to "cleanse the land for His people," but most of his warnings concern the annihilation that awaits a future Hebrew nation that would stray to serve other gods. The parallel between the two dooms, Canaanite and Israelite, is explicit, and is underlined by close verbal reminiscences. Israel too will suffer the massacre of its men and women, children and old people, and terror (*'emah*) will reign. That unusual word occurs rarely in the scriptures, but it is exactly the term used by Rahab to describe the feelings of the Canaanites facing Joshua's armies. The terror that Canaan experiences today, Israel might suffer tomorrow, unless Hebrews learn from the horrible example of their predecessors.[31]

No Other Gods

UNFORTUNATELY, WE CAN'T CONSIGN all the tales of ethnic conflict and slaughter to the realm of literary invention. In particular, we cannot dismiss the reality of *herem* warfare. It is credible to think of a historian inventing a tale of massacre or annihilation, perhaps to explain the utter destruction of a city that had become an archaeological ruin ("and from that day to this, no man or woman has lived in that place"). But that is quite different from the wholesale creation of an institution that must have been known, at least in premonarchical days.

Unless something like *herem* was a known reality, it would have had no plausibility for readers. Nations did ban other cities or tribes, and on occasion the nation of Israel did "devote" enemies to God, killing every man, woman, and child with utter fanaticism. In the late eighth century, the prophet Micah assumed that his listeners knew what he meant when he imagined the people of a divinely inspired Israel defeating their oppressors and *devoting* their ill-gotten gains to God, using the language of ritual warfare.[32]

But acknowledging the existence of YHWH warfare is quite different from accepting the highly organized no-exceptions practice described in Deuteronomy and Joshua, with all the ritual rules and prohibitions that would have been all but impossible to enforce in practice. Israeli scholar Moshe Weinfeld concluded that "the law of *herem* in Deuteronomy, then, is a utopian law that was written in retrospect," although "utopian" is an odd word in the context. The mode of warfare credited to Joshua owes much to Near Eastern realities at precisely the time that Deuteronomy was being constructed. Particularly striking are the parallels with the ruthless Assyrian campaigns between 750 and 630 BCE, which used massacres and terror tactics to demoralize potential enemies. The Deuteronomistic authors are taking a kind of institution they know from their contemporary world, and retrojecting this to an imaginary conquest era.[33]

Biblical writers of the eighth and seventh centuries were living through a religious and cultural revolution, and they rewrote history to reflect these circumstances. Even if we take the conquest out of the picture, the rigid agendas of those writers surface in many other texts, and in contexts where they are almost certainly depicting contemporary reality. A culture that fantasized about how it should have massacred its rivals in the distant past was unlikely to tolerate any departures from its radical ideals in the present day. The consequence was violent religious intolerance, and that again is consecrated in scripture. At many points, the teachings recall the most confrontational words of the Qur'an, and on occasion, they go far beyond them.

Again, it is Deuteronomy that lays down the harshest and most specific rules for defending monotheism at the point of a sword. Chapter 13 lists detailed rules for punishing any individual or family who advocates following the gods of neighboring peoples. Such a perverter of God's laws must be killed. "Show him no pity. Do not spare him or shield him"—not even if the perpetrator is your brother, your wife, or your child. If a whole Israelite town succumbs to an alien religion, then it has in effect gone over to the Canaanites, and it must be subject to *herem*: kill everyone and everything in that town, and then symbolically kill every material object. Collect all the plunder you have taken, and burn it as a sacrifice to God. The town should be left as a ruin and never be rebuilt. Treat it like Ai.[34]

Reputedly inspired by Deuteronomy, Josiah launched a religious purge that gave the temple clergy everything they had asked in destroying rival shrines and cult practices, and establishing a rigid monotheistic orthodoxy. The second book of Kings describes his campaign in loving detail:

> [H]e put down the idolatrous priests, whom the kings of Judah had ordained to burn incense in the high places in the cities of Judah, and in the places round about Jerusalem; them also that burned incense unto Baal, to the sun, and to the moon, and to the planets, and to all the host of heaven. . . . And the altars that were on the top of the upper chamber of Ahaz, which the kings of Judah had made, and the altars which Manasseh had made in the two courts of the house of the LORD, did the king beat down, and break them down from thence, and cast the dust of them into the brook Kidron.

Josiah smashed sacred images, desecrated shrines, cut sacred groves, and burned the bones in tombs. He "slew all the priests of the high places that were there upon the altars, and burned men's bones upon them, and returned to Jerusalem." Unlike the original conquest, these events were recorded accurately by near contemporaries and firsthand observers if not by participants: this really happened. The Bible holds Josiah out as a role model for holy behavior, even a new Moses. The account of his reign concludes, "And like unto him was there no king before him, that turned to the LORD with all his heart, and with all his soul, and with all his might, according to all the law of Moses; neither after him arose there any like him."[35] Nobody did it better.

Through such accounts, God is shown as furious at the existence of any other form of religion in the land. If the covenant between God and his people is analogous to marriage, then these alien practices represent adultery, a whoring after foreign gods. God is not just outraged that his people follow such practices, but also that they tolerate the existence of the rival faith. Live and let live is clearly not an option. Nor, assuredly, is worship and let worship.

In the modern world, the closest parallel to such a policy would be among the most extreme Islamist sects, whose standard campaign platform proposes rooting out alien religious practices and symbols. Some radical Egyptian Muslims dream of destroying the pyramids and other ancient glories, of blowing up the Sphinx. The most sensational example of such image-breaking occurred in Afghanistan, where in 2001 the Taliban government destroyed every vestige of the magnificent Buddha statues at Bamyan, which had survived for fifteen hundred years. The act was condemned globally as an obscene act of cultural vandalism and religious intolerance. Few Christian or Jewish critics realized just how squarely the Taliban's action fitted with what God was said to have commanded explicitly, and frequently, in their own sacred texts.

No Other Wives

OTHER TEXTS REFLECT THE xenophobic agenda that became so deeply entrenched during Josiah's era. Difficult to date exactly is the story of Phinehas, who won God's approval for murdering the mixed Israelite/Midianite couple. Although the story is set before 1200 BCE, it reflects the concerns and nightmares of a much later generation. Scholars date it to the Priestly level of the biblical tradition, which might mean a sixth-century date, not long after Josiah's time. The story itself carries a familiar message of absolute separation from surrounding peoples, a prohibition to be enforced by lethal force if necessary. As so often in the Old Testament, a religious threat is closely linked to sexual mixing.[36]

We have no idea whether Phinehas really did exist, and it is difficult to imagine any future archaeological or literary find that could settle that question one way or the other. But even if he never lived, the author or editor of Numbers believed that he should have done—that he should have carried out a killing like that described—

and that later generations should view him as a role model. As we will see, the story has alarmed commentators through history, especially among Jewish scholars, who warn of the perils of individual vigilantism; but Phinehas has nevertheless inspired many imitators.

This concern with ethnic mixing and intermarriage surfaces repeatedly in the Bible, most viscerally in the xenophobic books of Ezra and Nehemiah. Both texts reflect a similar historical situation—namely, the return of Israel to the Holy Land in the fifth century, after years of exile in Babylon. Ezra is a priestly scribe and Nehemiah a faithful Jew whom the Persians appoint as governor of Judea. Both men have to clean up a land that has been ruined, physically but also morally. They restore the city of Jerusalem, rebuild the walls, and rededicate the temple.[37]

But they also have to repair Israelite society, and that means removing the foreign influences. By this point, foreigners in the land have come to be seen as a defiling presence, by dint of what they are, rather than for any action they take. For the authors of both books, mixed marriages and miscegenation represent an ultimate horror, a decisive act of treason against Israel's God. Ezra is appalled to find that the Jewish elite have intermarried extensively with the local peoples and share their religious practices. Local rulers alert him that

> the people of Israel, and the priests, and the Levites, have not separated themselves from the people of the lands, doing according to their abominations, even of the Canaanites, the Hittites, the Perizzites, the Jebusites, the Ammonites, the Moabites, the Egyptians, and the Amorites. For they have taken of their daughters for themselves, and for their sons: so that the holy seed have mingled themselves with the people of those lands.[38]

What we call multicultural, Ezra calls abomination. He tears his hair from his head and his beard, and rends his clothes. But he soon

leaps into action, beginning an inquiry—we might say, an inqui-
sition—to identify all the men who have taken foreign wives. The
book's happy ending occurs when these men send away their wives
and half-breed children. The book of Nehemiah, similarly, ends
with his boast that he "cleansed them from everything foreign."[39]
This is not a popular sermon text in modern churches, nor is either
Ezra or Nehemiah a favorite of Bible study groups.

COMMANDS TO KILL, TO commit ethnic cleansing, to institutional-
ize segregation, to hate and fear other races and religions . . . all
are in the Bible, occurring with a far greater frequency than in the
Qur'an. Apart from Moses and Joshua, we find Josiah the persecutor
and Phinehas the racial assassin, not to mention the quest for racial
purity in Ezra and Nehemiah. We can argue what the passages in
question mean, and certainly whether they should have any relevance for later ages. But the words are there, and their inclusion in
the scripture means that they are, literally, canonized, no less than
the war passages are in the Muslim scripture.

CHAPTER THREE

Words of the Sword

*Fight in the cause of Allah those who fight you, but do not
transgress limits; for Allah loveth not transgressors.*

—QUR'AN 2:190 (YUSUF ALI TRANSLATION)

IN TERMS OF ITS bloodthirsty and intolerant passages, the Bible
raises considerably more issues than does the Qur'an. Some Bible
passages justify genocide and multigenerational race war; the Qur'an
has nothing comparable. While many Qur'anic texts undoubtedly
call for warfare or bloodshed, these are hedged around with more
restrictions than their biblical equivalents, with more opportunities
for the defeated to make peace and survive. Furthermore, any of
the defenses that can be offered for biblical violence—for instance,
that these passages are unrepresentative of the overall message of the
text—apply equally to the Qur'an.

When noting the scarcity of impossible or unpalatable texts in
the Qur'an, I stress that I am talking about that scripture alone,
rather than the later works that explained or elucidated it. By this,
I mean the Hadith (the reputed sayings of Muhammad) and the
later body of commentaries (known as the Tafsir). These later works
matter immensely for understanding the overall pattern of the reli-

gion, but they must be used carefully as means of approaching the original scripture.

Not just in Islam, commentaries and later interpretations distort readers' ideas about what exactly the original text contains. When Americans hear the phrase "the separation of church and state," many assume that it occurs in the U.S. Constitution, which it does not. It actually comes from a later letter by Thomas Jefferson, and the words may or may not accurately reflect the guiding principles of the Constitution itself. Similarly, Muslims often take ideas from the commentaries and read them back into the Qur'an itself. To take one grotesque example, many ordinary believers think that a passage in the Qur'an describes Jews being transformed into apes and pigs; as I will show below, that reading is false. This understanding stems from one tradition in the Tafsir, which has entered folklore.

If we do take those other sources, the Hadith and the Tafsir, into account as ways of understanding the Qur'an, then in fairness we should have to look at the entire contents of the Church Fathers for interpreting the Christian Bible, and the Talmud for the Hebrew Bible. If we did that, then alongside all the spiritual and cultural splendors of those works we could certainly find some obnoxious and unpalatable materials, some of which attack other faiths. But if instead we compare like with like, scripture with scripture, rather than how passages have been used by later generations of believers, then the Qur'an is in no sense a bloodier or more warlike text than the Bible—either the Hebrew Bible or the larger text beloved by Christians. Indeed, that Islamic text has far fewer passages demanding to be confronted or accommodated.[1]

In that sense, the Qur'an does not pose as many ethical difficulties as the Bible. This claim does not represent a kind of apology for Islam, a defense of its religious claims. In fact, one might even argue the opposite. As I will suggest, the disturbing features of the Bible reflect a much greater antiquity than that of the Qur'an, revealing complex dialogues with many cultures over time—interactions that ultimately created the essential foundation for the universalism of the Qur'an and of early Islam. In terms of its spiritual authority, the fact that the Qur'an is so straightforward—so lacking in extreme violence, in fact—is at once its strength and its weakness.

Degrees of Violence

To ILLUSTRATE THE DIFFERENCE between the two scriptures, we can divide the troubling texts into a crude (and highly impressionistic) three-part classification system. I base this both on the seriousness of the difficulty such texts pose for modern readers and on the danger that these texts might actually inspire violence or hatred among their readers.

TABLE 2
CLASSIFYING VIOLENT AND
DISTURBING SCRIPTURES

Category
1. *Extreme*
    Texts that call for direct violence against particular races or ethnic groups
    Passages that demand or sanction the extermination of rival groups
    Calls to annihilate enemies
2. *Alarming*
    Texts commanding or justifying acts of violence, whether by groups or individuals
    Calls for warfare in the name of God
    Appeals for racial hatred and segregation

3. Disturbing

Texts threatening savage violence or brutal punishment against the enemies of the faith, but in the supernatural realm

The Bible abounds with Category 1 ("extreme") texts, most egregiously in Deuteronomy and Joshua, while the Qur'an has nothing strictly comparable. That raw statement may sound surprising, given that it is so difficult to prove a negative, but we can say this with confidence. Through all the centuries of controversy between Islam and its enemies, Christian and Jewish critics have devoted intense effort to finding Qur'anic texts that expose the brutal nature of that faith, and they find many to parade. None, however, damns whole races, inflicts hereditary curses, or issues a command to exterminate. Nothing in the Qur'an teaches the evil of a particular race or ethnic group; so consequently, no such group is targeted for destruction. Islam has no equivalent to the Amalekites, nor does the Qur'an offer a historical record of struggle against such a people. No Qur'anic passage teaches that enemies in warfare should be annihilated or exterminated, and there is no equivalent to *herem* warfare. The Qur'an does not teach principles of war without mercy, or propose granting no quarter.[2]

Those statements are counterintuitive, given the widespread belief that the Qur'an is laden with vicious condemnations of Jews—not just as individuals, but as an evil race. The Qur'an, in this view, is rife with "Jew hatred." Clearly, this is a critical charge, but it is untrue. Because this is such a major issue, I will deal with it at length in a separate section later in this chapter.

A God of Terror?

THE QUR'AN HAS PLENTY of Category 2 ("alarming") texts, which give divine sanction to warfare. Remarkably few of these passages, though, demand softening or accommodating for a contemporary world. The main question is whether we grant the justification for warfare and armed violence in certain circumstances, which virtually all advanced societies do, and which in practice is the position of all the world's major religions. If we allow that point, then the Qur'an is no worse than the Bible. Both scriptures describe worlds in which people who claimed to be following God engaged in military conflict with enemies and persecutors. Most of the Qur'anic texts teach that warfare must be practiced according to established rules—rules that are far removed from those of Joshua.[3]

The Qur'an emerged in times of war, and those ancient conflicts and controversies shaped the text. The God of the Qur'an commands his followers to fight their enemies, to defeat and conquer them, and to use violence and subterfuge where necessary. We can also trace degrees of acceptance of violence depending on the state of the Muslim community at the time a given revelation was issued. As an example, the earlier Meccan suras are more conciliatory than the later Medinan texts, which were received when Muhammad was the theocratic ruler of a viable statelet.[4]

But acknowledging the military theme is quite different from presenting the religion of the Qur'an as one of mindless violence, of incessant aggression and conquest. When Islam's modern critics ransack the Qur'an for passages suggesting that violence and bloodshed permeate the text, they are hard-pressed to do so without some sleight of hand. The film *Fitna* quotes warlike verses, interspersed with the voices of modern victims of terrorism from New York City, Amsterdam, and Madrid.[5] It quotes for instance sura 8:60:

> Prepare for them whatever force and cavalry
>> you are capable of gathering
> To strike terror
> To strike terror into the hearts of the enemies,
>> of Allah and your enemies.

The film then follows this verse with a wrenching tape of an emergency call from the World Trade Center, suggesting that terror *and terrorism* are integral to Islam. But the verse in question refers to confronting enemies on the battlefield and goes on to stress that if your enemies are open to making peace, then you should be open to peace. If their peace offers are deceptive, then Muslims should be on the lookout for that as well. That is a prescription for regular warfare against opposing armies, not for terrorism. And, as we have seen, the Bible also speaks of "terror" as an effective weapon of war.

While the Qur'an permits warfare, it also lays down rules. The lengthy suras 8 and 9, *al-Anfal* and *at-Tawba,* give the clear scriptural foundation for understanding jihad as actual warfare, as opposed to more generalized struggle. In the notorious Sword Verse, 9:5, *at-Tawba* instructs believers that once the months of truce are completed, they should attack idolaters, *mushrikun,* those who associate anything else with God in worship. Kill them, capture them, besiege them, ambush them wherever you get the chance. Also in this sura is verse 29, the so-called Tribute Verse, which (at least as interpreted by later commentators) calls for non-Muslims to accept a subordinate social status, symbolized by the payment of a special tax.[6]

In the intolerant and militaristic atmosphere of the fourteenth century, such verses were expounded in still more hard-line ways by great Muslim commentators such as Ibn Taymiyya. One of his pupils, Ibn Kathir—one of the most influential scholars of Tafsir—developed the Sword Verse still further:

Do not wait until you find them [idolaters and infidels].
Rather, seek and besiege them in their areas and forts, gather
intelligence about them in the various roads and fairways so
that what is made wide looks ever smaller to them. This way,
they will have no choice, but to die or embrace Islam.[7]

But even the Sword Verse commands that those enemies be offered the chance to repent and change sides. If they join you, if they
pray and give alms, let them go. Sura 47 again tells Muslims to meet
their enemies bravely, to strike off their heads, and to bind captives,
and *Fitna* quotes this as a "hateful verse"; however, the fact that
there *are* captives indicates that we are not talking about a war of
extermination. In fact, the text continues, "Then grant them their
freedom or take ransom from them, until war shall lay down her
burdens." At least some of the defeated survive to fight again.[8]

Rarely does the Qur'an contemplate the destruction of a city to
the point of utter obliteration, of razing it to the ground. But when
such an event does occur, God warns the inhabitants, giving them a
last clear chance to mend their ways, to surrender to his commands:
doom is not inevitable. Only then, if its people resist, does destruction overcome the city.[9] That pattern closely follows the humane
military code that Jewish thinkers evolved through the centuries,
but it contrasts with many original biblical texts.

Hellfire

ONLY IN WHAT I have classified as Category 3 ("disturbing")
passages—condemnations of sinners and unbelievers to eternal
punishment—does the Qur'an offer a pattern that is strictly comparable to the Bible, and especially to the Christian scriptures. But if
threat of hellfire pervades the Qur'an, do such texts pose a danger
of actual violence in the real world? Although much of the Qur'an

envisions Muslims struggling against unbelievers in conflicts that fall short of actual warfare, the stress on hell and damnation suggests that Islam so demonizes its enemies that the faithful will inevitably be driven to fight against them. Throughout history, some Muslims and Christians have found that consigning enemy souls to eternal flames is a useful preparation for literal warfare against such groups. And yet some of the world's most devotedly apocalyptic movements also tend to be pacifist in the worldly sphere, contenting themselves with simply contemplating the destruction of their foes: God will act in his good time, and it is not for mere humans to preempt him.

Critics of Islam easily find Qur'anic verses that preach enmity toward unbelievers, and in many cases, these infidels are threatened with the pains of hell. One popular exhibit on this theme is verse 4:56, in which God threatens to roast his enemies with fire, and when their skins are thoroughly burned, he will supply them with new skins so that they can start over. The passage is indeed gruesome, but it draws entirely on a biblical and specifically Christian vision of a fiery eternity of suffering for sinners and unbelievers.

In this instance, the Qur'an has much closer parallels with the New Testament than the Old. For much of the period covered by the Old Testament, the Hebrew world had little sense of an afterlife: that concept became prominent only after 400 BCE or so, the period between the writing of the Old and New Testaments as they exist in their canonical form. In that era, and especially after 170 BCE, Jewish apocalyptic literature produced many accounts of the afterlife, together with gruesome visions of the punishment of sinners. Nascent Christianity drew heavily on these works, and hellish visions pervaded the religious worldview of Jesus and the early church. If we are to denounce the Qur'an for its hellfire fantasies, then we have to lay the blame with the Judeo-Christian traditions from which the Muslim text draws. Moreover, the Qur'an's warnings of hell are overwhelmingly directed not against infidels or any particular race or sect, but against sinners of whatever creed. The Muslim inferno is reserved primarily for those who skimp on charity: those who show no kindness to the orphan; those who fail to compete with each other in feeding the poor; those who love riches, and seize the inheritance of the weak.

None of the Qur'anic warnings of fire and brimstone are too shocking when set aside the New Testament. The fact that Western critics are so appalled by the Muslim text means that they have forgotten the religious roots of their own culture. This amnesia is hardly surprising, given that few mainline churches dwell on Jesus's hellfire preaching, his vision of an afterlife where the worm dies not and the fire is not quenched.

One of the New Testament's most uncomfortable passages occurs in Matthew's Gospel, when Jesus tells the story of a farmer who sows his field. An enemy secretly sows tares (weeds) among the good seed, and the two types of plant, the good and the noxious, grow up together. Rather than try to separate the two, the farmer tells his laborers to let them grow to completion, so that wheat and weeds can be separated at the harvest. As Jesus explains,

> The field is the world, the good seed are the children of the kingdom, but the tares are the children of the wicked one. The enemy that sowed them is the Devil; the harvest is the end of the world; and the reapers are the angels. As therefore the tares are gathered and burned in the fire, so shall it be in the end of this world. The Son of Man shall send forth his angels, and they shall gather out of his kingdom all things that offend . . . and shall cast them into a furnace of fire: there shall be wailing and gnashing of teeth.[10]

Jesus's hearers might have understood his words in varying ways. Did "children of the wicked one" refer to evildoers, or did it perhaps encompass all Gentiles? In either case, the passage disturbs modern sensibilities, as the evildoers in the story seem to have no choice in their fate. They are evil *of their nature.* Some influential Christian thinkers have taken this text to mean that some sinners are fated to damnation from their birth, or even that they are predestined to hell from the creation of the world, so that no earthly decisions that they make can affect their fate. But whether they have any free will in the matter or not, the final destination for sinners, according to Jesus himself, is horrific destruction in supernatural fire.

If hellfire texts are more obvious in the Qur'an than the Bible, the difference is one of quantity rather than substance. In other matters, however, the Qur'an has the advantage, in that it teaches an exclusivism based on religious loyalties and faith, rather than on race. It is always open to unbelievers to change their minds, to cease being infidels, and to join a global faith that, in theory, acknowledges no distinctions of race or class.

Abrogation

LET US ASSUME, THOUGH, that the Qur'an does contain particularly bloody passages that grossly offend the sensibilities of the modern world. Readers of the Qur'an, like those of the Bible, can still debate whether such scriptural texts applied only to the time they were written, or if they have lasting or even eternal application. Does the call for war against unbelievers have an expiration date? Qur'anic commentators through the centuries have assumed that suras such as *at-Tawba* remain valid, and have used these passages as the foundation of a whole theology of holy warfare. But the text itself does not demand that interpretation, or even suggest that the commands to fight extend beyond the specific circumstances of the internecine Arabian battles of the 620s. Some modern scholars insist that the Sword Verse is directed not against all infidels in general, but against specific groups of pagan enemies of the early Muslim community, foes who were notoriously aggressive and devious, but who

are now long dead and gone—quite as extinct, in fact, as the Amalekites. Throughout Muslim history, commentators have delighted
in extracting symbolic and allegorical meanings from such verses,
particularly those exhortations to fight and conquer.[11]

The Qur'an does provide convenient escape routes for readers
wishing to adapt particular messages to later circumstances, alternative interpretations that are not available to strict followers of the
Bible. In the New Testament, Jesus explicitly denies that the Law
can be adapted or edited—"not one jot or one tittle . . . till all be
fulfilled."[12] From earliest times, though, Qur'an commentators have
recognized that different verses carry different weight, because they
originated in different situations in the life of Muhammad and the
nascent Muslim community.

Where problems and contradictions do arise, human readers must wrestle with them in light of the divine authority of the
Qur'anic text, but there are well-known instances in which some
verses countermand or overrule others. The best-known example
involves the so-called Satanic Verses, in which Muhammad seemed
to grant toleration to the cults of three pagan Meccan goddesses. A
later revelation reversed this doctrine. God warned believers that
Satan always attempted to contaminate the sacred scripture with
sinful words, which could and must be overturned: "God renders
null and void whatever aspersion Satan may cast; and God makes
His messages clear in and by themselves."[13]

Historically, commentators have used the idea of abroga-
tion in what many modern observers would consider the wrong
direction—namely, by using later, more hard-line verses to overrule earlier Meccan passages that taught tolerance of other faiths.
Crucially for later Muslim teaching, commentators singled out the
Sword Verse as a trump card outweighing any revelations that suggest a live and let live attitude to other faiths, or urge that there
be no compulsion in religion.[14] But again, these are the ideas of
commentators. The Qur'anic text itself gives no warrant that the

Sword Verse should overrule other words, and some of Islam's great-est modern thinkers condemn the idea. One daring advocate was Mahmoud Muhammad Taha, a scholar executed in 1985 for his opposition to Sudan's fundamentalist regime. For Taha, the moder-ate and tolerant Meccan suras represent the ideal vision of Islam, and those suras were overruled—temporarily—by the exigencies of the political situation that Muhammad encountered in Medina. Because that emergency situation has long passed, said Taha, the Meccan texts should now shape the faith in a democratic modern society. Egyptian scholar Nasr Abu Zaid urged that the Qur'an be read as a cultural product, a literary work that reflected the values and beliefs of the Arabs at the time of its composition. Unlike Taha, Abu Zaid escaped execution, although he had to flee into European exile.[15]

Presently, the ideas of Taha or Abu Zaid currently represent a minority perspective, but who can predict how matters may change in a decade or two? There is no reason why future commentary and interpretation should not reverse the rigorist reading of the text and move to new understandings.[16]

The Qur'an and the Jews

WHAT ABOUT CHARGES THAT the motif of anti-Semitism runs through the Qur'an, that the whole text is founded upon "Jew hatred"? This belief circulates widely in Internet denunciations of Islam, and it has been elaborated in several recent books. Writer Andrew Bostom, for instance, seeks to describe *The Legacy of Islamic Antisemitism* and asserts that this tradition is rooted in the Qur'an.[17] Although I believe writers like Bostom exaggerate the centrality of anti-Semitism to Islamic history, they rightly draw attention to a genuine current of anti-Jewish sentiment and activism within Muslim cultures. Muslim–Jewish relations were not always and everywhere as sunny as they were for some limited periods in the history of Moorish Spain, and real acts of bigotry and even mass murder did occur. Anti-Semitism was not an imported newcomer to the Middle East in relatively modern times, a by-product of European racist propaganda.[18]

Recent writers can easily find genuinely ugly texts in Islamic history, including a handful from early stages of the religion. According to the hadith collection known as *Sahih Bukhari,* Muhammad declared,

> **The last hour would not come unless the Muslims will fight against the Jews, and the Muslims would kill them until the Jews would hide themselves behind a stone or a tree, and a stone or a tree would say: "Muslim, or the servant of Allah, there is a Jew behind me; come and kill him."**[19]

The words may or may not be historical, in the sense of having been uttered by Muhammad himself. However confident Muslim scholars are about the authenticity of the Hadith and their transmission over time, the historicity of these stories is questionable, and many reflect conditions prevailing in the Muslim world decades or centuries after Muhammad's time. But whether or not Muhammad ever said such a thing, the fact remains that this quote and other sayings are included in a collection that enjoys religious authority, and they have gained new influence in modern times. This particular hadith even appears in the 1988 Covenant of the Palestinian Hamas movement.[20] The reputed saying is undeniably anti-Semitic, in the sense of supporting an ideological system of hatred based on race and ethnicity. In its association of Jews with the End Times, the passage recalls potent themes in medieval Christian anti-Semitism, the kind of teachings that drove pogroms.

But if a few passages in the Hadith are venomously anti-Jewish, the Qur'an itself has none such, and claims to the contrary need to be read very carefully. Muhammad clearly did have serious conflicts with the Jews who made up a sizable share of the population of Arabia in his day, and on occasion those Jews were some of his fiercest foes. (At other times, his relations with Jews were cordial.) That opposition mattered so much because Jewish groups were potent foes who could have posed a grave threat to his mission. On at least two occasions in the then-recent past, Jewish forces in the Middle East had launched destructive military campaigns against religious enemies (specifically, Christians)—in southern Arabia in 523 CE, and again in Palestine in 614. In the 620s, Jews were among the serious enemies that Muhammad had to fight in the process of establishing his new regime. Only by a long stretch, though, can engaging in warfare against armed Jewish forces be classified as anti-Semitic of its nature.[21]

Muhammad was acutely sensitive to his religious conflicts with Jews. Because he saw himself as the successor to the great Jewish prophets of old, Muhammad was shocked to find that Jews did not accept his claims, and he denounced those contemporary critics as enemies of the divine message he thought he was charged to deliver. The Qur'an declares that the Jews are the most stubborn in their resistance to the message preached by God's prophet Muhammad, and are nothing like as open as the Christians.[22] The scripture records conflicts and controversies with specific Jews in Arabia around 620 CE, but only through the eyes of dedicated faith can we read the resulting tirades as condemnations of the Jewish race, or of Jews in later generations. In fact, the Qur'an's customary tone toward Jews runs so contrary to the visceral hatred of the hadith passage quoted earlier as to raise grave doubts about the authenticity of that tale. It does *not* represent the opinion of the Muhammad who claimed to declare the divine words in the Qur'an.

Complicating the picture is the vexed question of the sources that may have contributed to the final structure of the Qur'an. Historians have long known that Islam emerged within Jewish and Christian cultural environments, and scholars increasingly see the breach between the different traditions—and the emergence of Islam as a separate faith—as a lengthy and uneven process spread over several decades. Seventh-century followers of Muhammad spoke of themselves generally as Believers, a label that could apply to a wide variety of monotheists, and only later did the more exclusive term "Muslim" emerge. This complex history is strongly reflected in the Qur'anic text. While faithful Muslims recoil from any suggestion that the Qur'an draws on earthly influences, many modern scholars believe that both Jewish and Christian texts and traditions underlie large portions of the eventual scripture. Among those were rabbinic commentaries that, among other things, recounted stories of Moses and his battles with the faithless Hebrews of his time, backsliders whom he variously denounced and cursed. Some of the Qur'an's most hair-raising condemnations of Jewish sinners probably come from this exact stratum of tales, in which Jewish writers recorded prophetic condemnations of fellow Jews.[23]

The Myth of Jew Hatred

To understand the Qur'an's denunciations of religious rivals, we can usefully look at the Bible and the countless remarks in the Old Testament about Gentiles—"the Nations"—and all the dreams of a utopian world in which the nations would recognize the supremacy of Israel's God. Read in context, these passages form part of a magnificent universalist vision of a world ordered by peace and justice. When the words are taken in isolation, anti-Semitic agitators use them to depict Judaism as a religion pledged to world domination. That is rather the same process that befalls the Qur'anic texts.

None of the Qur'an's alleged manifestations of "Jew hatred" are convincing as expressions of systematic racial hatred. Critics of the Qur'an cite verse 2:61 as a foundational text for Islamic anti-

Semitism, and some later Islamic commentators did indeed take the words in this sense. The passage supposedly describes the Hebrew ingratitude against Moses, which leads to divine punishment. According to some commentators, "humiliation and wretchedness" are accordingly stamped on the Jews as a race. But here is the full passage, with its sequel:

> [Moses] said: Would ye exchange that which is higher for that which is lower? Go down to settled country, thus ye shall get that which ye demand. And humiliation and wretchedness were stamped upon them and they were visited with wrath from Allah. That was because they disbelieved in Allah's revelations and slew the prophets wrongfully. That was for their disobedience and transgression.
>
> Lo! those who believe (in that which is revealed unto thee, Muhammad), and those who are Jews, and Christians, and Sabaeans, whoever believeth in Allah and the Last Day and doeth right, surely their reward is with their Lord, and there shall no fear come upon them neither shall they grieve.[24]

Using a common literary device, the Qur'an sets contrasting verses alongside each other. The first condemns one group for behaving in a particular way; the second blesses those who do right. The first group receives wretchedness or hellfire; the second wins rewards and Paradise. It is a gross misreading to take only the first of such pairings as if they condemned the whole group, without noting the parallel verse that is essential to understanding the scripture. In this instance, the follow-up verse promises God's rich rewards to those who believe in Muhammad's message—but also to Jews, Christians, and Sabaeans, provided they do what is right. These other believers need know neither fear nor grief, and certainly not humiliation nor wretchedness. The passage does not contemplate the damnation or denigration of any race. This is scarcely a charter for "Jew hatred."

The closer we look at the passage, in fact, the clearer we see its origins in the Hebrew tradition. The curse is not laid on all Jews, but only on those who resisted Moses, the disobedient ones who rejected God and his revelations. The Qur'anic account precisely echoes those Old Testament passages that describe the horrors inflicted on those who rebelled against Moses in the wilderness, a theme relished by later rabbis.

The People of the Book

In order to make such texts look vicious, anti-Islamic critics systematically exaggerate the Jewish element in the passage. Commonly, the texts in question address the People of the Book (or the People of the Scripture, *ahl al-Kitab*), a generic term that encompasses Christians, Jews, and sometimes members of other faiths, who are clearly distinguished from *mushrikun*, idolaters. Often, though, the passages concerning *ahl al-Kitab* are misquoted as if addressed solely to Jews.

The verse 3:112, regularly quoted by modern-day polemicists, offers an example. It offers grim prognostications for those who oppose the message of Islam:

> **Ignominy shall be their portion wheresoever they are found**
> **save [where they grasp] a rope from Allah and a rope**
> **from men. They have incurred anger from their Lord, and**
> **wretchedness is laid upon them. That is because they used**
> **to disbelieve the revelations of Allah, and slew the Prophets**
> **wrongfully. That is because they were rebellious and used to**
> **transgress.**[25]

Describing the People of the Book in general, this passage warns of ignominy and wretchedness for those rebels who disbelieve God's word. It has no specific anti-Jewish intent.

Bostom cites several Qur'anic verses to illustrate "the Jews being associated with Satan and consigned to hell," but none in fact need carry that message. One verse, 98:6, warns that "those who disbelieve, among the People of the Scripture and the idolaters, will abide in fire of hell. They are the worst of created beings." (And the passage cites "People of the Scripture" rather than specifically Jews.) The next verse promises, though, that "those who believe and do good works are the best of created beings." Jews, like Christians and Muslims, will be judged not by their claims to belong to a particular religion or ethnic group, but by how well they obey God's laws.

In another supposed warrant for anti-Semitism, God recalls the gifts he gave the house of Abraham, including the scripture and the divine wisdom. According to verses 4:54–55, among those Jews "were [some] who believed therein and of them were [some] who disbelieved. Hell is sufficient for [their] burning." Jews will be condemned to hell if they fail in faith, but will be rewarded if they hold fast. These are precisely the same terms offered to believers of all traditions.[26]

Also demanding careful reading is the notorious passage in the Qur'an's Sura 2, in which God recalls transforming sinners into despicable apes. The text is a prime case study for modern debates over the literal truth of the Qur'an. Did God really perform a magical transformation, in which living human beings were turned into apes? Liberal Muslims use the passage to show that the Qur'an contains figurative language and metaphor, while fundamentalists insist that God in fact performed a real miracle. For Western readers, though, the question is less the quality of the special effects than the identity of the victims. Believers in the "Jew hatred" motif usually describe the evildoers as Jews, and many Muslims through the centuries have accepted that interpretation. But the text does not support it. Although the story comes in a passage describing Moses and the children of Israel, the victims suffer for the sin of Sabbath-breaking. God proclaims, "Ye know of those of you who broke the Sabbath, how We said unto them: Be ye apes, despised and hated!"

For this, they are made "an example to their own and to succeeding generations, and an admonition to the God-fearing." They are punished for sin, not for Judaism. In fact, they suffer for a sin that centuries of rabbinic tradition also categorized as singularly grievous.[27]

Some Qur'anic commentators have indeed used these and other texts to attack Jews, to present them as a condemned race, destined for hell. But in so doing, they are going far beyond the natural sense of the text. The Qur'an offers nothing vaguely as explicit as the New Testament passages in which Jesus himself, who is for Christians the incarnation of the Divine, speaks so furiously against "the Jews." It is the Jesus of the New Testament who calls his enemies the children not of Abraham but of the Devil, the Father of Lies. That same Jesus denounces the Jews of his day, warning that "this generation will be held responsible for the blood of all the prophets that has been shed since the beginning of the world."[28] He was not condemning all Jews in any racial sense, but was rather attacking rival factions and leaders in his day. And that is the model we find in the Qur'an.

The Pseudo-Qur'an

Some of the Qur'an's critics, notably Andrew Bostom himself, are serious scholars who argue on the basis of diligent readings of scripture, commentaries and historical documents. Although someone might argue with their conclusions, their scholarship demands respect. Quite different, but just as influential, are the popular critics who have in effect created a whole alternative version of the Qur'an, using flagrant misreadings and misrepresentations of the actual text. This pseudo-Qur'an actually recalls another milestone in the history of bigotry—namely, the pseudo-Talmud that used to circulate in bygone decades, when anti-Semites forged a series of scabrous and pornographic passages that they attributed to the Jewish tradition.

A glance at the Internet will produce dozens of verses in which the Qur'an allegedly damns Jews and commends terrorism, and these passages reverberate around websites and blogs. The fact that the same verses occur so frequently and in more or less identical language strongly suggests to any nonexpert that these words are authentic, and readers rarely take the trouble to verify them. Most such passages, though, are simply bogus. In some cases, an individual might have deliberately forged a verse for polemical purposes, but in others, no dishonest intent was involved. Perhaps someone originally paraphrased a text, which somewhere through the process of transmission acquired quotation marks, leading later readers to believe that this was indeed a faithful Qur'anic translation. Those later recipients then circulated the text even more widely, believing that they were furthering the cause of truth. But whatever the intent, we now have a whole pseudo-Qur'an that appears to be directed chiefly to vicious attacks on Jews.

I offer some of the uglier examples:

Sufficient for the Jew is the flaming fire![29]

In 2010, a Google search of this phrase yielded forty-six citations. This is in fact a bastardized version of Qur'an 4:54–55, which I discussed earlier. The actual passage says that some Jews believed the revelations while others disbelieved, and hell is the portion of those unbelievers. The Qur'an does not consign Jews to hellfire on the basis of race or religion.

Allah made the Jews leave their homes by terrorizing them so that you killed some and made many captive.[30]

As it stands, this passage calls forth images of Muslims engaging in ethnic cleansing of Jewish families, and stresses the potent buzzword "terror." This is reportedly a quotation from Qur'an 33:26, which records how some of the People of the Book joined the war against the early Muslim community. God, however, brought them down from their strongholds or fortified places, and they fled in fear, so that Muslim armies confiscated their property. The passage describes a victorious war against Jewish military forces, not acts of persecution.

> **We will not remove a Jew from the punishment. They know the shameful thing that awaits them.**[31]

The verse quoted is at best a tendentious paraphrase of the actual text, purportedly Qur'an 2:96. The actual verse comes in the middle of a denunciation of Jews who have failed to live up to their covenant with God. Such people might want to live for a thousand years, the text says, but even if they did, it would not save them from punishment for their sins. According to the authentic Qur'an, the Jews who will be judged will fall prey to God's anger not because they are Jews, but because of their sin and lack of faith.

> **The Jews are devoid of sense. There is a grievous punishment awaiting them. Satan tells them not to believe so they will end up in Hell.**[32]

This verse is commonly cited as Qur'an 59:14, which is useful to know, as otherwise it would be impossible to find similar words in an actual text of the Qur'an. Sura 59 condemns those People of the Book, whether Christians or Jews, who stubbornly fight the Muslim community after they have been defeated and driven out. This muleheadedness proves, says the Qur'an, that they must have no sense. At best, the quoted verse is a very rough abridgment of the whole sura, rather than any specific verse, with the customary substitution of "Jew" for the more general non-Muslim enemy implied here.

In different ways, each of these verses is a poisonous distortion of the Qur'an's actual words. The tragedy is that uninformed observers will take these bogus pseudo-scriptures as faithful reflections of the text. In reality, the Qur'an has nothing that need be taken as a condemnation of Jews, or of any ethnic group.

Books and Their Times

IF THE QUR'AN'S CONTENT is so much less offensive than that of the Bible, should we regard that as an argument for the superiority of the religion based on that text? We can debate the relative appeal of the different faiths, but the lack of Joshua texts or extermination orders in the Qur'an really does not offer strong support for Muslim claims. In fact, the Qur'an's attitudes toward warfare and bloodshed illustrate not so much its moral superiority as its rootedness in one particular historical era—that is, in the lifetime of Muhammad.

The Bible is a book that grew organically over many centuries: perhaps thirteen hundred years from the oldest passages of the Pentateuch to the conclusion of the New Testament. In that time, the various books drew together the ideas and assumptions of many different eras and civilizations, and in some of those eras, ideas of ethnic cleansing and massacre were seen as acceptable. Whether or not these theories were ever literally applied, they were reflected in the religious teachings of their day, some of which eventually made it into the Bible. However unpalatable portions of the text may be to modern ears, they testify to the book's antiquity and the long process of debate and dialogue that produced the Bible as we know it. The Bible is a building of many stories.

The Qur'an, in contrast, is strictly a work of its time. It is a one-story structure. For better or worse, the Qur'an assumes as a given the political values of the Christianity of the late ancient and early Byzantine world, including assumptions about the toleration of deviance and the enforcement of morality. So much that shocks modern Western readers about the Qur'an actually derives from the Roman Christian world at the time of Muhammad, including the brutal physical punishments, the crucifixions and beheadings. The Qur'an reflects the strident rhetoric common to interfaith controversies in the Middle East around 600 CE. The views found in that scripture are no worse than the policies of most states and empires then in existence, and are usually, by the standards of the time, generous and open-minded. Few Christians at the time would have dared suggest, as the Qur'an does, that there should be no compulsion in religion.[33]

In terms of attitudes toward violence and conflict, the Qur'an reflects the ideas of legitimate warfare on the fringes of the great world empires in the early seventh century, however consistently it tries to interpret them in humane and reasonable ways. That religious world rejected the association of faith with race or ethnicity, and so, naturally, does the Qur'an: hence the lack of extermination passages. The Middle Eastern world had very different ideas on these matters in 600 CE than it had in 700 BCE. Deuteronomy and Joshua grew from the earlier era; the Qur'an, from the later.

Much of what modern Westerners may admire or fear about Qur'anic faith stems from the Christianity of the seventh century as it was interpreted in Arabia, and also, to a lesser extent, the Judaism of that time. But in either case, modern observers are responding to ideas that grew out of the Bible, and the long centuries of debate and discussion over that text. If the Qur'an seems more universalist or humane in its outlook than the Bible, that is because it depends on ideas that the biblically based faiths themselves had evolved and familiarized around the then-known world. In its relative humanity, the Qur'an dates itself to a precise and limited era.

PART II

The Inheritance

The issue then cannot be whether or not genocide is intrinsically good or evil—its sanction by a holy God settles that question.

—Eugene Merrill, Dallas Theological Seminary

But one might object that, if the Qur'an is no worse than the Bible in terms of its violent words, then surely it differs from that book in terms of the effects it has had in the real world? Modern Jews and Christians assume that, while the Bible's dark texts are dead letters, the Qur'an's warlike words remain vividly alive as a force driving extremism. Historically, though, the differences are not clear-cut.

CHAPTER FOUR

Sons of Joshua

It often seems necessary that a people of markedly inferior type
should vanish before a people of superior potentialities, since there is
a point beyond which racial mixing cannot go without disaster.

—WILLIAM FOXWELL ALBRIGHT, FOUNDER
OF MODERN BIBLICAL ARCHAEOLOGY

DESPITE ITS MORAL DIFFICULTIES, the conquest account was
fundamental to the tradition of Jewish and Christian biblical
interpretation—the whole narrative of God's choosing a people and
giving them a land. In turn, that model supplied the essential framework of Christian belief. On many occasions too, the conquest stories inspired or justified actual violence by believers in that tradition.

Even in modern times, plenty of religious thinkers are prepared
to take these stories at face value, and some justify the underlying
theology of annihilation. Still today, some theologians accept that
God commanded genocide and ethnic cleansing, so that it is no
business of mere mortals to challenge these decrees. However such
writers hedge their accounts, however they specify that the conquest instructions were a once-and-for-all event that can have no
influence on later ages, their commentaries provide classic justifica-

tions for genocide—justifications that in their details precisely echo the language and rhetoric of twentieth-century Holocausts.

Heirs of Conquest

IDEAS OF EXODUS AND conquest are the inescapable foundations of biblical religion. They echo through the Psalms, which for centuries provided the fundamental structure of praise and worship among both Jews and Christians. Still today the psalms are central to Christian worship, even in liberal-inclined churches that have conscientiously purged the historical accounts of massacre:

> [God] drove out nations before them
> and allotted their lands to them as an inheritance;
> he settled the tribes of Israel in their homes.[1]

> He gave them the lands of the nations,
> and they fell heir to what others had toiled for.[2]

Usually, the religious heirs of Moses and Joshua celebrated these events as a saga of the birth and growth of a nation, but without details of the bloodshed. Psalm 136, for instance, hymns God's great deeds, for which his people must ever thank him forever, and among these acts we hear that the Lord God

> slew famous kings
> *for his mercy endureth for ever*
> Sihon king of the Amorites:
> *for his mercy endureth for ever*
> Og the king of Bashan
> *for his mercy endureth for ever*
> And gave their land for an heritage
> *for his mercy endureth for ever.*[3]

And yet, at least according to Deuteronomy, when Moses's forces defeated Sihon, they also killed all his subjects—every man, woman, and child.

Other biblical authors were frank about the violence. In the fifth century BCE, Nehemiah recalls the peoples displaced in order to make the new Israel:

> You gave them kingdoms and nations, allotting to them even the remotest frontiers. They took over the country of Sihon king of Heshbon and the country of Og king of Bashan.
> . . . Their sons went in and took possession of the land. You subdued before them the Canaanites, who lived in the land; you handed the Canaanites over to them, along with their kings and the peoples of the land, to deal with them as they pleased.[4]

Jesus and Joshua

CHRISTIANS, LIKE JEWS, INHERITED these memories of exodus and conquest. From earliest times, Christians believed that the Old Testament was foreshadowing their own narrative. Old Testament stories and events prefigured the New, offering a series of models or types—hence the concept of "typology," which I will explore more fully in chapter 8.[5]

Old Testament passages shape the narrative structure of the four Gospels, in which many words and actions attributed to Jesus are grounded in older prophecies or exemplars. All the evangelists, for instance, borrow from Old Testament passages to shape their accounts of the crucifixion. Few stories in the Gospel accounts of Jesus lack an Old Testament parallel or precedent, and the resemblances are all the more apparent when we read that older text in the Greek translation that the evangelists would have known best. This assimilation of Old and New laws can puzzle modern readers of the Bible, who are used to seeing the Old Testament as the Hebrew Bible, the foundational text of Judaism, while the New Testament is the core scripture of Christianity, with a radical break separating the two. Through most of the Christian era, faithful believers knew that the Old Testament was entirely their scripture, every part of which prefigured the coming of Jesus Christ. Jesus was the new Abraham and Moses, the new Elijah and Joshua.[6]

Christians found by far their most important "types" in the story of the movement from Egypt to Canaan. This ancient saga was now read in terms of the Easter story, of the crucifixion and resurrection. For Christians, Jesus was Moses, who saved his people and brought them out of the land of Egypt. In baptism, Christians passed through death into life, just as the ancient Hebrews had passed through the Red Sea. Rooted as they were in Jewish tradition, the first Christians confidently placed their own faith in the context of that older story of redemption and salvation, and that meant drawing heavily on Deuteronomy. Deuteronomy, in fact, is one of the portions of the Old Testament most extensively cited in the New, the third most heavily used text after Psalms and Isaiah.[7] The Law on which Jesus meditated fully included Deuteronomy, and that book may well have loomed larger than any other in his mind. When Jesus went into the desert, the Devil tempted him with three questions, and each time Jesus responded with a text from Deuteronomy.[8]

But Jesus was also Joshua, the successor of Moses, and the one who actually led the Israelites into the Promised Land. Jesus himself was named for that great judge; indeed, the names are the same in the Greek that was the language of many Jews in the Second Temple era, between about 300 BCE and 70 CE. When Jews translated the scriptures into Greek in the third century BCE, creating the so-called Septuagint, Joshua's name appears as *Iesous,* exactly the form used for Jesus in the Greek New Testament. This resemblance can shock modern readers, seeing *Iesous* credited with all those bloodthirsty acts during the conquest of Canaan. Intellectually, we know that Jesus is not ordering the massacre of civilians, but the usage is still unnerving.

Early Christian writers, though, reveled in the parallels: one *Iesous* did this, another did that. If the Easter story recalls the flight from Egypt, then the movement toward Canaan becomes a symbol of the earthly progress toward heaven. Jesus, like Joshua, brought his people over the Jordan into a land flowing with milk and honey. Augustine's *City of God* stressed that Moses led the people out of Egypt, but only Jesus led them into the Promised Land. Augustine's Syriac contemporary Theodoret wrote that just as *Iesous*/Joshua led the people into the Promised Land after the death of Moses, "[a]fter the end of the Law, our *Iesous*/Jesus came and opened the Kingdom of Heaven to his holy people."[9]

The conquest story permeates the New Testament. Paul, of course, was originally Saul, named for the great king who warred against the Amalekites. He repeatedly quotes Deuteronomy in his letters, while the book of Acts reports a sermon in which Paul tells how God "overthrew seven nations in Canaan and gave their land to his people as their inheritance." Also in Acts, the first Christian martyr, Stephen, tells how "our fathers under Joshua brought [the Tabernacle] with them when they took the land from the nations God drove out before them." Even Rahab, the Jericho woman who sheltered Joshua's spies, became a significant figure in early Christian thought, as a symbol of faith and hospitality. She had a claim to rank as the first Gentile convert, the forerunner of the many Gentiles now joining the emerging church. Rahab was after all a non-Jew—a Canaanite, indeed—who accepted the Hebrew God and his people, and whose subsequent marriage made her an ancestor of King David, and ultimately of Jesus. She is one of a handful of Old Testament women cited regularly in early Christian writings.[10]

The Clay and the Potter

MODERN READERS MIGHT PUZZLE over the total Christian assimilation of the conquest epic, in which Israelites overcame and slaughtered heathens of other races. Surely, the problems abound. Why were early non-Jewish readers, Greeks and others, not more disturbed by the racial exclusivism as much as the violence? Seeing themselves as the new Chosen People, though, Christians found in the Old Testament tales the principles and rules by which they should live. Christians through the centuries have happily recited texts exalting Israel (commonly read as "the church") over "the nations." When encountering passages in which God told the Israelites to massacre the natives of Canaan, few Christians have thought to put themselves in the position of the victims rather than the conquerors. Making the passages more palatable, many Christians interpreted the Bible in an allegorical way. Commentators found no moral objections to the conquest tales when the Canaanites or Midianites destined for extermination represent sins or evil impulses, rather than real people.

But throughout Christian history, some readers have turned to the conquest tales as *history,* and have labored to confront the issue of destroying real cities and real races. Judging from the number of Church Fathers who tried to address such concerns, the issue had worried some Christians from early centuries. If you took the stories literally, how could the God of Jesus, the God of love and forgiveness, have demanded such ruthless behavior?

Just how lively these debates were emerges from the writings of Theodoret, a fifth-century commentator who exercised wide influence in the Eastern church of his time. In his *Questions on the Octateuch,* he provided a detailed exegesis of the books of Judges, Joshua, and Ruth, as well as the traditional five Books of Moses. Theodoret was addressing questions that actually did arise in the minds of his contemporaries, so that the "questions" that structure his book are more than a mere literary device: they represent serious difficulties that people had with the texts. Often, what strikes a modern reader is just how concerned these early believers were with biblical passages that modern counterparts tend to gloss over. Why, they asked, did Moses command his people to devote Amalek to total destruction? Why did God harden the hearts of Joshua's enemies, to bring them to defeat and slaughter? "There are those who accuse the prophet [Joshua] of cruelty for slaying everywhere without exception and crucifying the kings"—so why did he act like this?[11]

While many Christian apologists have presented the violence in symbolic and spiritual terms, other thinkers over the centuries have indeed accepted the material and historical reality of the conquest and have explored its moral problems. Some, moreover, have produced thoughtful arguments, however much those arguments now disturb modern believers. Normally, such apologists have deployed two main themes, which coexist uneasily:

1. God is an absolute sovereign who is the standard of right and justice; thus whatever he commands is by definition just, however wrong it may seem to human beings. The conquest is a test of human faith in God's power and goodness.
2. The native peoples of Canaan were so overwhelmingly evil that exterminating them was an act of justice.

The first of these theories repudiates any need for a justification for God's decision, while the second tries to provide an explanation that would satisfy human criteria.[12]

Commonly, theologians have despaired of finding answers that could satisfy human reason. Rather, they have invoked God's absolute, inscrutable, wisdom and might, his arbitrary power to do as he wished with his creation. They have often returned to an image from Paul's letter to the Romans, in which the apostle compared

God to the potter who could do as he chose with his clay, and it was not for the vessels that he shaped to complain about their fate.[13]

Augustine: Obeying Orders

On this issue as on so much else, by far the most influential commentator was Augustine of Hippo, who stressed God's absolute sovereignty and righteousness. No matter how wrong an act might seem to human eyes, if God ordered it, it could never be wrong and thus had to be obeyed.

Augustine's responses emerged from his long debates with the Manichaean sect, to which he had once belonged. Although Manichaeans had a potent theology of their own, based on an eternal conflict between the forces of light and darkness, much of their popular appeal stemmed from a rationalistic attack on the Old Testament. If, as they believed, the Old Testament revealed the acts of an evil, inferior deity, then it was not surprising that this text was so full of blatant acts of injustice and immorality. Defending the Old Testament became a primary task for Christian apologists.

Augustine's most celebrated opponent was a Manichaean leader named Faustus, a fellow North African, who pointed out flagrant contradictions between the Pentateuch and the teachings of Jesus. As Augustine protested, "Faustus blames God in the Old Testament for slaughtering thousands of human beings for slight offenses, as Faustus calls them, or for nothing." He "speaks of Moses as commanding and doing many cruel things."[14] To modern eyes, Faustus was making a solid case for the prosecution. Augustine's response, the *Contra Faustum,* was a detailed defense of the Bible. Yes, said Augustine, many of the acts described seem cruel or vicious, but they can be defended in various ways. As we will see, Augustine argued that many of the most extreme stories have to be understood allegorically; but even if we did not use this approach, he said, God still remains uncondemned. If the violent actions were done in obedience to God, that fact entirely justified them.

For ancient readers, one of the most troubling biblical stories told how, when the Hebrews left Egypt, they looted the treasures of their Egyptian masters. Involvement in such a theft made Moses seem like a bandit chief rather than the leader of a liberation struggle. Why did he do it? For Augustine, not only did Moses not sin in doing this, "but it would have been sin not to do it. It was by the command of God, who, from His knowledge both of the actions and of the hearts of men, can decide on what every one should be made to suffer, and through whose agency." God is absolute, and his standards above those of men—very much, in fact, like the Allah portrayed in the Qur'an. For Augustine too, God "commands nothing but what is most just."[15]

When we accept this principle, all the wars and conquests fall into logical place, and that insight led Augustine to draw influential conclusions about the legitimacy of war and violent action. In judging any war, he said, we have to know the authority by which it takes place. "When war is undertaken in obedience to God, who would rebuke, or humble, or crush the pride of man, it must be allowed to be a righteous war." But Augustine also held that "only obeying orders" provides a solid defense against participating in a wrongful war. In some cases, he said, a righteous man might fight in an unrighteous worldly cause, but even so, he is blameless: "It may be an unrighteous command on the part of the king, while the soldier is innocent, because his position makes obedience a duty." If that is true of human affairs, "how much more must the man be blameless who carries on war on the authority of God, of whom every one who serves Him knows that He can never require what is wrong?"[16] Although this was not his primary intention, Augustine was laying firm foundations for a Christian theory of just war, and in a way that would make excellent sense to later Muslim theorists of jihad.

Reformers: Enacting God's Judgment

THE ARGUMENT FOR GOD'S arbitrary sovereignty became central to the Protestant theologies that emerged during the Reformation of the sixteenth century. In fact, many Protestants drew strength from exactly those elements of the stories that most appall moderns, especially the incomprehensible nature of God's commands. Like Augustine, John Calvin used some of the thorniest conquest stories to make his most sweeping theological arguments. Calvin's last major work, in fact, was a commentary on the book of Joshua (1563–1564), which one admirer termed his "dying bequest to the church." For later Christian generations, that legacy has been a mixed blessing. Calvin used the Old Testament massacres as prime exhibits of his theology, and his interpretations haunted much later Protestant and Puritan thought.[17]

Basic to Calvinist theology was the idea of God's choice of a people for himself, a decision that could not be resisted or challenged. Through original sin, humanity was utterly fallen and consigned to damnation, and that fall, that depravity, polluted all human perceptions. We recall Christ's parable of the wheat and the tares growing up together side by side, until they finally came to judgment, and there was precious little a tare could do to alter its destiny. A man could live according to the highest ethical standards, benefiting society and perhaps even saving innocent lives, but none of those achievements could bring salvation unless that person was predestined to be saved. Not even deliberately pledging oneself to Christ and his church would contradict this verdict. By human standards, such a theology might appear monstrously unjust, even diabolical; but that very perception, said Calvin, just showed how flawed human values and attitudes were, when set against the perfect justice of God.

Human beings had no basis to complain of God's harshness under any circumstances, even when he eliminated whole nations. Calvin was not saying that massacres or genocide were normally permissible—far from it: "Had the Israelites gratified their own lust and rage in slaughtering mothers and their children," such behavior "would have been barbarous and atrocious cruelty," what we would today call a war crime.[18] But such language could never be applied to any—*any*—act commanded by God. The best Christian response in such circumstances was rather to give humble thanks that God's incredible patience had allowed the deity to tolerate the existence of other peoples whose sins were equally bad.

This attitude was tested perfectly when dealing with the killing of children, a behavior that repulsed even those accustomed to the harsh rules of war in early modern Europe. But for Calvin, children too were born in sin and merited damnation quite as much as their parents, unless God had made the gracious and arbitrary decision to save them. Calvin challenged any notion that humans could judge or condemn God's acts:

> Certainly any man who will thoroughly examine himself, will find that he is deserving of a hundred deaths. Why, then, should not the Lord perceive just ground for one death in any infant that has passed from its mother's womb? In vain, shall we murmur or make noisy complaint, that he has doomed the whole offspring of an accursed race to the same destruction; the potter will nevertheless have absolute power over his own vessels, or rather over his own clay.[19]

Calvin was saying that a whole race might be damned to the point of meriting total destruction, and that if it reached such a state, it would be actively sinful to resist God's command to eliminate it. "Though, in our judgment at least, the children and many of the women also were without blame, let us remember that the judgment-seat of heaven is not subject to our laws."[20]

Even Calvin, though—a man not normally afraid to follow any argument to its dreadful conclusion—offered another point that softens his basic theme about divine justice. Yes, God commanded the slaughter of the peoples of Canaan, but these natives had also deserved it because of their appalling sins. For Calvin, the question was not why God had wiped out those people, but rather why he had put up with such dreadful sinners for so long: "Who will now presume to complain of excessive rigor, after God had so long delayed to execute judgment? If anyone object that children, at least, were still free from fault, it is easy to answer that they perished justly, as the race was accursed and reprobated."[21]

Calvin exercised a lasting influence, not just on the sectarian groups that we call Puritans, but on mainstream Protestant churches across Europe and North America. Later writers turned gratefully to his suggestion that the Canaanites had eminently deserved their fate by their outrageously sinful behavior. Around 1700, for instance, the Welsh Presbyterian pastor Matthew Henry closely followed Calvin in a series of biblical commentaries that are still in print to this day. Henry operates on the assumption that if God chose to wreak such appalling vengeance on a city, that can only have been the result of extreme provocation. They must have asked for it. Henry offers this commentary on the annihilation of the city of Ai: "God, the righteous Judge, had sentenced the Canaanites for their wickedness; the Israelites only executed his doom. . . . Especial reason no doubt there was for this severity to the king of Ai; it is likely he had been notoriously wicked and vile, and a blasphemer of the God of Israel."[22] The king's notorious wickedness is Henry's own invention, however, and has no biblical grounds.

Defending Literalism

SUCH INTERPRETATIONS CARRY LITTLE weight today for mainstream believers, even for many conservatives. Moreover, any knowledge of recent history raises deep suspicion about any characterization of whole races as pernicious or sinful, and certainly about any suggestion that a people is unworthy to exist. When we read biblical accounts of the unparalleled evils of Israel's enemies, we easily recognize the propaganda that regimes direct against their unpopular minorities.

Yet many Christian thinkers, usually evangelicals, still deploy these once-familiar arguments. Largely, this defense of the conquest arises from a need to defend biblical authority. Since the rise of critical Bible scholarship during the nineteenth century, liberals have believed that biblical statements can and must be judged against the findings of history and science. Literalists reject this approach, fearing that undermining the credibility of any part of scripture weakens the authority of the whole, and leaves individuals to judge the Bible by the standards of later eras. In that case, they argue, religious doctrine would become wholly relative and subjective. As a result fundamentalists have to defend the truth of every part of scripture, however unpalatable.

In the case of the conquest, literalists have a hopeless choice. They can avoid the moral dilemmas posed by the massacres by saying that these events did not happen in anything like that way; and if they were to choose that course, they would have plenty of fine scholars, archaeologists as well as textual critics, to back them up. Unfortunately, that approach would make nonsense of any claims of biblical infallibility. Alternatively, they can accept wholeheartedly that the massacres did happen as described, and then grapple with the theological issues and paradoxes raised by God's command of genocide. Among other points, literalists somehow have to reconcile those divine statements with God's later words of love and forgiveness. Either way, Canaanites and Amalekites pose a threat to biblical literalists no less severe than they once posed to ancient Israelites.

Damned Races

AT LEAST SINCE THE mid-nineteenth century, conservative Christians have striven to answer the attacks of skeptics and secularists on the issues surrounding the conquest, but their attempts have been deeply problematic. Among other issues, apologists justified the Bible in terms that could all too easily be applied to modern-day instances of racial conflict and annihilation. Central to the new apologetic was the theme of racial evil, and the idea that some races were so evil, so depraved, that their extermination was a moral imperative. When we read such arguments, which proliferate from the 1860s onward, we inevitably think of the encounters that Euro-Americans were in those very years having around the globe—with Africans, American Indians, Aborigines, and others—and how those bloodless religious texts could have had an all-too-direct impact on real world affairs.[23]

Christian attitudes interacted closely with new and controversial scientific views. From the 1860s, under the influence of Darwinism, Anglo-American thought moved toward hereditarian views—that is, seeing heredity as the dominant force shaping the lives of families and communities. In 1877, R. L. Dugdale popularized these views with his study titled *The Jukes*, which examined a supposedly depraved and degenerate family of thieves and beggars who were regrettably allowed to pass on their genes. In 1883, English scholar Francis Galton coined the word "eugenics" for the new science that would promote healthy biological stock while curbing the reproductive potential of the unfit. Eugenic ideas reached their height of political influence in the early twentieth century.[24]

Some Christian leaders enthusiastically adopted and promoted eugenic thought, but the pattern of influence was by no means all in one direction. Even before scientific eugenic ideas reached their full development, similar themes of doomed heredity could readily be found in the tracts and sermons of Christian thinkers, as they justified the slaughter of Amalekites and Canaanites, and these ideas influenced scientific discourse. For all their pretensions to scientific objectivity, eugenic thinkers themselves drew on their religious backgrounds, while the widely quoted religious activists prepared the way for the mass acceptance of full-fledged eugenic thought after 1900.[25]

At least by the 1860s, Protestant preachers were regularly framing their arguments in biological or medical terms, comparing the Bible's damned races to a cancer or tumor that had to be removed for the sake of the healthy organism. In 1867, popular London preacher Jonathan Bayley suggested that the Canaanites

> had fallen into such polluting abomination, such foul, loathsome and detestable wickedness that no reformation was possible. Hence they needed to be exterminated for the good of mankind. They were like incurable ulcers in the great body of humanity and to save the race these must be cut off. The Israelites were the executioners of providence. . . . The good of the human race required the extirpation of a tribe too vile to be continued.[26]

A few years later, Massachusetts clergyman John W. Haley produced his *Examination of the Alleged Discrepancies of the Bible,* a tract that still continues to be reprinted. Haley agreed that the evil races of the Bible were so bad that any reasonable society would have felt the need to wipe them out. For the Amalekites, the destruction had to be total, including the last toddler:

Besides, had the women and children been spared, there would soon have been a fresh crop of adult Amalekites, precisely like their predecessors. Or suppose merely the children had been saved; if left to care for themselves they must have miserably perished of starvation; if adopted and reared in Israelite families they might, *from their hereditary disposition and proclivities to evil* have proved a most undesirable and pernicious element in the nation. It was, doubtless, on the whole, the best thing for the world that the Amalekite race should be exterminated.[27]

These words appeared in 1876, a year before Dugdale exposed the alleged horrors of the Juke family.

By far the most popular apologist in the Anglo-American world was the revivalist R. A. Torrey. Among other achievements, it was Torrey who edited the collection of conservative theological essays known as *The Fundamentals,* which gave its name to the whole fundamentalist movement. In 1900, he published an analysis of *Difficulties and Alleged Errors and Contradictions in the Bible,* which was intended to give ordinary believers an arsenal of arguments with which to defend themselves against liberal and rationalist critics. The book is invaluable for what it tells us about the nature of theological debate at this time, the kind of antireligious arguments pressed by street orators, village atheists, and radical pamphleteers. Among the obvious difficulties that Torrey needed to explain: "The Antiquity of Man According to the Bible and According to Science," "Joshua Commanding the Sun to Stand Still," and, of course, "The Wholesale Slaughter of the Canaanites by God's Command."[28]

This last issue posed as significant a stumbling block to faith, as it had in Faustus's time. As Torrey admitted,

There are few things in the Bible over which more intelligent readers have stumbled, and over which infidels have more frequently gloated and gloried, than God's command that certain people should be utterly exterminated, sparing neither sex nor age. . . . How can we reconcile any such appallingly harsh commands as these with the doctrine so plainly taught in the New Testament that God is love?[29]

Torrey turned back to Augustine and Calvin in asserting that God the Creator can rule as he wishes, and rather than blame God, we should be grateful that he does not visit on us modern-day sinners the fate he inflicted on the Canaanites. Moreover, these ancient people really were singularly vicious. Wholesale massacres are appalling, yes:

> But there is something even more appalling than this. That is that the iniquity of any people should have become so full, their rebellion against God so strong and so universal, their moral corruption and debasement so utter and so pervasive, even down to babes just born, as to make such treatment absolutely necessary in the interests of humanity.

> [The Canaanites] had become a moral cancer threatening the very life of the whole human race. That cancer must be cut out in every fiber if the body was to be saved. Cutting out a cancer is a delicate operation, but often it is the kindest thing a surgeon can do under existing circumstances. The kindest thing that God could do for the human race was to cut out every root and fiber of these grossly wicked people.

That certainly meant killing the women, for "depraved women are more dangerous than depraved men."[30]

His argument meshed precisely with the language of the most radical wing of the eugenic movement:

> Anyone who has had experience with the children of the depraved knows how persistently the vices bred for generations

in the ancestors reappear in the children even when they are taken away from their evil surroundings and brought up in the most favorable envionment.

Canaanite children were just bad seed. For Torrey,

> The extermination of the Canaanite children was not only an act of mercy and love to the world at large; it was also an act of love and mercy to the children themselves. . . . Even today, I could almost wish that all the babies born in the slums might be slain in infancy, were it not for the hope that the church of Christ would awake and carry to them the saving gospel of the Son of God.[31]

The Holocaust Era

NOT JUST AMONG STRICT fundamentalists, asserting the literal authority of the Old Testament logically demands defending at least one unequivocal incident of genocide. We see this response in the writings of William Foxwell Albright, one of the most influential figures in the archaeology of Israel/Palestine, and a chaired professor at Johns Hopkins University. He dominated his scholarly field from the 1930s through the 1960s, mentoring a whole generation of brilliant scholars. Through works both scholarly and popular, he shaped how ordinary Christians in the English-speaking world understood the biblical record.[32]

Albright was the great exponent of biblical archaeology, a project aimed at verifying the truth of the scripture, rather than just pursuing the academic study of a region and an era. Although not a strict literalist, Albright held that archaeology confirmed the textual accounts found in the Old Testament, and he believed in both the Israelite conquest of Canaan and the destruction of that region's native societies and peoples. Albright regarded these massacres as quite justified, describing the Canaanite genocide as not just inevitable but desirable. Racial replacement was part of the process of historical progress and evolution. As he wrote, the treatment of the Canaanites was "no worse" than the Turkish genocide of the Armenians, and just as "inevitable" as the Euro-American slaughter of indigenous Indian peoples. Apparently, he regarded these analogies as a justification for the ancient massacres: everybody did it.[33]

Albright's arguments are multiply intriguing. Whom exactly was he thinking of when he imagined the markedly "inferior type" vanishing before the advance of "superior" peoples? Such remarks were not uncommon for an American of his generation—he was born in 1891—and they usually referred to various tribal or "primitive" nations falling back before white domination: indigenous peoples in North and South America, Pacific Islanders, Australian Aborigines, and African Bushmen. As a committed Zionist, he was also thinking of the Arab peoples of Palestine, whose existence he scarcely acknowledged. At best, Arabs provided colorful scenery for the expanding Jewish settlements.[34]

The irony, of course, is that in his arguments for ethnic cleansing and historical evolution, he was speaking exactly the contemporary language of the deadliest enemies of the Jews he so idolized. In 1940, he published a popular text titled *From the Stone Age to Christianity,* a study of the historical development of monotheism, in which he wrote,

It was fortunate for the future of monotheism that the Israelites of the conquest were a wild folk, endowed with primitive energy and ruthless will to exist, since the resulting decimation of the Canaanites prevented the complete fusion of the two kindred folk which would inevitably have depressed Yahwistic standards to a point where recovery was impossible.

Monotheism, he believed, could never have survived the continuing presence of the dreadful Canaanite religion, marred as it was by "orgiastic nature worship, their cult of fertility in the form of serpent symbols and sensuous nudity, and their gross mythology."[35] Albright then noted how other Canaanites settled North Africa, where they became the Carthaginians. And here too, their worsethan-worthless religion, with its "cult of sex," led to the annihilation of that people by "the immensely superior Romans."

This passage was published in 1940, just when Europe was falling under the rule of another group of self-proclaimed "superior Romans," based in Berlin. They too boasted of their "primitive energy and ruthless will to exist," and were equally determined to extirpate any "markedly inferior" races who stood in the path of their historical progress. Albright, though, saw nothing troubling in that analogy, and his text reappeared unchanged in a new edition published in 1957, a decade after the Nuremberg Trials. His comments would make sense as a form of veiled pro-Nazi sentiment, were it not for the source. But if Albright was not defending Nazi policies, as he assuredly was not, it is astonishing that he proved unable to think through the implications.

Defending Genocide

EVEN AMONG MODERN EVANGELICALS, respectable scholars echo Albright's views on the conquest, though without the racist and eugenic subtexts. In fact, it would be difficult to think of another area of scholarship, certainly in the realm of religion, where the theory of genocide has so many active defenders.

Christian and specifically evangelical scholars are well aware of the difficulties of the texts in Joshua and elsewhere, and many agonize over them: in recent years, a number of books and journals have devoted special attention to the dark passages. But such concerns are notably absent from much of the standard literature on the conquest era. When not actively defending the massacres, some commentators scarcely pursue the implications. One commentary written as recently as 2000 includes a section on the campaign against Ai, jauntily titled "Ai Spy."[36]

While some scholars speak frankly of the conquest in damning modern terms, others deny just as firmly that such negative language is appropriate. Apologist Paul Copan, for instance, objects that "ethnic cleansing suggests a racial hatred, which just is not behind the injunctions to kill Canaanites. . . . [T]he Israelites did not determine themselves to be the in-group, who in turn demonized the out-group and then destroyed them."[37] I find that reading profoundly counterintuitive.

In 2003, the respected evangelical press Zondervan published a thoughtful book under the provocative title *Show Them No Mercy*. This was a symposium of four scholars on the Canaanite genocide (which all accepted as a broadly accurate historical account) and what that event implied for modern understandings of the Bible. The debate became acrimonious. One scholar, C. S. Cowles, argued passionately for a radical discontinuity between the Old and New Testaments, and denied that a Christian could reconcile the genocide with his or her faith. He asked, "Can we imagine the God revealed fully and finally in Jesus ordering the killing of children and infants? At any time? In any place? For any reason?"[38] For Cowles, the human face of *herem* warfare could never be Jesus, but is rather Osama bin Laden. If that view meant challenging or invalidating the authority of some Old Testament texts, so be it.

But Cowles was an isolated voice. The other three scholars all protested his attempt to treat the bloodier passages of the Old Testament as less than authoritative. Indeed, other participants presented views that would have been familiar to Calvin or Matthew Henry. Speaking decisively for biblical continuity was veteran evangelical scholar Eugene Merrill, who denied that the genocide command could be regarded as in any sense evil or immoral. Such terms could not be applied to God, he asserted. For Merrill, the design underlying the policy is "beyond human comprehension, but one that is not for that reason unjust or immoral."[39]

Moreover, argued Merrill, the conquest war was thoroughly justified, as the Canaanites had no right to be in the land that they had occupied the past few centuries, and which they continued to hold regardless of a divine promise (of which they had not heard). They were "squatters on the land of promise, and furthermore would lead Israel into idolatry and moral decay." Canaanites were rebels against God, and their destruction was necessary to safeguard the future of Israel. In fact, said Merrill, the holy war carried on by Joshua and others was highly effective, and we must recognize "the pedagogical value of Yahweh war," the assertion of divine sovereignty.[40] The Hebrew annihilation of some cities carried a "shock and awe" effect for its neighbors.

So could the God of Jesus ever have commanded the slaughter of infants? In Merrill's view, he not only could, but had. Another participant agreed that we humans had no basis on which to describe any acts or commands of God as evil. Even when dealing with genocide, a term that all participants accepted, "there simply comes a point in which human reason must bow to the divine and recognize that his ways are truly not ours and his thoughts are truly above our own."[41]

Genocide on the Net

ACTIVIST AND EXTREME FORMS of religion have found a secure home on the Internet, where Islamist and jihadist sites proliferate. But both Christians and Jews also use the Net to present harrowing material: the biblical massacres continue to fascinate popular evangelists and apologists. Usually, Christian authors recycle Torrey's century-old arguments, although their passionate commitment to modern Zionism adds a contemporary edge to their arguments. When they discuss the struggles of the ancient Hebrews, they are clearly thinking of the contemporary situation of the state of Israel, viewed through the lens of the Israeli hard right. Comments about ancient Canaanites merge uncomfortably with attitudes toward contemporary Arabs and Muslims.

Many of these evangelical ministries assume that Canaan's older native peoples must have been uniquely vicious and sinful. Because the Bible says little about specific sins attributed to the Canaanites, preachers are able to let their darker speculations run free. One site asserts that:

> The sins of the Canaanites were at the boiling point, and Joshua was to completely destroy them lest Israel inherit their evil ways. Some of the abominations happening in the land were temple prostitution, father and son committing sexual acts with the same prostitute, child sacrifice, homosexualities, idolatry, and on and on.[42]

Such commentators assume, wrongly, that the kind of violence portrayed in Joshua must have been standard for the ancient world, and should not be judged by gentler modern standards. One Internet-based ministry, *JesusWalk*, warns,

> We get in trouble when we try to impose a twentieth Century ethic in a Bronze Age situation. . . . In fact, genocide was common in the Bronze Age. . . . Israel was a threat to all the people of Canaan. Unless she destroyed them, she would be destroyed herself. . . . It was kill or be killed.[43]

The old medical and biological analogies also circulate. Just within the past few years, one Baptist scholar defended the Canaanite genocide with the words, "Like a surgeon, God removed the cancerous growth of Canaanite depravity in order to promote the longevity of his people."[44] Another online ministry lists the sins and horrors that the Bible attributes to the Canaanites, and urges Christians not to be disturbed at God's wise judgment in extirpating this dreadful race. "If the cancer remains, Israel will not survive. For Israel's survival, the Canaanites will have to go." However, adds the author, at least the slaughtered children would find a happy ending in the afterlife. "The one bright spot in this sordid story is that God removed an entire generation of Canaanite children and took them to such a [loving] home . . . His home."[45]

WHATEVER WE THINK ABOUT the theology found in such accounts, no commentator who accepts the literal truth of the Canaanite genocide should discuss it without reference to the scholarly literature addressing modern acts of mass killing. If the arguments are unacceptable when applied to twentieth-century Armenians or Jews, then they are no better when used of ancient Canaanites.

CHAPTER FIVE

Warrant for Genocide

*I have pursued mine enemies, and overtaken them:
neither did I turn again till they were consumed.*

*I have wounded them that they were not able to
rise: they are fallen under my feet.*

—PSALMS 18:37–38

*I question whether the Spaniards would have murdered
so many millions in the Indies had they not thought
they might have used them like the Canaanites.*

—MATTHEW TINDAL, ENLIGHTENMENT SKEPTIC

IN THE POLITICAL REALM too, tales of slaughter wielded a long
influence over both Jewish and Christian traditions. Both faiths
cherished a glorious vision of a divinely chosen people that sought
to accomplish God's purposes in this world, until the process was
eventually fulfilled in a messianic age. But for both, the process involved enemies who had to be overcome, and sometimes that meant
inflicting real destruction upon material human foes. Later believers learned to frame their enemies in cosmic terms, to see them as

evil forces, with the implication that they could not in the long run stand up against God's will, or God's people. Such a doctrine gave its upholders a sturdy faith in the justice of their cause, which translated into firm courage on the battlefield. The Bible lends itself naturally to doctrines of holy war.

Distinctively Christian readings of the Bible, and the political lessons people have drawn from such readings over the centuries, matter so much because for over fifteen hundred years it was Christian rather than Jewish kingdoms that battled for supremacy in Europe, and Christian empires that spanned the globe. The fact of chosenness gave divine authorization to subjugate and evict the former inhabitants of conquered lands. Among nations rooted in Protestantism—the English, Americans, Dutch, and Germans— believers came to view rival races as utterly evil, to the point that, in extreme instances, these enemies should be utterly destroyed. The Bible gave the West its vocabulary for genocide.

Wars of the Covenant

ALTHOUGH EVANGELICAL WRITERS JUSTIFY bygone acts of religious violence, virtually all writers in this tradition stress that the Canaanite genocide was a one-of-a-kind event that could not and must never be repeated in the modern world. Eugene Merrill could not make this point more strongly: "The genocide sanctioned by scripture was unique in its time, place and circumstances. It is not to be carried over to the age of the church."[1] But historically, such clear distinctions have not been universal. Throughout the history, at least some Christians have regarded themselves as heirs to the promises made to the former chosen people, the Hebrews; and for many, that inheritance has included a set of attitudes toward enemies and persecutors.

Christian doctrines of holy warfare emerged slowly. In the earliest Christian centuries, believers maintained a strong suspicion of the Roman state and secular law—and, more particularly, of the military. At least until the fourth century, Christians had strong doubts of the legitimacy of serving in the armed forces. This situation changed, of course, once the Roman Empire accepted Christianity, and Christian rulers began waging war in the name of God. At that point, church leaders sought biblical passages that could sanctify their efforts, and often they found them in the Old Testament references to Canaanites and Amalekites.

The Amalekite story carried considerable weight because of parallels that early Church Fathers identified between Moses and Christ. Moses kept his arms raised during the battle with the Amalekites, to secure God's blessing in the struggle; Jesus spread his arms on the cross to defeat the forces of sin. When Christianity became the religion of kings and states, the analogy provided the basis for a whole theology of sacred warfare, which influenced conduct up to modern times. In this reading, clergy imitated Moses by spreading their arms in prayer, while secular generals performed the role of Joshua, going out to smite Amalek. Clerics liked the analogy because it gave them a precise and indispensable role in the struggle.

Already by Charlemagne's time, around 800 CE, kings and prelates were exhorting each other to fulfill their proper role in the combat with Amalek, whose precise identity shifted according to need. Pagan enemies were ideal, but the foe's religious status was flexible. When Pope Urban II launched the first Crusade in 1095, he told Christian warriors, "It is our duty to pray, yours to fight against the Amalekites"—in this case, the Muslims. Other conquest-era stories helped form the church's military ideal. When clerical writers deplored the trains of loose women who accompanied Crusading forces, they found an obvious solution in the book of Numbers. Why could these women not be disposed of as efficiently as Phinehas had removed the Midianite woman who tempted the Hebrew armies?[2]

Holy War versus Just War

IN LATER CENTURIES, HOLY war texts claimed Christian victims. The popular rediscovery of the Bible at the end of the Middle Ages reversed what had been an impressive trend over several centuries to humanize and civilize warfare. In terms of its practical consequences for Christendom's armed conflicts, the return to the Bible was very bad news.[3]

The ugly example of the Crusades may make it sound absurd to describe medieval warfare as civilized, but in fact scholars and church leaders had made real progress as the Middle Ages advanced. They developed humane doctrines of just war, which limited and specified the proper causes that states could invoke to launch war (*jus ad bellum*). Theorists tried to limit the practical conduct of war, reducing unnecessary violence and destruction, and offering protection to non-combatants and civilians (*jus in bello*). [4]

By the late fifteenth century, these ideas were widely acknowledged, however often the rules were broken in practice. But as dissenting sects began reading the Bible for themselves, they challenged these ideas as unreasonably limiting how pious believers should be able to fight. For true believers, just war theory was wrong precisely because it limited the opportunity for all-out holy war. Zealots resented the tight restrictions that the more humane theory placed on who exactly could initiate violence: according to just war tenets, only a properly constituted legal regime could declare war. The new Bible believers knew that, on occasion, ordinary Christians needed to take the laws of war into their own hands. Every man should be his own Joshua, his own Phinehas. Throughout such theorizing, parallels with contemporary Islamist thought are evident.

The emerging Protestant movement found its military models in the wars of Moses and Joshua. The well-armed Taborites of fifteenth-century Bohemia, radical proto-Protestants, denounced their Catholic neighbors as "Moabites, Amalekites . . . whom they deemed it their duty to extirpate." Extreme rhetoric became dangerously commonplace during the Reformation that burned through Germany in the 1520s. Denouncing rabble-rousing preachers, Martin Luther complained that "our dear prophets have chattered thus into the minds of the people, 'Dear people, God has ordered his people to beat Amalek to death.' Misery and tribulation have come out of this sort of thing." According to taste, Amalek could be aristocrats, landlords, Catholics, Jews, or other Protestants with whom one disagreed.[5]

In the Old Testament, early Protestants found powerful support for their doctrines—support that was at once theological, social, and political—and times of crisis brought violent texts to the fore. Protestantism, like Islam, was born in war, in the seemingly endless conflicts that rent Europe between 1550 and 1648, and that often threatened to result in a total Catholic victory. The conquest stories taught a generation fighting for its survival that God's elect would always triumph, no matter how overwhelming the odds. Calvinists developed a potent theory of resistance against unjust rulers, usually framed in Old Testament terms, as theologians justified tyrannicide, the assassination of unjust rulers by godly zealots.[6]

In the 1550s, Scottish Protestant firebrand John Knox turned naturally to the story of the Amalekites, those "who troubled the people of Israel passing up from Egypt." The enemy nation was utterly destroyed, "man, woman, infant, suckling, oxen, cattle, camels, and asses—and finally, all that lived in that land." Catholic persecutors should take note: "Terrible should be the remembrance hereof to all such as trouble or molest such as would follow the commandment and vocation of God, leaving spiritual Egypt (the kingdom of Antichrist) and the abomination thereof." Looking at the nation's Catholic queen, Mary, he prayed that "God, for His great mercy's sake," should stir up a modern-day hero, a Phinehas. That was an unequivocal call for assassination.[7]

Reformers developed a radical doctrine of religious-based war that abandoned just war theories and restraints. The most important theorist was Heinrich Bullinger, a Swiss reformer now largely forgotten, but hugely influential across the Protestant Europe of his day. His famous sermon "On War" sought to revive *herem* warfare as a practical reality. Bullinger imagined a special category of war that a magistrate or ruler might command

> **upon men which are incurable, whom the very judgment of the Lord condemneth and biddeth to kill without pity or mercy. Such were the wars which Moses had with the Midianites, and [Joshua] with the Amalekites. . . . [These are] the wars that are taken in hand for the defense of true religion against idolaters and enemies of the true and catholic faith.**

The Bible showed how such wars should be fought, believed Bullinger: "The laws of war are recited in the 20th chapter of Deuteronomy, both profitable and necessary. . . . Moreover, in every place of the scripture, these laws of war are still bidden to be kept." If a city fell into idolatry, then it "should be set upon with warriors and utterly razed," according to the provisions of Deuteronomy. Bullinger was formulating what we might today call a far-reaching theory of Christian jihad.[8]

English Puritan writers of the 1620s and 1630s further developed bloodcurdling theories of neo-*herem,* which aimed to supersede just war notions. William Gouge used the Exodus passage on the Amalekites to argue that religious wars were not just *permissible* for faithful Christians, but *required.* War could be holy: "For a soldier to die in the field in a good cause, it is as for a preacher to die in a pulpit." Gouge—an apt name, in light of his opinions—expanded just war theory to justify aggressive conquests, provided they were for motives of "maintenance of truth and purity of religion." As precedent, he cited the Israelite expansion into Canaan.[9]

Gouge was by no means the most bellicose Puritan of this era. Some writers went beyond merely justifying the act of holy warfare, demanding that it should be as savage and indiscriminate as the conflicts of the Bible. In 1626, Thomas Barnes proclaimed,

> **The stretching out of the sword to blood requires the putting on of a kind of cruelty; as we see in Samuel, who hewed Agag in pieces without any show of compassion; as we see in Joshua, who hanged up the five heathenish kings without any compassion.**[10]

For Barnes, neither mercy nor compassion should limit the impact of holy war. Like many Puritans, he cited Saul's example because it so perfectly illustrated the theme of covenant that was fundamental to Calvinist thought. Saul violated the covenant, and perished accordingly.

Catholics and Amalekites

ENGLISH WRITERS WERE SO important because their nation was a leader in colonial and imperial expansion: Gouge and Barnes were cherished writers in New England. British military culture, moreover, was thoroughly grounded in religious and biblical values. Puritan warlords recognized themselves in biblical accounts of Joshua and Gideon, and that self-understanding had disastrous consequences for their enemies, whether English Royalists or Irish Catholics. The civil wars of the 1640s killed perhaps a quarter of a million across the four nations of the British Isles.[11]

Oliver Cromwell himself, the effective dictator of England through the 1650s, identified wholeheartedly with Gideon, and saw his enemies as Midianites or Amalekites. When a former ally was reluctant to go along with Cromwell's extremism, the general chided him for his timidity: "Be not offended at the manner of God's working," wrote Cromwell. "Perhaps no other way was left. What if God accepted the zeal, as he did that of Phinehas, whose reason might have called for a jury!" Sometimes, correct procedure and legal niceties had to give way to direct godly action against the Midianite foe. The specific issue under debate at this time was the execution of England's King Charles I in 1649, the act of regicide that horrified the European political world. For Cromwell, as for other English Puritans in those years of crisis, the core question was, What Would Phinehas Do?[12]

If even the king was vulnerable, woe betide other nations and peoples. Catholics were special targets of Puritan vengeance, because of their infuriating claims to Christian status. As any good Protestant of the era knew, Catholics served the pope, who was the Antichrist foretold in the book of Revelation. If Anglo-Scottish settlers in Ireland saw themselves as a new Israel, then the Catholic natives who opposed them must be Amalekites and Canaanites, with all the curses appertaining to those names. Hatred between the two faiths reached terrible heights following the 1641 uprising in which Catholics tried to annihilate Protestant communities. Protestant writer Daniel Harcourt complained, "How dearly the Israelites . . . paid for their cruel mercy in not extirpating the idolatrous Canaanites."[13]

Protestants vowed not to repeat that mistake. When Cromwell reconquered Ireland in 1649, he drew on the example of Amalek to justify the massacre of the entire population of defiant towns such as Wexford and Drogheda. Other commanders were no less ferocious—particularly Scots Presbyterians, immersed as they were in Calvin's thought. When generals flinched from slaughter, their clerical chaplains drove them on. In one battle, General David Leslie's chaplain threatened him with all "the curses which befell Saul for sparing the Amalekites" unless he killed every single prisoner of war. Leslie exacted a grim revenge when he saw the chaplain

ankle deep in the blood of slaughtered prisoners. At last, gloated
Leslie, the preacher had got his fill of blood.[14]

Cromwell's religious attitudes poisoned Anglo-Irish relations
for centuries afterward. When English biblical commentators discuss the Israelites' enemies, it is often difficult to tell whether the
authors are thinking primarily of those ancient conflicts, or of the
Irish Catholics of their own day. As late as 1885, respected Anglo-
Irish evangelical A. R. Fausset published a commentary on Judges that
showed no qualms about annihilating pagan races: "The law to do
so was evidently from God, the righteous judge, not man; and the
divine aim was to exterminate idolatry and its attendant pollutions."
Although Fausset felt that the Hebrews had erred, their mistake
was not in massacring the Canaanites but rather in leaving some
breathing. He could only explain this excessive liberalism by assuming that the Israelites had succumbed to decadence: "Compromise,
indifference to the honor of God which idolatry insults, indolence
and love of gain, made Israel content with imposing tribute, even
when strong enough to have extirpated them." Not coincidentally,
this meditation on racial-religious supremacy appeared exactly as
Irish Protestants, like Fausset himself, were dreading the prospect
of an Irish Home Rule bill, which would allow the nation's loathed
Catholics a place in government.[15]

By 1700, England's own religious divisions were ceasing to
cause actual domestic bloodshed (Ireland was always a different
matter), but God's Elect continued to find countless Canaanites to
fight overseas. Later generations of soldiers and colonialists faced
enemies who lacked even the notional Christian qualifications of
Irish Catholics, and who thus could easily be compared to Canaan's
native peoples.

Critics at the time easily understood just how convenient the
biblical texts were for any state trying to legitimize aggressive expansion. In 1730, deistic skeptic Matthew Tindal wrote a blister-
ing attack on mainstream religion in his *Christianity as Old as the*

Creation, which cited the political abuses that strict fundamentalism could spawn:

> **What prince can ever want a pretence of going to war, and totally extirpating those he invades, when he sees Saul was commanded by God to destroy the Amalekites, men and women, infants and sucklings, ox and sheep, camel and ass, for an injury done four hundred years before?**

Already at this early historical moment, Tindal is sensitive to the imperialist implications of the biblical text. If a nation lacked territory, he asked, might they not think

> **what the Israelites did to the Canaanites a good precedent; and that they might invade a neighboring idolatrous nation, that never did them the least harm; and extirpate not only men and women but even their innocent infants in order to get possession of the country?**[16]

He referred specifically to the Spanish conquests in the Americas, which at the time represented the paradigmatic case of racial extermination, comparable to the Jewish Shoah in modern thought.

Like other commentators on the conquest wars, Tindal uses the word "extirpate," which needs some explanation. The word, first coined in the 1530s, suggests total removal. The Latin word *stirpes* meant the root or trunk of a tree, and thus to extirpate meant to root out, to pluck out the stem. To extirpate a people, then, meant not just to cause them terrible damage, but to end their biological existence. Extirpation was identical with "genocide," a word not coined until the 1940s. Centuries before that point, though, Protestant Bible readers not only knew the concept of genocide, but believed that in certain circumstances such behavior might be an absolute imperative commanded directly by God.

Amalek in America

BIBLICAL NOTIONS OF EXTIRPATION influenced colonial America from the earliest days of the settlement. In a tract publicizing the new Virginia settlement, Robert Gray expressed the hope that Indians might accept Christianity, but if they did not, biblical commands were clear: "Saul had his kingdom rent from him and his posterity because he spared Agag . . . whom God would not have spared; so acceptable a service is it to destroy idolaters, whom God hateth."[17]

When John Winthrop described the covenant relationship between God and the emerging New England, he warned of the dreadful consequences that would follow if the colonists betrayed their oath:

> When God gives a special commission, he looks to have
> it strictly observed in every article. When he gave Saul a
> commission to destroy Amalek, he indented with him upon
> certain articles, and because he failed in one of the least, and
> that upon a fair pretense, it lost him the kingdom which should
> have been his reward if he had observed his commission.

Although Winthrop was not specifically discussing the new colony's relationship with the pagan natives of the land, the parallels with Saul's massacre would soon become apparent. With no sense of irony, Winthrop's harrowing text bears the mild title *A Model of Christian Charity*.[18]

As New England's relations with the Native Americans deteriorated, so biblical analogies strengthened. For Cotton Mather, the Pequot Indians who attacked the colony in 1637 were "these Ammonites [who] perceived that they had made themselves to stink before the New-English Israel."[19] If they were Amalek, then their villages and families must be wiped out. In 1662, pioneering American poet Michael Wigglesworth commemorated the winning of "a waste and howling wilderness." Eventually, God destroyed those natives who had sought to harm his people:

> **Those curst Amalekites that first**
> **Lifted up their hand on high**
> **To fight against God's Israel**
> **Were ruin'd fearfully.**[20]

Winthrop's example came to the fore again in 1675, when New England faced another destructive war against the native peoples. In his history of the conflict, Increase Mather reported plots against the "English Israel" by "the Heathen People amongst whom we live, and whose land the Lord God of our Fathers hath given to us for a rightful Possession." He reported many battles against "the uncircumcised." In using that term, Mather was not, of course, referring to their actual medical state—the English did not circumcise either—but rather comparing the Indians to the enemy races that opposed the ancient Israelites. Reporting one defeat, he wrote, "This day Amalek prevailed over Israel! For Moses' hands were not held up, as should have been!"[21]

Cotton Mather, son of Increase, elaborated these ideas. In his history of the settlement, the *Magnalia Christi Americana,* Cotton Mather recounted the "Wars of the Lord" with all enemies, with heretics within and Indians without. He celebrated Winthrop as the American Nehemiah, the leader who kept the holy people both safe and separate from pagan foes. In 1689, the younger Mather told soldiers about to fight the Indians that they were the soldiers of Moses and Joshua, and like so many clerics before him, he promised to pray for the Christian army "while you are in the field with your lives in your hands against the Amalek that is now annoying this Israel in the wilderness."[22]

Over the next century, themes of racial war resurfaced in each new conflict. In a sermon preached in Boston in 1704, Henry Gibbs celebrated "the mercies of God in extirpating the enemies of Israel in Canaan"—specifically, in his American Canaan. As Theodore Roosevelt reported the western expansion, "Many of the best of the backwoodsmen were Bible-readers. They looked at their foes as the Hebrew prophets looked at the enemies of Israel. What were the abominations because of which the Canaanites were destroyed before Joshua, when compared with the abominations of the red savages whose lands they, another chosen people, should in their turn inherit?"[23] In the 1770s, British-allied Indians proved some of the deadliest foes of the emerging American nation. In response, American soldiers and political leaders turned to familiar biblical language of holy warfare. Even the humane Benjamin Franklin noted the devastation that rum had caused among the natives, and wondered "if it be the design of Providence to extirpate these savages in order to make room for the cultivation of the earth."[24]

Americans were a new Israel, for whom the language of covenant and election was quite appropriate. Ezra Stiles termed George Washington the American Joshua. When Washington died, the preachers eulogizing him differed only in whether he might better be compared to Joshua or to Moses himself. Both Franklin and Jefferson wanted to see the biblical exodus and the journey to the Promised Land prominently represented on the new nation's great seal. Jefferson's second inaugural address appealed to "that Being in whose hands we are, who led our fathers, as Israel of old, from their native land and planted them in a country flowing with all the necessities and comforts of life."[25] Such ideas segued naturally into the Manifest Destiny theory proclaimed in the 1830s, the vision that Joshua's people should spread over the whole Promised Continent, sweeping away any Canaanites in their path.[26]

Christian Empires

AMERICANS WERE FAR FROM unique in these opinions, and in their religious grounding. British imperialists understood the concept of extirpating primitive races, such as Australian Aborigines. Such language was not usually applied to more "advanced" communities like the peoples of India, however, unless and until they resisted occupation in ways that the British thought barbaric. When the British faced a widespread native rebellion during the Indian Mutiny of 1857, their generals resorted to memories of Cromwell, and to Joshua before him. Even London's sober *Times* newspaper recalled the Amalekites, warning that the rebels' treachery could be purged only by mass bloodshed. Facing what was in part a Muslim jihad, the empire replied with the language of Christian holy war.[27]

Preachers and religious writers created the thought-world that made an Amalekite solution thinkable in India and elsewhere; and in turn, the practical experiences of empire supplied those same religious activists with examples through which to interpret the scripture. Discussing the Old Testament's racial massacres in 1884, Presbyterian scholar Edward Curtis drew modern imperial comparisons. Yes, he conceded, the treatment of the Canaanites seemed harsh, but the "terrible surgery" was necessary to suppress outrageous evil. "Cromwell applied a little of a similar kind; the Indian Mutiny made men desire more," he noted. According to Curtis, many of his contemporaries would have favored the "complete annihilation" of the Muslims who had slaughtered Balkan Christians in the 1870s. For Curtis, the more heartily modern Christians came to accept the idea of extirpation in their own time, the easier it was for them to understand Joshua in his; and vice versa.[28]

Other Protestant cultures evolved their own ideas of "covenant," and with them, comparable attitudes to the native peoples they encountered. The Dutch presence in southern Africa dates from the mid-seventeenth century, and over the decades the region offered refuge to other Protestants dispossessed from Europe. The Calvinist ideas that permeated Afrikaaner society became even stronger when settlers were forced to migrate to new territories deep in the continental interior. In 1838, the Afrikaaners defeated a fearsome Zulu army at the Battle of Blood River, which the victors interpreted as a divine rescue equal to anything that God had granted ancient Israel. Regular commemorations of Blood River began in the 1860s, when clergy preached on the text: "And Moses built an altar, and called the name of it Adonai-nissi." Biblically literate listeners knew how the passage continued: " . . . the LORD will have war with Amalek from generation to generation." The Amalekite label now adhered to Zulus, and more generally to all black Africans.[29]

For the next century and a half, Afrikaaner religious and political theory founded itself wholly in the idea of Israel conquering and building up Canaan as a special land subject to divine covenant, with the anniversary of Blood River as a day of national sanctity, the Day of the Covenant. Part of the covenant was a belief in strict separation from the heathen peoples of the land, a ban that applied especially to sexual relations. In 1938, Afrikaaners commemorated the original trek with a reenactment, which became the basis of a new hard-line white nationalism and a policy of separateness, apartheid. From 1948 through 1994, an Afrikaaner-dominated Nationalist Party ruled South Africa, as apartheid became the focus of worldwide protests. The party found its strongest popular support in the Reformed (Calvinist) churches, where sermons regularly taught doctrines of strict separation and racial supremacy. When Nationalist leaders were not viewing black Africans as Amalekites, they described them more conveniently in the language of the ancient Gibeonites. Africans were destined to be hewers of wood and drawers of water, and should be educated accordingly.[30]

Vernichtung

AMONG GERMANS TOO, WE can trace biblical origins for the language of extermination that became so pervasive during the Holocaust. As in the Dutch case, the story involved the application of biblical concepts to the encounter with black Africans.

Like English-speakers, Germans too knew the idea of extirpation or uprooting, and used the related verb *ausrotten*. This term was consecrated in Luther's great Bible translation of 1545. Not necessarily implying "uprooting" whole peoples, it could be used for cutting an evildoer off from the people, or even for tearing up pagan sacred groves.[31] But Luther did use the word to mean destroying races and nations. While English translators reported that God had "cast out" the seven nations of Canaan, Luther's readers knew that these races had been *ausgerottet*. In later Bible commentaries, enemy races encountered during the conquest were subjected to *Ausrottung*.

German scholars also used another word—namely, *Vernichtung*, or "annihilation"—which was the term for the total destruction under the biblical code of *herem* warfare. *Vernichtung* was the word used in the Elberfelder Bible translation and commentary published in 1871. In Judges, the Hebrew text includes the name Hormah, which is derived from *herem:* the Elberfelder translator renders it as *Vernichtung*. The word implies not just total destruction, but destruction carried out under divine command. The term, later so notorious, appears in the context of Old Testament warfare. In 1897, Jewish scholar Ludwig A. Rosenthal wrote of "the extermination order [*Vernichtungsbefehl*] against Amalek," and the term is used in other commentaries. German scholars of the early twentieth century discussed the total *Vernichtung* of the Canaanites.[32]

Both these biblically resonant words, *Ausrottung* and *Vernichtung*, entered mainstream political usage during the age of imperial expansion and racial conflict. (These were the very years in which

Anglo-American Christians were finding biological justifications for destroying the Canaanites.) In 1870, Friedrich Engels argued that the continued Irish resistance to the British Empire could not be suppressed except by the extermination, *Ausrottung,* of the suppressed race.[33] Engels, of course, was imagining such a scenario as an ultimate nightmare, but other contemporaries saw annihilation as a viable policy, and they drew their terminology from the Bible and its commentaries.

From 1884, imperial Germany expanded its drive to build a great colonial empire in Africa, and like the British and Dutch before them, they justified their acts in terms of spreading the gospel. Cooperating closely with the churches, colonists drew on biblical imagery, which shaped their response to native resistance. The bitterest conflict emerged in South-West Africa, in what is now Namibia. In 1904, the Herero and Nama peoples launched a widespread rebellion, which the Germans met with extreme brutality. They took no prisoners, massacring women and children; African rebels, in contrast, laid down strict limits about which of their enemies might be singled out for attack. German forces acted under a *Vernichtungsbefehl,* the extermination order issued in 1904 by General Lothar von Trotha. The word was intended to recall biblical precedent, and individual German soldiers thoroughly understood the connection. Seeing a murdered child, one major noted that their orders specified that "nothing living was to be spared": everything that breathed must perish. Ultimately, 80 percent of the Herero people died. Even after these tribes were largely destroyed, German policy toward other groups remained unchanged. In 1912, German soldiers and militia turned their attention to the Bushman peoples, who were subjected to what press and officials described as a policy of *Ausrottung.*[34]

Colonial experience established the concept of racial destruction in German military and bureaucratic circles, leaving an inheritance for the next generation. In 1939, Hitler publicly warned of the *Vernichtung* of the Jewish race in Europe, and a death camp like Auschwitz was a *Vernichtungslager*. In their private conversations, however, German leaders preferred to speak of the policy being directed against the Jews as *Ausrottung*. In a speech to SS leaders in 1943, Heinrich Himmler discussed the *Ausrottung* of the Jewish people. Leaders such as Himmler radically distanced themselves from Christianity and despised Christian doctrine, but the Bible gave them the language they needed.[35]

And the People Said "Amen"

IN THE PAST HALF century, Christianity has spread widely in nations of Africa and Asia where the faith is a new planting, and where believers are discovering the Bible for the first time. Usually, when emerging churches read about the evils of Amalek or the Canaanites, they are happy to explore these names as allegories, as symbols of evil impulses to be fought and overcome.

Usually, but not always. In some cases, modern Christians find in these passages justification for real acts of violence against living human beings—rival nations or communities. In the heated politics of modern Nigeria, pastors and prophets invoke biblical stories that can have chilling outcomes. In 1999, a controversial Pentecostal prophet denounced the Nigerian president in words that sounded worryingly specific. God allegedly declared that "[Olusegun] Obasanjo is not your messiah. He is King Agag and the prophetic axe will fall upon his head before May 29." The government took the prophecy seriously enough, given Nigeria's history of assassination and political mayhem, and the prophet was later arrested.[36]

The same story about King Agag and his Amalekite foes featured in a catastrophic context in 1994, during the Rwandan genocide. The Hutu people had determined to annihilate their Tutsi rivals, and they eventually killed perhaps eight hundred thousand. Many of the most determined leaders, the *génocidaires,* drew on Christian inspiration—some in fact were clergy—and they turned to predictable portions of the Bible. Stirring his flock to violence, one pastor preached on 1 Samuel 15:

> He compared the Tutsis to the Amalekites, and said Saul was rejected by God because he failed to exterminate all of the Amalekites. He said "If you don't exterminate the Tutsis, you'll be rejected. If you don't want to be rejected by God, then finish the job of killing the people God has rejected. No child, no wife, no old man should be left alive." And the people said "Amen."[37]

ACTS OF RACIAL VIOLENCE and extermination have complex causes, and no one could blame the bloody texts of the Bible alone for any particular massacre or battle, still less a massive world-historical phenomenon such as the Shoah. The texts are there, but for most readers they are counterbalanced by other, much better known passages that teach a completely different message. No simple chain of causation leads from the existence of a text to a given historical act. Nonetheless, the conquest passages were available when commanders wanted to justify barbaric crimes by presenting them as the divine will.

CHAPTER SIX

Amalekite Nightmares

The opposition of the race of Amalek to the light of Israel is intrinsic, and it has no remedy but annihilation, in order to clear the path of Jewish history of its greatest obstacle.

—RABBI ABRAHAM ISAAC KOOK

THE CHRISTIAN RECORD OF using scripture to justify violence is well known, and the Muslim one much better so. Far less known is the tradition within Judaism of using a particular interpretation of scripture to understand violence and warfare and, on occasion, to drive militant activism.

Although heirs to a common biblical tradition, Jews and Christians historically placed a different emphasis on the bloody texts. While Christians viewed the charge to conquer Canaanites and Amalekites as a warrant for imperial expansion and warfare, Jews saw Amalek as a pervasive force of ultimate evil, a universal foe that needed to be combated in each generation. Such a view is dualistic, in imagining a struggle between absolute forces of good and evil. Through the cumulative disasters of Jewish history, such a doctrine often provided a valuable tool for making sense of pogroms and persecutions, and giving a cosmic meaning to human suffering. Usually, Amalek was (and is) conceived as a spiritual enemy, but on occasion, the struggle against Amalek has meant engaging in acts of direct action and violence in the real world, even acts of vigilantism and extremism. This tradition is today rooted within a network of communities, institutions, and movements.

Of course, this view represents only a small fraction of Jewish thought, whether in Israel or further afield: the vast majority of Jews would be appalled to find that such ideas existed, and would condemn them if they did. Nevertheless, extremist Jewish thinkers have cultivated a theology that justifies violence, and they have done so on the basis of authentic scriptural texts. In the modern state of Israel, readings of such texts—the Amalekite curse, the tale of Phinehas—fuel political controversy, and books such as Numbers and Joshua are at the heart of everyday politics. Whether one is a Jew or not, to be described as an Amalekite or even an ally of Amalek is today a deadly insult, and one that can have lethal consequences.

Holy War

THE IDEA OF WARFARE, holy or otherwise, normally demands the existence of a state, and for most of the past two millennia, no Jewish state existed. But Jewish traditions of holy warfare did not die after the fall of the old kingdom and the exile in Babylon. In the 160s BCE, the Maccabean family led a nationalist revolt against the occupying forces of a Hellenistic pagan empire. When the Maccabean leader Judas took the city of Caspis, he "made unspeakable slaughters," so that a nearby lake ran red with blood: an admiring historian compared his attack to Joshua's seizure of Jericho. The Maccabean (Hasmonean) dynasty ruled from 140 through 37 BCE, and some kings fought as religious leaders, to the point of forcing neighboring peoples to convert to Judaism. Although the kingdom eventually fell under Roman control, such militaristic piety inspired the nationalists who finally launched their great revolt against Rome in 66 CE.[1]

During the long eras of occupation, religious writers continued to dream of holy warfare that would drive out all Gentile invaders. Among the scroll collection found at Qumran, the War Scroll envisages the Sons of Light engaging in a massively destructive holy war against the *Kittim* (pagan) occupiers. Inevitably, the conflict recalls the formal structures of YHWH warfare, although updated to take account of contemporary Roman tactics.[2] The sense of a near-terminal national crisis created a passion for apocalyptic literature, with its vision of an ultimate cosmic war of the forces of good and evil. Such texts, which became common over the next two centuries, borrowed freely from biblical visions of *herem* warfare, and these in turn had a profound influence on Christian apocalyptic.[3]

The tradition of *herem* continued to influence practical politics on those occasions when popular risings again created Jewish states, however transient. During the great revolts against Rome, Jewish forces tried to annihilate or expel all Gentile communities from the land. In the seventh century, a similar impulse stirred a total war against Palestine's Christian population, leading to mass killings.[4] Although we cannot be sure about the specifically religious motivation, this may well have been the last instance in which any Jewish force tried to implement the Deuteronomic war code in its full force. In later centuries, the *herem* or ban became a religious interdiction, a strict rabbinic prohibition comparable to excommunication in the Catholic Church. The daring seventeenth-century thinker Baruch Spinoza was subject to a nonlethal *herem* of this sort.

The idea of holy warfare was a potent reality in the Second Temple era, and the spontaneous vigilantism associated with Phinehas became all the more popular during the Jewish subjection to Hellenistic and Roman empires. The book of Sirach or Ecclesiasticus (a second-century-BCE text) cited Phinehas as "third in glory" after Moses and Aaron. When Mattathias, father of Judas Maccabeus, assassinated Greek royal officials and initiated the national uprising, the Book of Maccabees compared him to Phinehas. Likewise,

Phinehas was the role model for the fanatically anti-Roman Zealot movement, the *Kana'im*.[5]

Long after the fall of Jerusalem, Jewish thinkers lauded Phinehas as an exemplar of devoted service to God's cause. According to a Targum (an elaborated translation) on the original passage in Numbers 25, God promised, "I will make Phinehas the angel of the covenant, that he may live forever to proclaim redemption at the end of days." As a messianic figure, Phinehas overlapped with Elijah in popular belief. Such a tradition kept alive the option of violence in God's cause: "If a man sheds the blood of the wicked, it is as though he had offered a sacrifice." One Talmudic text lists the most severe violations of holy law, which demanded immediate violent retaliation by a latter-day Phinehas, described as *Kanai ben Kanai*—a Zealot, the son of a Zealot—who would appease God's anger. Among these ultimate offenses for Jews is sex with a Syrian (Gentile) woman.[6]

The Eternal Amalekite

READING THE VIOLENT TEXTS posed many problems for later Jewish scholars, who found here a God that radically contradicted their image of a just and loving deity. As I will describe, they struggled to find means of softening the accounts in order to prevent latter-day zealots imitating this ancient violence. Some of their solutions were obvious enough; others, more ingenious. Even if God did command violence against the Canaanites, for instance, this was of no possible relevance to later generations, as the Canaanites had ceased to exist.[7]

But the Amalekites posed a very different problem of interpretation. Moses, we recall, went far beyond merely placing a curse on Amalek. Rather, he quoted God's two clear declarations on the subject: he, God personally, promised eternal struggle against Amalek, and he swore to blot out that nation's name. Far from being a mysterious isolated story in scripture, that theme surfaces repeatedly in Jewish lore and tradition.[8]

One highly respected figure in modern Orthodox Judaism is Rabbi Norman Lamm, chancellor of New York City's Yeshiva University, who presents a moral conundrum. Just suppose, he says, that a young Jew goes to a rabbi to report that, based on infallible genetic evidence, he can prove that his neighbor is a direct descendant of the Amalekites. What should the rabbi advise the young man? Should he tell him to follow the biblical command by executing his neighbor? If he did so, what would distinguish that rabbi from the Islamist mullahs who justified the September 11 attacks?[9] Rabbi Lamm was obviously not suggesting that an actual modern rabbi would ever face such an agonizing case of conscience, if only because no such absolute genetic proof of Amalekite descent could ever be found. Rather, he was using the example to explore an apparent contradiction between an explicit command of the law, and the overwhelming power of morality as it has shaped Judaism over the millennia. For one thing, the Amalekite passages flatly violate later Jewish thinking about the rules of humane warfare. We seem to be confronting "a blatant case of law versus morality," a moral and intellectual problem Lamm did his scholarly best to unravel.

But the author was unquestionably right in his basic assumption, that a powerful Jewish tradition commanded eternal enmity against a particular race, and ordered the use of violence in that conflict. Apart from the Exodus passage, the Amalekite theme surfaces in the interpretations of the book of Esther. That work tells the story of the evil counselor Haman, who plots to kill the Jews, but is prevented by the wise Mordecai and the good Queen Esther. The book has many oddities: this is for instance the only biblical book never to mention the word "God," while it also marks the first literary appearance of the word "Jew." But the story has always been a favorite, commemorated in the popular festival of Purim. Jews worldwide know Purim as an opportunity for celebration, for dressing up and general silliness. Even the sober Talmud commends the custom of drinking wine until you can no longer tell the difference between "Arur Haman!" (Cursed be Haman) and "Barukh Mordekhai!" (Blessed be Mordecai).[10]

A casual reader would miss the linkage between the book of Esther and the Amalekite mythology. The book identifies Haman as an Agagite, probably referring to his place of origin, but later tradition understood the word to mean that he was a descendant of King Agag, and thus an Amalekite. When Esther is read today, Jewish listeners use loud groggers to make noise whenever Haman's name is mentioned, in a literal fulfillment of the command to "blot out the name of Amalek." In the Midrash, Haman recounts the whole story of Moses and Joshua from an Amalekite viewpoint, culminating in the killing of "my ancestor Agag . . . and so [Samuel] inflicted on him an unnatural death." In retaliation for that ancient killing, Haman would now pursue the vendetta against all living Jews, pursuing exactly the kind of eternal war against Israel that God claimed to be waging against the Amalekites. Orthodox synagogues read the account of Saul and Agag on the Sabbath before Purim.[11] Esther, in this reading, tells a story of transgenerational race war, which manifests itself in ferocious bloodletting that features not at all in modern Purim celebrations.[12]

Quite apart from the words of scripture, the message was reinforced by the very greatest minds of Judaism. According to the Midrash Rabbah, when the Israelites entered the Promised Land they had to obey three key commandments—namely, to blot out the memory of Amalek, to set a king over them, and to build a temple. The Amalekite clause ranked first.[13] In interpreting these commands, Jewish sages have reached some far-reaching conclusions. The Mekhilta, an interpretation of Exodus, raises the hatred of Amalek to cosmic proportions, declaring that "neither the name nor the throne [of God] is complete until the seed of Amalek is destroyed." In the twelfth century CE, Maimonides urged Jews always to remember Amalek's attack on Israel in the wilderness: "We are to speak of this at all times, and to arouse the people to make war upon him, and bid them to hate him, and that hatred of him be not weakened or lessened with the passage of time." The conflict with Amalek would follow civilized rules: Jews were to demand that Amalek accept the universal laws handed down to Noah and pay a special tax to the Jewish people, so that their lives would be spared. But if they refused these offers, then Maimonides took seriously the prospect of a future war that would literally, rather than spiritually, pit the forces of Israel against Amalek.[14]

Other sages used the story of Agag as a warning against excessive scruples in obeying God's clear commands. Later generations, they said, should not "be righteous overmuch." Some commentators warned that excessive moral tenderness would cause even more harm in the long run. In the words of Rabbi Simeon ben Lakish, "Whoever acts compassionately where cruelty is called for will act cruelly when compassion is required."[15] Moral qualms should never get in the way of undertaking violence if and when one believes that God has commanded it; and in such extraordinary circumstances, compassion is an act of blasphemous disobedience.

Jewish sages through the centuries strove mightily to avoid the inhumane implications of those arguments, and the perilous idea of attributing hereditary blood-guilt to any group whatever. Talmudic scholars argued at length whether Amalekite descendants could not just be tolerated, but might actually be permitted to convert to Judaism. While some thought not, they faced a powerful counterargument from the tradition that descendants of Haman himself had learned Torah! However explicit the scriptural texts, believers could not avoid reading them through evolving ideas of faith and justice. Yet despite this noble tradition, the darkest concept of Amalek as a deadly enemy would often resurface to shape attitudes in the worldly sphere.

Interpreting Amalek

BUT IF AMALEK IS to be hated from generation to generation, which particular individuals should be the target of that loathing? It has been at least two thousand years since a specific tribe or nation claimed that ethnic label. At least from the time of the Roman Empire, Amalek has been a free-floating designation that in particular eras has been applied to the deadliest enemies of the Jewish people, and specifically to any nation that makes a concerted effort to conquer or destroy the Jews. Rabbis used Amalek as a code to designate the Roman Empire, just as the Christians of that era disguised Rome under the title of Babylon. In 1898, Palestine's chief rabbi refused to meet the visiting German kaiser because of a tradition that the Germans were descended from Amalek—and that was long before Germany identified itself so powerfully with anti-Jewish causes.[16]

Later generations of Jews applied the name to Christian persecutors, and of course to the German Nazis. If they want to destroy us, said Jewish thinkers, they must be Amalek. When an Israeli court sentenced Nazi mass murderer Adolf Eichmann for his role in the Holocaust, he appealed for clemency to that nation's president. In 1962, president Yitzhak ben-Zvi denied the petition, quoting in his reply Samuel's words to King Agag: "As your sword bereaved women, so will your mother be bereaved among women." Eichmann must die, like other Amalekites before him.[17]

Amalek was and is far more than a codeword or an insult. As a force of supernatural evil, Amalek became a close parallel to the Christian notion of the Antichrist. Both ideas claimed at least some scriptural basis, but they enjoyed vastly different degrees of attention at different times and places. For most believers in most cultures, the ideas were distant or irrelevant; but both titles, Amalek and Antichrist, came to the fore in times of stress and crisis, when they became intimately linked to apocalyptic themes of the final cosmic struggle. Both images served to teach believers that their sufferings had an ultimate significance in the divine plan, and that God would eventually intervene to vindicate his own. Secure in this knowledge, believers gained the courage to resist oppression, by armed force if necessary. But viewing one's enemies in these supernatural terms could have dire consequences for the conduct of real-world warfare. If your worldly enemies are literally of the Devil, then there is little need to treat them humanely.

The New Israel

IN MODERN TIMES, THE idea of Amalek faded for most Jews, at least as long as persecution stayed safely remote. A potent tradition spiritualized Amalek, identifying it not as a people but as an evil tendency—one that would remain until the messianic age and the time of redemption. In the United States, for instance, that interpretation prevailed among most non-Orthodox Jews, while few ordinary nonexpert believers even knew the relevant passages.

But the Amalek theme reemerged powerfully in segments of twentieth-century Judaism, as the Jewish people passed through a series of revolutionary changes that were often catastrophic—the Holocaust itself, the uprooting of East European and Middle Eastern communities, and the turmoil surrounding the birth of the state of Israel. In its origins, Zionism was a secular movement with a powerful socialist element, which coexisted uneasily with far more determined religious activists. Over time, though, those activists grew in numbers and influence, and their supernatural worldview became a potent factor in the politics of the new state. For the first time in centuries, religious radicals found themselves in a political state in which they stood a realistic chance of establishing their views as state policy.

One guiding force in modern Jewish Orthodoxy was Rabbi Abraham Isaac Kook (1865–1935), first Ashkenazic chief rabbi under the British Mandate for Palestine. In contrast to the secular Zionists, Rav Kook freely used supernatural language to demonize actual or potential enemies. He bemoaned the "stupid" policy that led the Jews to fail to exterminate altogether the native inhabitants of historic Canaan, and that led to the Canaanites' evils infecting the Jewish people. Nor did he think such harshness demanded apology:

> Why did we deal with them cruelly? We cannot imagine
> how dark and base the world would have become if not for
> this cruelty of ours, just as we cannot imagine how evil and
> reprehensible it would have been but for the pure illumination
> of the Lord's Light and Ways, with which we enlightened [the
> world] through our historical progress.[18]

Reading these words, Simone Weil, a later convert to Catholic Christianity, suggested that if Kook's views had prevailed in any actual historical society, they would have meant doom for any rival religions that existed under Jewish rule. Kook was presenting a charter for persecution at best, genocide at worst.[19]

Kook's many pupils and followers soon acquired great influence. In 1924, the rabbi founded a Jerusalem yeshiva, or seminary, Mercaz haRav, which has up to the present day produced some of the most extreme Jewish activists. His tradition was kept alive by his son, Tzvi Yehuda Kook, who taught that the Jewish return to the Holy Land promised to inaugurate the messianic age. For the Kooks and their disciples, modern Jews were literally living in the End Times of the old cosmic order.[20]

Radical and apocalyptic ideas reached a wide public as the growing Orthodox religious element in the Israeli population became more prominent. The most extreme wing of contemporary Judaism is the *haredim*—literally, those who tremble before God—who are commonly described as the ultra-Orthodox. Today, Israel is home to perhaps seven hundred thousand *haredim,* or one-eighth of the nation's Jewish population. Perhaps a half million more *haredim* live in the United States. Because their families tend to be very large, *haredim* represent an ever-larger proportion of the Jewish population both in Israel and worldwide. Within twenty years, they could easily represent 30 percent of Israel's Jews, a hugely influential bloc in a powerful (and nuclear-armed) nation. By 2050, *haredim* will be approaching majority status.[21]

A Land to Conquer

RELIGIOUS POLITICS GAINED NEW force after the Six Day War of 1967, when Israeli forces conquered the city of Jerusalem and the West Bank of the Jordan. Israel now came to rule the whole of old Palestine, and both Jews and Christians viewed these events in apocalyptic terms. The 1967 war gave a massive boost to evangelical Christian involvement in American politics. Many Jews too, especially among the ultra-Orthodox, saw a fulfillment of biblical prophecy and gained new hope for an imminent messianic age.[22] Israel's 1977 election marked a new era of rightist and fiercely nationalist governments, who allied with extreme religious parties. Extremists dreamed of reconstructing the Israeli state on the basis of Halacha, Jewish ritual law, in a close parallel to the Sharia state sought by Islamists. One militant in this cause was Rabbi Mordechai Eliyahu, a former member of an extremist "zealot" group, who in 1983 became Israel's Sephardic chief rabbi.

In this heady atmosphere, religious Jews moved to occupy and settle the conquered lands in obedience to God's command. Some argued that the divine mandate stretched even further, to lands currently occupied by Jordan and Syria. The settler movement Gush

Emunim (the Bloc of the Faithful) became a major force on the Israeli far right, and its members found their primary inspiration in
the Kooks. Also on the hard right were other militant and military-
oriented groups, which have usually been U.S.-derived and U.S.-
funded, notably the followers of Rabbi Meir Kahane. Meeting protests or violence from Arab residents, settlers and their supporters
formed a paramilitary underground, which undertook terrorist attacks.[23] Militant groups seek not only the expropriation of non-Jewish
land, but the expulsion ("transfer") of non-Jews from what should be
a pure Jewish state. The ultra-Orthodox use two biblical analogies
to justify such policies. In dealing with the peoples of the land, the
Palestinian Arabs, they turn to the texts about driving out the tribes
of ancient Canaan. When such schemes encounter resistance, as they
must, enemies are reframed in still darker terms as Amalek.[24]

Such activities cause real alarm among moderate and liberal Israelis, who constitute the vast majority of the population. Israeli
media, in fact, do an excellent job of exposing and confronting
Jewish extremism, especially when it promotes violence. The Israeli
government has through the years banned the most extreme factions as overtly terrorist, racist, and antidemocratic.[25]

The extremism of such groups can surprise Westerners who
think of Israel only as a bastion of liberal democracy. When Western observers discuss Middle Eastern affairs, they often use the
Israeli-founded Internet source MEMRI, the Middle East Media
Research Institute, which collects and translates the most shocking and homicidal statements of Muslim leaders and activists.[26]
MEMRI performs a valuable public service, allowing Islamists to
condemn themselves out of their own mouths. Lacking in these
explorations of "Middle East Media," though, are any comparable
selections from Israeli or Jewish activists, which offer many parallels
to these outrageous statements. It is difficult to find a sentiment uttered by Islamist agitators that does not have an exact parallel on the
far reaches of Jewish extremism.

Arabs as Amalekites

FROM THE EARLY DAYS of the new state, Israeli leaders spoke of Arab enemies as Amalek, but without the sophisticated theological agenda of later years. In 1956, even the secular-minded David Ben-Gurion responded to threats from Egypt's leader Gamal Abdel Nasser by declaring that "the hosts of Amalek from north, east and south, who are now concentrating on the other side of our border, [will not] be able to subdue us." Ben-Gurion harked back to Joshua as the founder of the Jewish military tradition, suggesting that Israel could expect a revival of those age-old battles. When Israel developed ballistic missiles in the 1960s, they bore the name Jericho, recalling Joshua's triumph: today, that country's Jericho-3 missiles are the mainstay of its nuclear forces.[27]

Such ancient analogies were still more common among extreme nationalists such as Menachem Begin, who saw Jewish history as a constant struggle against the forces of Amalek. In his vision, Arabs had inherited the Nazi right to bear this title. Rabbinic leaders, meanwhile, developed a theology to support the rhetoric. In the lead-up to the 1967 war, Amalek theory was restated and further broadened by Joseph Ber Soloveitchik, the heir of a prestigious rabbinic dynasty. Responding to the prospect of a new war against Arab states, Soloveitchik declared that "when a people emblazons on its banner, 'Come and let us cut them off from being a nation, that the name of Israel may no longer be in remembrance,' it becomes, thereby, Amalek." Gush Emunim statements concur that "in every generation there is an Amalek."[28]

Such ideas became standard fare for the settler movement after 1967. Extremists described Arabs as Canaanites and Amalekites, whose only possible position within the Israeli state would be as humble tributaries or subject peoples. This is close to the subordinate status of *dhimmi*s, or protected peoples, which radical Islamists seek to impose on all non-Muslim residents in Muslim-ruled societies. One leader of the Jewish settler movement proclaimed, "The Palestinians are Amalek. We will destroy them. We won't kill them all. But we will destroy their ability to think as a nation." When Palestinian leader Yasser Arafat died in 2004, a federation of hard-right Jewish religious leaders celebrated the death of "the Amalek and the Hitler of our generation."[29]

Biblical analogies circulate far from the lunatic fringe. Conservative rabbi Jack Reimer, for instance, is a highly respected mainstream U.S. figure who in the 1990s had some well-publicized interactions with Bill Clinton. In 2006, though, Reimer invoked the Amalek idea as a means of understanding contemporary political realities. Although he was not attacking Muslims or Arabs in general, he described his conviction that

> Islamic Fundamentalism, or, as some people prefer to call it, "Islamo-fascism," is the most dangerous force that we have ever faced and that it is worthy of the name: Amalek. We must recognize who Amalek is in our generation, and we must prepare to fight it in every way we can. And may God help us in this task.[30]

Name-calling has consequences. Some activists went far beyond Reimer in applying the Amalekite label to Palestinians in general, and if that perception was true, then these enemies must be fought and eliminated. Such rhetoric is remarkably commonplace in Israel's extreme right, although activists differ on whether they mean mass killing or total expulsion. In 1980, the student magazine of Bar Ilan University included an incendiary article by a rabbi under the title "Genocide: A Commandment of the Torah." The author foretold that "the day is not far when we shall all be called to this holy war, to this commandment of the annihilation of Amalek"—namely, the Palestinians. Another rabbi writing in support of the violent settler underground used the same ethnic analogy, before quoting the passage from Numbers 33 in which God commands the expulsion of "all the inhabitants of the land."[31]

Although we are discussing ideological and religious claims, the issue of whether the Palestinians are in fact Canaanite in any scientific or ethnic sense is controversial. (As far as I know, nobody claims Amalekite blood.) Genetically, much of the Palestinian Arab population has local roots dating back to prehistoric times, and undoubtedly has some ancestry among the Canaanite peoples who occupied the land before Joshua, as well as among older Jewish populations. Some Palestinians themselves stress their Canaanite genealogy, in order to reinforce their claims as deep-rooted ancient owners of the land. Other Arab thinkers warn, though, that the Canaanite affirmation is dangerous, because it meshes with Jewish claims about the age-old racial struggle for the Holy Land. Whatever the ethnic realities, one ironic consequence of Zionism has been to cause Arabs to define themselves as Canaanites, restoring a national identity that had been absent from the world for millennia.[32]

Sacred Violence

ACTIVIST INVOCATIONS OF AMALEK become acutely more intense in Israel during periods of crisis and armed conflict. One such escalation of rhetoric occurred during the second Intifada, the Palestinian uprising that began in 2000. In 2001, Hebrew University law professor Eliav Shochetman published a controversial essay on the "Contemporary Lessons from an Ancient Midrash." The text in question involved Saul's questioning of God's extermination order, which called forth the rebuke, "Be not righteous overmuch." Shochetman warned modern Israelis to avoid any tendency toward compassion that could prove destructive in the long term: "One must fulfill the commandment of the obliteration of Amalek even, if in terms of his feelings, it seems cruel." Although Shochetman rejected a racial campaign against Arabs as such, he urged a total "Amalekite" war against organizations hostile to Israel.[33]

Such ferocious language reached new heights following a 2008 attack by a lone Palestinian who killed several teenage students at the Kook-founded Mercaz haRav yeshiva. Responding to the incident, some religious leaders used overtly racist rhetoric. Extremist rabbi Mordechai Eliyahu declared that "the life of one yeshiva boy is worth more than the lives of a thousand Arabs." For Mois Navon, an alumnus of Mercaz haRav, the students had been "mercilessly gunned down by a raging beast called Amalek." Yisrael Rosen, a highly regarded Orthodox leader, wrote that mere humans could not "flee from this Divine commandment [to fight Amalek] even if we hide under the wings of 'the family of nations' and even if the commandment is difficult for us to bear and we have been discouraged." In such a struggle, the only real sin would be excessive compassion:

> Those who slaughter students poring over their Torah, those who rain Qassams [rockets] down indiscriminately on men, women, old and young, babes and sucklings—those who hail the destruction of Israel and dance on the blood, are Amalek in our generation. . . . [O]nly with hostility, and by conquering our humane emotions that are contrary to that, will we be victorious.[34]

When Israeli armed forces invaded the Palestinian territory of Gaza in 2009, rabbis accompanying them were well stocked with pamphlets and propaganda expounding the war in religious/racial terms, and framing the confrontation in the biblical language of reconquest. Rabbi Eliyahu justified actions that might lead to the death of Arab civilians, quoting a ruthless passage from Psalm 18: "I have pursued mine enemies, and overtaken them: neither did I turn again till they were consumed."[35]

The extremist subculture has driven religiously motivated acts of terrorism by individuals and small groups. Scholar Elliott Horowitz has traced a strand of Jewish religious violence against Arabs and Muslims, but also against Christians of any ethnic background. Such attacks usually occur at or near the feast of Purim. Apart from commemorating the defeat of Haman's Amalekites, the feast also involves a casting off of restraints and restrictions. Some ultra-Orthodox, particularly students at extremist yeshivas, insult Christian clergy in the streets, spitting on the priests or on the crosses they bear, which they define as "abominations."[36]

The most notorious manifestation of ethnic violence occurred on the day of Purim, the 14th of Adar, in 1994, when U.S.-born doctor Baruch Goldstein entered a mosque in the city of Hebron and massacred twenty-nine Arab worshippers with an automatic rifle. The attack cast a long shadow on regional affairs. Among other things, it galvanized support for the most extreme activists of the Palestinian Hamas, and it directly inspired the organizers of the later suicide bombing campaign. Although utterly condemned by Israeli authorities, Goldstein was a hero to Jewish extremists, who memorialized "the holy Baruch Goldstein" in a plaque near his grave.[37]

Jews as Amalekites

JEWISH EXTREMISTS DO NOT confine their campaigns to attacking Arabs and Muslims. As Rabbi Lamm observed, in trying to show the moral and intellectual perils of the Amalek doctrine, the concept is infinitely expandable. Lamm deliberately takes the argument to a "bizarre and absurd conclusion." First, Jews are commanded to destroy the literal people of Amalek; but then they must strike at those other peoples whose behavior is like that of Amalek—that is, every nation under the sun that has ever demonstrated anti-Semitism. But even then, with the globe half-emptied, true zealots would have only just begun, as they would then turn their attention to secular

Jews. Next would come the turn of religious Jews whose faith is not quite what the strictest Orthodox think it should be. Actually, in terms of their condemnations, rather than of actual violence, that is a fair description of how some extremists have escalated the biblical commands.[38]

As the ultra-Orthodox have grown, so they have become ever more strident in denouncing mainstream or secular Jews who, they believe, fall short of the theocratic standards that are demanded of the new Israel. Particularly sensitive are violations of the Sabbath and definitions of Jewish conversion that fall short of the strictest standards of Orthodoxy. Moreover, any talk of conceding sovereignty over the least part of Greater Palestine is regarded as an ultimate treason. Although most such controversies are peaceful (though contentious), they have demonstrated a real potential to ignite violence between Jews. The most extreme example to date occurred in 1995 when an ultra-Orthodox assassin murdered Israeli Prime Minister Yitzhak Rabin, whom he hated for his role in peace negotiations with Arab states. When in 2005 Israel was considering a partial removal of settlements, Mordechai Eliyahu warned that "any Prime Minister in Israel who would dare to damage the Land of Israel or disengage from further parts of it will find himself disengaging from this world."[39]

Extremists customarily use the Bible to justify their acts. *Haredim* engage in intimidation and mob actions against secular Jews, stoning cars being driven on the Sabbath and beating their drivers. The ultras cite the example of Phinehas, who likewise witnessed a blasphemous act that threatened the nation, and who undertook instant direct action. In turning to Phinehas, they echo Rav Abraham Kook. In the words of a modern admirer, "Rav Kook explained that the Torah does not ordinarily approve of such acts of zealotry. Only if they were discharged purely for the sake of Heaven are they sanctioned." Of course, that "only" gives a huge amount of leeway to individual activists to decide that their cause is that of God.[40]

Phinehas's example resurfaced in national politics in 1996, when Israel's Sephardic chief rabbi denounced Reform Jews for their departures from orthodoxy. He cited Zimri, the victim of Phinehas's righteous wrath: "Zimri was the first Reform Jew who contended it was possible to assimilate the People of Israel through conversion [of non-Jews]." While the rabbi denied advocating violence, he fully endorsed Phinehas's acts: "As a result of Zimri's actions, there was a plague on Israel. It is written that Phinehas understood drastic steps were needed to stop the plague."[41]

Jews, evidently, could become Amalekites or Midianites. At least since the early twentieth century, some Orthodox rabbis have applied the Amalekite label to Jewish secularizers, and modern *haredim* have continued that identification. When the Israeli government threatened to conscript yeshiva students into the armed forces, *haredi* newspapers denounced the regime as Amalek. When Israeli activists sought to organize Gay Pride demonstrations, *haredim* called for a War Against Amalek, which took the practical form of vandalism and street riots.[42] Visiting extremist settlers in 2004, U.S. journalist Jeffrey Goldberg heard the Amalekite taint being applied even to then–Prime Minister Ariel Sharon, whom most regarded as a hard-line Zionist in his own right. For one settler woman, though, "the Amalekite spirit is everywhere. It's not just the Arabs. . . . Sharon isn't Amalek, but he works for Amalek. . . . Sharon is forfeiting his right to live."[43]

Like the invocation of Phinehas, such Amalekite comparisons could be lethally threatening. In 2000, a typical controversy was raging between the *haredim* and the government, with Education Minister Yossi Sarid as the lightning rod of ultra-Orthodox protest. Sarid was denounced in fiery terms by Rabbi Ovadia Yosef, one of Israel's most prestigious religious figures and the spiritual adviser to the powerful far-right religious party Shas. Rabbi Yosef, in other words, is not a marginal crank. Speaking shortly before Purim, he compared minister Sarid to Satan before asking,

> [How] long do we have to suffer this wicked man? God will
> extirpate him, the way he will extirpate Amalek. Cursed is
> Haman, cursed is Yossi Sarid. He will be uprooted from the
> seed of Israel. Just as revenge was wrought on Haman, so it
> will be wrought on him.

Secular Israelis condemned the inflammatory terms of the attack, as
did non-Orthodox religious leaders.[44]

Think Amalek

THE EXTREMIST FOCUS ON biblical images of evil makes it exceedingly difficult for Israeli governments to contemplate any compromise peace that would yield sovereignty over any part of Palestine.
From the radical-right stance, such a concession would not only
mean negotiating with Amalek, but actively collaborating with it.
Also dangerous is the ultra-Orthodox determination to remove vestiges of that enemy alien authority on Jewish land, including the
Muslim sacred sites on what Jews call the Temple Mount in Jerusalem. Jewish extremists have repeatedly plotted to destroy such
cherished sites, including the Dome of the Rock and the al-Aqsa
mosque. Such an attack, if successful, would likely provoke a massive global reaction against Israel, a wave of fury that could destabi-
lize and radicalize moderate Muslim nations. The resulting situation
could only be described with the religious language of apocalypse.
Speaking of Iran, Benjamin Netanyahu has reasonably warned that
a "messianic apocalyptic cult" should never control nuclear weapons, but that term surely applies equally to some extremists on the
Jewish far right.[45]

The idea of Amalek, with its visions of apocalyptic struggle,
might yet contribute to far-reaching global confrontations. As the
state of Israel has maintained absolute military supremacy within

the Middle East, both Israelis and their enemies understand that this position could be challenged only by weapons of mass destruction, which conjure visions of apocalyptic confrontation. Once a nation has decided that an enemy does not follow reason or self-interest, but is an agent of cosmic evil, the prospects for peace become remote, whether that evil is framed in terms of Amalek or the Antichrist. If, for instance, Israel decides that Iran has assumed the role of Amalek, then that enemy becomes a symbol of all that is evil in humanity, and one that must be fought and defeated, at whatever cost.

FOR JEWS, AS FOR Christians and Muslims, the critical fact is not the existence of bloody scriptures, but rather the uses to which they are put within the evolving tradition of the religion. The scriptures that incite some to violence are quite familiar to other readers, who nevertheless draw totally different conclusions. The fact that a minority of activists derive harsh and violent ideas from the scriptures of Judaism, or any other faith, has no implications whatever for evaluating that religion, or the texts on which it is based.

PART III

Truth and Reconciliation

The greater our homage for the Scripture, the more
decided must be our condemnation of what the
truth of Scripture itself teaches us to condemn.

—AUGUSTINE

*For two thousand years, the lethal commands that God reportedly issued
in the time of Moses and Joshua have gravely troubled believers, to the
point that some at least have revolted against the whole idea of scriptural
authority. So strong has the reaction been, so widespread, that we must
ask an obvious question: Why is it not universal? To the contrary, why
do so many believers seem so untroubled about living with the texts?
How have they dealt with the moral and theological dilemmas?*

CHAPTER SEVEN

Judging God

Among the detestable villains that in any period of the world have disgraced the name of man, it is impossible to find a greater than Moses, if this account be true. Here is an order to butcher the boys, to massacre the mothers, and debauch the daughters!

—THOMAS PAINE

AT LEAST SINCE THE Enlightenment, the horrors of the conquest of Canaan by the Israelites have served as prime exhibits in the trial and condemnation of the Judeo-Christian God. A. A. Milne, better known for describing the world of Winnie the Pooh, made an astute theological point:

> The Old Testament is responsible for more atheism,
> agnosticism, disbelief—call it what you will—than any book
> ever written: It has emptied more churches than all the
> counter-attractions of cinema, motor bicycle, and golf course.[1]

More recently, a number of so-called New Atheist authors have mocked what they regard as the absurdities of religion. Reading the Old Testament, Richard Dawkins, Christopher Hitchens, and Sam Harris find not a source of inspiration or a model for conduct, but rather a catalyst for horror and bafflement. How, they ask, can any sane person reconcile such atrocities with a belief in a just or loving God?

That question is anything but new. Contrary to the claims of modern-day secularists, it is not only an enlightened modern-day audience, armed with the tools of historical criticism, which notes the moral difficulties in the Bible. At many points over the past two thousand years, readers have been so repelled that they rejected the unfathomable divine commands, to the point of repudiating orthodox faith. If asked how they possibly could reconcile the very different images of God found in various parts of the Bible, many believers through history have answered simply: perhaps they can't.

Jewish philosopher Martin Buber reported meeting an observant Jew and confessing to him that he could not accept the story of Saul and Agag. "Nothing," wrote Buber, "can make me believe in a God who punishes Saul because he has not murdered his enemy." He was startled to find that, far from condemning his skepticism, his more traditional-minded friend shared his qualms. Buber continued, "There is in the end nothing astonishing in the fact that an observant Jew of this nature, when he has to choose between God and the Bible, chooses God: the God in whom he believes, Him in whom he can believe."[2] Among both Jews and Christians, that kind of response, a willingness to choose a particular concept of God over the scriptural text, has long been a powerful force driving alternative forms of faith and eventually reshaping mainstream perceptions.

For those through history who spurned the God of Moses and Joshua, different responses were possible. One was to reject the Bible altogether, as well as any religion that claimed to be rooted in such atrocities. But within the Christian tradition, some struggling believers adopted what they believed to be a more nuanced attitude, distinguishing between the repugnant texts of the Old Testament and the more acceptable books. In terms foreshadowing modern debates over the Qur'an, at least some Christians tried to tear the hateful passages from their own scripture, and to reconstruct the religion based on what remained.

Some radicals held that the different biblical texts clash so much that they constitute two different scriptures, proclaiming two distinct Gods. The atrocities of the Bible are cherished texts for atheists, secularists, and enemies of Western religion; but they also fostered the views of the Gnostics, the Dualists, and other long-powerful movements that tried to stay within the Christian fold. Moreover, the struggle to reconcile different texts inspired some to seek solutions far short of the extreme heretical movements. If not driven to invent different gods, Christians for centuries have been forced by the dark passages to seek the limits of their belief in biblical authority, and of the Bible as a revealed scripture. By forcing theologians to come to terms with modern challenges, these texts have sparked critical changes within Christianity.

Dark Father

MANY SELF-DESCRIBED CHRISTIANS WHO condemned Joshua's God have tried to remain faithful followers of Jesus, a feat that puzzles both infidels and orthodox Christians alike. Yet historically, this option enjoyed wide popularity, to the point that we can properly describe it as a whole alternative form of Christianity. God, for these other believers, is Goodness and Light, a description that could never be applied to the deity that slaughtered the people of Canaan and Midian.[3]

These alternative Christians are known by various names, and it is easy to get lost in the maze of heresies, movements, and "-isms" that litter accounts of church history—all the varieties of Gnostics, Cainites, Sethites, Dualists, and others. As the Christian Great Church developed, the newly defined orthodox saw those other believers as deadly rivals for the loyalty of the faithful. But for all the attention that Gnostics have received in recent years, all the theories that scholars have advanced to explain their appeal, much of the strength of alternative Christianities lay in their attempt to explain the nagging contradictions of the Bible.[4]

Many early Christians encountering the New Testament believed they had found a radical disconnect with large portions of the Old. From a very early stage within the Jesus movement, some drew an absolute distinction between the good God of the New Testament, who was revealed in Christ, and the inferior and capricious deity of the Old Testament, who proclaimed himself as YHWH. Various sects gave this older God different names—some called him Ialdabaoth, others referred to the Craftsman, or the *Demiourgos* (Demiurge). No ancient thinker ever actually named him the Dark Father, but that *Star Wars*–resonant image (Darth Vader) gives a fair idea of his character.[5]

Gnostic sects created complex mythologies to explain how these different Gods had come into existence. They stressed the process of illusion or deception through which the lesser deity had fooled humanity into believing that he was absolute and indeed the One True God, and had subsequently convinced whole peoples of that silly creed. Gnostics—literally, "those who know"—were the ones who had freed themselves of the delusion. Usually, this division was associated with a deeply pessimistic view of the material world, which was the creation of the lesser God.

For Gnostic believers, Christ revealed the world of Spirit, and came to free his followers from the snares of the material creation and its God. By definition, the idea of a conflict between the Gods of the Old and New Testaments involved an absolute rejection of Judaism and the Jewish law. In the second century, the Syrian Gnostic Saturninus taught that "the God of the Jews was one of the angels. . . . Christ came to destroy the God of the Jews, but to save such as believe in him; that is, those who possess the spark of his life." Gnostics assumed and exaggerated the radical newness of Jesus's message, while darkening as best they could the substance of the old Law.[6]

For these critics, the Old Testament was a cancer demanding radical surgery. By the frank admission of his followers, the old God was a murderer who had killed the Egyptians in the Red Sea, who had commanded the mass slaughter of Canaanites and others. Some early movements so thoroughly rejected this deity that they venerated those biblical figures who rebelled against him, including Cain. Jesus was another in a long line of insurgents struggling against that old God, the lord of *this* world. For the Syrian teacher Cerdo, around 130, Christ came "to abolish the rule and the tyranny of the Demiurge who made the world."[7] Of course the books of Moses and Joshua were atrocious and shocking: their God was a devil in all but name.

Two Bibles

AMONG EARLY ADVOCATES OF a two-God theory, the most celebrated was Marcion, who came from Pontus in what is now northern Turkey. Even his deadliest foes admit his prominence in the Christian community: about 140, he almost became bishop of Rome.[8]

His views were truly radical. Marcion found in the Old Testament a God who was "the author of evils," one who was seen "to take delight in war, to be infirm of purpose, and even to be contrary to Himself." Marcion pointed out logical contradictions and improbabilities throughout the Old Testament, applying rational analysis to a text he found absurd. God forbade idolatry and the making of graven images; he then ordered Moses to erect the bronze figure of a serpent in order to safeguard the Israelites in the wilderness—and so on.[9]

The main thrust of his critique was on moral grounds, directed against a God who acted like a capricious tyrant. Marcion loathed the idea of God hardening the hearts of his victims, making them commit evils for which he could then punish them. Marcion had a clear preference for those on the losing side in the Old Testament, those who appeared as the villains and victims of the Hebrew narrative. He taught that Christ's death had brought salvation to "Cain, and those like him, and the Sodomites, and the Egyptians," while the good characters of the Old Testament did not achieve salvation: not Abel, not Noah, none of the patriarchs or prophets who had gullibly followed the lesser God.[10]

Troubled by his failure to reconcile the Old and New Testaments, he turned to two sayings attributed to Jesus: "A good tree cannot bring forth evil fruit," and "No man puts a piece of new cloth on an old garment." Through such words, thought Marcion, Christ was proclaiming that his gospel could not be reconciled with the Old Testament. Christianity must free itself of that pernicious pseudo-scripture and become an entirely new creation. To lay the foundation of this new religious order, Marcion prepared a new Bible—one that omitted the whole Old Testament and much of what we think of as the New.

Marcion's influence was immediate and powerful. For one thing, it was probably his version of the New Testament that galvanized the mainstream church into declaring exactly what the authentic canon actually was. Moreover, the number of tracts written against Marcion and his school from all parts of the Christian world suggests just how widespread his followers were, and how far his influence extended.

Gnostic and Marcionite sects lingered for centuries in the Middle East, and the survivors easily identified with the new religion of Manichaeanism. The third-century prophet Mani was a radical Dualist, teaching an absolute division between Light and Darkness. He saw Christ as a leader of the forces of light in the perpetual war against darkness and matter. Mani closely followed

Marcion in his critique of the Old Testament, and the two relied on a similar corpus of Bible passages. Mani, like Marcion, mocked the notion of a united and harmonious Bible:

> **Some good God of the Law! He spoiled the Egyptians, expelled the Amorites, Girgashites and other nations and gave their land to the children of Israel. If He said, "Thou shalt not covet," how could he give them other people's land?**[11]

Apart from Mani himself, the movement's most famous representative was the North African Faustus, whose attack on mainstream Christianity called forth Augustine's tirade, the *Contra Faustum*.[12]

For over a thousand years, Manichaeanism held the status of a fully fledged world religion. During the Middle Ages, Dualist/Gnostic sects and churches operated across Eurasia, literally from France to China, preaching a Jesus who had come to redeem the world from the homicidal Creator God of the Pentateuch.[13]

In terms of their influence on later Christians, the views of Marcion, Mani, and Faustus have had a mixed history. In its overt form, Marcionism has few followers today. Certain other early forms of alternative Christianity have proved attractive to modern thinkers seeking avidly for new and more relevant interpretations of the Judeo-Christian message. Marcionism, however, has experienced no such revival. Marcion's rejection of the material world resonates poorly with a modern audience searching for religious teachings that affirm sexuality, rather than condemn it. His condemnation of the Jewish God naturally implies anti-Semitism and racial hatred.[14]

Yet Marcion continues to exert a real influence among millions who have never heard his name.[15] Marcionism is in evidence whenever ordinary Christians imagine the Old Testament God as a ferocious, vengeful, and judgmental figure, the smiter of Amalekites and the issuer of Thou Shalt Nots, while the New Testament deity is the doting Father of the Jesus who gave the Sermon on the Mount.

Such a view makes it easy to dismiss the dark passages as part of the Jewish Old Testament, supposedly a sinister and bloody past that has now been swept away by Christian light. So potent is Marcionism, so overwhelming the temptation to contrast and separate the Old and New Testaments, that every Christian generation has to fight anew the battle against Marcion's ghost.

The Rise of Reason

SOME REJECTED THE OLD Testament God; others began by asking just why his reported acts sometimes shocked and repelled us. Throughout Christian history, the fact that believers have been troubled by passages in the Old Testament has in itself proved a critical theological insight. On what basis dare we mortals criticize the reported deeds of God, the source of all right and truth? What is the basis of our moral conscience? If the Bible truly speaks the words of the Creator and Judge of all, then it is not fitting for any mere creature to respond with anything other than humble gratitude and respect, and the fact of being shocked at the Bible's stories is itself a grave intellectual sin. Pots do not criticize potters. Yet many who have claimed to follow Jesus have rebelled against those scriptures, claiming an inspiration higher than the written word itself.

As we have seen, the idea of unquestioning acceptance of God's sovereignty became a fundamental part of Reformation thought. Intellectual approaches were transformed from the end of the seventeenth century on, as Catholics and Protestants wearied of decades of warfare and fanaticism. What changed was not so much the attitude to the ferocity of biblical violence—both Augustine and Calvin knew that such acts were appalling by the standards of their own age—but rather the sense that humanity could legitimately pass judgment on words and acts attributed to God. Christians laid claim to moral standards that allowed them to perform just such criticism: to judge the

Bible by some higher standard. This belief provided the foundation for all modern forms of liberal or progressive Christianity.[16]

Supporting the idea of such a universal standard were new concepts of "natural law," the ancient idea that common principles of justice remain valid in all times and places. Natural law theory was revived in the seventeenth century, particularly through the work of Dutch polymath Hugo Grotius. Grotius, the founder of modern international law, pioneered many modern ideas concerning war and peace. He claimed that such universal principles held true even if God did not exist, or existed but did not intervene in human affairs. So powerful was natural law, claimed Grotius, that "even the will of an omnipotent being cannot change or abrogate" it.[17]

In our own time, the idea of a universal law is revolutionary enough. It underlies all attempts to apply human rights principles across the borders of individual states, say, or to arrest generals or heads of state for crimes against humanity, even if those leaders had done nothing contrary to the written codes of their particular nations. But in the Enlightenment, natural law ideas reshaped attitudes toward biblical authority. If you believed in natural law, rooted as it was in reason and nature, then you had an absolute standard by which to judge the biblical text. And often, you found that Bible stories grossly violated the laws of nature.

Alongside natural law, there developed in the late seventeenth century the idea of natural religion, the belief that reason and experience were as accurate a guide to divine truth as was scripture. If our minds flinched at alleged divine commands, then we had at least as much right to put our faith in those spontaneous human feelings as in the words of scripture. God, in this view, speaks to his followers in different ways, of which revelation—scripture—is but one. Over and above the words of the text, God also wrote his law in human hearts, giving individuals the right and duty to evaluate scripture, and ultimately to choose which passages to accept, based on the dictates of reason.[18]

God Versus Law

THAT CONCEPT OF THE supremacy of reason initially emerged in Great Britain and the Netherlands. In the British context, the movement became known as Deism, named for the God (Latin, *Deus*) who created the world and established its basic rules and principles, but who did not interfere in the ordinary lives of its people. Humans could know the laws of God, which were also those of nature, and only superstition and priestly self-interest tried to conceal those facts with talk of mystery, revelation, and miracle. That idea is expressed by the title of John Toland's 1696 book, one of the core texts of the developing Enlightenment: *Christianity Not Mysterious: Or, A Treatise Shewing That There Is Nothing in the Gospel Contrary to Reason, Nor Above It.* If the scripture contained contradictions, or if its teachings flatly violated reason, then defending those texts was in itself a crime against both reason and religion. As Toland wrote, "To believe the divinity of scripture or the sense of any passage thereof, without rational proofs, and an evident consistency, is a blamable credulity." In establishing this principle, activists repeatedly used the Bible's notorious passages as potent evidence for the inadequacies of scripture.[19]

In 1730, Matthew Tindal published the most important systematic critique of biblical authority to date in his *Christianity as Old as the Creation,* which some have called "the Deist's Bible." Tindal was by profession a judge who took a special interest in international law and conflict, including matters of piracy and irregular warfare. He actually understood the arguments concerning conquest and occupation in a way that very few other biblical scholars ever had before, or would subsequently. He was also firmly rooted in Grotius's theories of natural law.[20]

We have already met Tindal denouncing the conquest texts as a possible justification for later militarism and imperialism, but his book went further in its complaints against the Bible's offenses against reason. He began with a simple principle: "that though the literal sense of the scripture be ever so plain, yet it must not stand in competition with what our Reason tells us of the nature and perceptions of God." Once a person accepted that idea, reading the Old Testament demanded a substantial process of weeding. In fact, he noted, so much in the Bible was topsy-turvy: "The holier men in the Old Testament are represented, the more cruel they seem to be." Reason demanded better. In fact, Tindal thought that the contradictions resulted from a kind of warped reason, or rationalized self-interest: "'Tis no doubt the interest of wicked priests to have God represented under opposite characters, and to give in one Testament rules contrary to those in the other that they, as it serves their turn, may make use of either."[21]

Tindal returned often to the conquest of Canaan. Not only were the violent acts of the conquest self-evidently atrocious, he believed, but every attempt to justify them dug deeper into flagrant absurdity. Perhaps, apologists speculated, God was using the Canaanites as a deterrent to others, so that other nations would learn not to commit the same crimes they had? But in that case, Tindal argued, God should have intervened in some miraculous way, to make it clear that the extermination was his act alone. He would not have used the Israelites, who had their own vested interest for grabbing the land. By the same token, God should have let the Canaanites know that they were being divinely punished, to prevent them resisting God's Hebrew servants. "Otherwise, would there not be two opposite rights at the same time: a right in the Jews by revelation, to take away the lives of the Canaanites, and a right in the Canaanites by the Law of Nature to defend their lives?"[22]

Anyway, said Tindal, in the process of punishing the Canaanites, the Israelites themselves had committed crimes against humanity:

If God would punish the Canaanites for acting contrary to the Law of Nature, would he in order to do this require the

Israelites to act contrary to the same Law, in murdering men, women, and children that never did them the least injury? . . . Would God in such a case choose a people as prone to idolatry as the Canaanites themselves?[23]

Together with the other Deists, Tindal had a profound impact on liberal Christians. Among other signs of his influence, he may be the source for Jefferson's famous phrase about "the pursuit of happiness" being a fundamental human right. His works also contributed mightily to legitimizing biblical criticism. One influential pupil was Hermann Samuel Reimarus, a founder of the German school of Higher Criticism. Reimarus followed Toland in mocking the standard orthodox justifications for the slaughter of the Canaanites. Who, he asked, would take seriously a claim that the Israelites were executing God's justice when the killers themselves profited so enormously from the act? Perhaps, said Reimarus, the Canaanites had been uniquely sinful, but our only evidence for that comes from the people who wiped them out, and who thus stood to benefit from offering such an explanation. Clearly, it's not only jaded modern observers who are sensitive to what sounds like familiar war propaganda in the biblical text.[24]

Rejecting God

WESTERN ATTITUDES TO SCRIPTURE were already in flux in Toland's time, and radical approaches became widespread as the eighteenth century went on. Deists argued that while God had created the world, religious scriptures and traditions were the product of human cultures, and were limited by the circumstances of their time. As scholarly investigation of the Bible developed, critics argued that the Bible had evolved over time, and that its earliest stages came from an era of extreme savagery. Modern-day believers, so said these critics, need not believe that the violent texts of the conquest era exercised any religious authority for later generations. Hearing such arguments, an orthodox believer might well retort, So you are morally better than God? And the skeptic would respond, If the Bible quotes God accurately, then yes indeed I am; and if it does not, why should I treat it seriously?

Such a critique was potentially devastating for any notion of biblical authority. Once we accept that human reason and modern ethical standards are the criteria by which the conquest texts are to be judged, then we can apply the same approach to any other part of the Bible—and to its moral and religious thought no less than its historical accounts. If Moses was in fact a mass murderer, why should any modern person heed his moral regulations? If whole books of the Bible could be discarded, why not shed all of them?

By the end of the eighteenth century, critiquing the flaws of organized religion moved to outright assaults on the whole idea of revealed religion or, in some instances, of any religion whatever. Activists proudly proclaimed themselves infidels, unbelievers, and indeed enemies of faith. Thomas Paine exemplified this tradition in the English-speaking world, in his controversial tract *The Age of Reason*. Some of Paine's most powerful arguments exploited the moral outrage that a modern readership would feel when encountering the Bible's tales of bloodshed. Reading such stories, which make up so large a portion of the Old Testament, "it would be more consistent that we called it the word of a demon, than the Word of God. It is a history of wickedness, that has served to corrupt and brutalize mankind."[25]

For Paine, the fact that Christians continued to treasure the Bible meant either that they had not read it seriously or, if they had done so, that they were morally blind. Imagine, he asked, that someone told you that one of your friends was responsible for "the cruel and murdering orders, with which the Bible is filled, and the numberless torturing executions of men, women, and children, in consequence of those orders." Surely, "you would have glowed with satisfaction at detecting the falsehood of the charge, and gloried in defending his injured fame." Yet Christians made no such effort to deny the crimes attributed to God: either they meekly accepted the truth of the tales, or they actively justified them. "It is because ye are sunk in the cruelty of superstition, or feel no interest in the honor of your Creator, that ye listen to the horrid tales of the Bible, or hear them with callous indifference."[26]

Paine's arguments long continued to influence atheists and secularists, and found a hospitable environment in the emerging Socialist and Communist movements. Nineteenth-century skeptics found new ammunition for their views during Europe's imperial expansion, as they saw the Bible being used so readily to justify conquest. In 1841, American infidel thinker C. G. Olmsted denounced the biblical account of the massacres in Canaan:

> No other cause is pretended to be assigned but such as the bloody saints, Cortez and Pizarro, gave for their extermination of the innocent and virtuous aborigines. They were of a different religion; their god had not the same name; they worshiped by different sacrifices.[27]

Infidels found the new imperial discoveries valuable in attacking the whole society that produced the supposedly infallible Bible, as they compared the Old Testament world with the primitive and tribal societies in Africa or the Americas. Given that the ancient Hebrew society was primitive and bloodthirsty, it was scarcely surprising to find the Israelites acting as horribly as their modern-day counterparts. Voltaire drew comparisons with the Hurons and Iroquois, who in their day were legendary for torturing and mutilating their victims. Yet compared with Joshua's Hebrews, the Indians were humane *philosophes*. Reading Bible accounts of the conquest, Voltaire mused, "If the author of this history had planned to make the Jews pariahs [*exécrables*] to other nations, would he have done otherwise?"[28] Mark Twain compared the invasion of Canaan with acts of rape, murder, and mutilation perpetrated by Native Americans during the bloody wars of the 1860s. After reporting the slaughter of a white family, he continued, "The Minnesota campaign was merely a duplicate of the Midianite raid. Nothing happened in the one that didn't happen in the other." If we could trace any moral differences between the two events, then Native Americans emerged better and more mercifully than Moses or Joshua.[29]

Neither Paine nor Twain saw any great need to wrestle with the Bible's internal conflicts—specifically, with the paradox of a loving God ordering genocide: it was all a primitive fable. In reality, they believed, there is neither God nor any higher law. Humans commit atrocities and massacres against each other, and invoke whatever higher authorities they have conveniently invented to justify their crimes. Scripture is a record of changing human perceptions as expressed in societies at different levels of evolution, and nothing more.

IN THEIR DIFFERENT WAYS, the critics—from Marcion to Voltaire and Paine, and on to Harris and Dawkins—were all asking excellent questions about the Bible, and about the authority of scripture. Much in the Bible does shock our sensibilities. Yet these questions have failed to destroy biblically based religions, or indeed to make much impact on them. While radical criticisms survive today, they represent an extreme minority perspective. For all the criticisms aimed at the Bible through the centuries, Christians not only survive but still constitute by far the world's most numerous religion. Atheists remain few, while Marcionites scarcely exist. At least in the United States, believers predominate massively, and even after decades of European secularization, the Bible still has many millions of followers on that continent.

Some observers are surprised to see faith flourishing as it does in a world founded so absolutely on the secular assumptions of science and technology. No less surprising, biblically based religions continue to boom despite the widespread popular acceptance of ideas of universal rights and natural law. Even if they could not express these theories as fluently as Toland or Grotius, most Westerners have fundamental beliefs about human rights, about the conduct of war, and about the unacceptable nature of unprovoked aggression, ethnic cleansing, and genocide. Yet most Christians and Jews see little difficulty in reconciling these views with the scriptures to which they adhere. Somehow, they have learned not to see that such books of blood exist.

CHAPTER EIGHT

Coming to Terms

Onward Christian soldiers, marching as to war!
—SABINE BARING-GOULD

SINCE THE REFORMATION, MANY millions of ordinary Christians have read the Bible attentively, and many have certainly encountered the accounts of the ancient holy wars. The vast majority, though, have neither rebelled against the horrific violence of those tales, nor found in those stories a warrant for endless aggression against their neighbors. Overwhelmingly, they have read the tales of Moses and Joshua as examples of sanctified military heroism, rarely paying much thought to the victims of those accounts. Most hotel rooms across North America contain a Bible placed there under the auspices of a Christian group that takes its name from Gideon, a warlord of the Hebrew conquest.

Several strategies allow believers to cope with an unpalatable passage. Much the most common approach is to read a passage as if it said something different from its obvious intent, to subject the text to an unconscious process of editing and rewriting. One variant of this method is to treat words as allegorical or mystical in nature, to remove any literal violence and gore. If these strategies fail, many readers find ways of removing the offending texts altogether, but without admitting that they have done so. They effectively pretend that the offending text is not there, by ignoring it or even removing it from public readings. One way or another, believers skillfully avoid having to confront bloody texts. They learn to forget.

At that point, we might well ask: So where is the problem? If in fact the texts are to all intents and purposes suppressed, have they not been rendered safe? The difficulty is, of course, that they still exist, and still form part of canonized scripture. Although they may evade mainstream attention at present, they continue to influence behavior among devoted fringe movements, and they will almost certainly shape emerging forms of faith. However hard readers try to avoid them, the texts of terror return to influence behavior in times of crisis. Try as we might to sterilize them, to edit them, to ignore them, they come back. Dormant is not dead.

When all else has failed, the only way of dealing with these scriptures is to accept them, to acknowledge their existence, and to learn to live with them.

Justifying Evil

WE ARE HARDWIRED TO edit reality. Memory and experience teach us what to expect from the world, but on occasion we encounter facts or situations that fail to mesh with those preconceptions. At that point, a part of the brain comes into play, the component popularly known as the mind's Delete key. (Its technical name is the dorsolateral prefrontal cortex, or DLPFC.) We suppress or inhibit unsettling anomalies, to the point that we honestly do not absorb or remember them. Within our brain, each of us has a personal censor. This does not mean that the development of moral consciousness slavishly follows some predetermined biological pattern, but we do have a natural tendency to ignore or underplay those things that do not fit our reality.

Whatever our particular religious or ethnic tradition, human beings are very good at explaining away wrongful actions performed by "people like us," while condemning identical behaviors undertaken by others. In an experiment undertaken in the mid-1960s, psychologist Georges Tamarin took a sample of Israeli children aged from eight to fourteen and asked their opinion of some of the genocidal passages in Joshua. What did they think of those policies? Strikingly, 66 percent totally approved, while 8 percent approved partially. Tamarin then gave the same test to another sample, but this time the story referred to an imaginary General Lin in a Chinese state three thousand years ago, rather than to events in Canaan or Palestine. This time, only 7 percent approved the actions, while the number of those totally disapproving grew from 26 to 75 percent.[1]

When such massacres are framed in the abstract—as acts committed by a faceless Chinese general or a Ugandan warlord, say—we have no problem calling them crimes against humanity. We might even add to the condemnation by assuming that such savagery is exactly what we might expect of "them," of primitive Africans or cruel Orientals. But when the culprits are venerated figures such as Moses and Joshua, and their acts are lauded in sacred scripture, the moral categories become much more complex. Believers make every effort to avoid trying to resolve the contradictions. They have to learn how not to confront unacceptable facts. In the context of this experiment, nothing suggested that Israeli youngsters were either more or less cynical than those of any other society.

How do people cope with things they do, or acts committed in their name, that they know to be wrong? Actually, several modern scholarly literatures try to address this issue. In the 1950s, social psychologists tried to explain how people manage to balance facts that flatly contradict each other—what the researchers termed cognitive dissonance.[2] Building on this work, other scholars tried to understand how people avoid having to come to terms with unpleasant moral and ethical realities. The key word in this avoidance process is *neutralization*.

A little background is in order. Criminologists had long debated how lawbreakers formed the deviant and countercultural values that led them to carry out their careers of crime and violence. In the 1960s, though, researchers found, to their surprise, that offenders were nothing like as deviant as they had believed. Criminals, in fact, shared quite normal values and aspirations, and knew quite well that what they were doing was morally wrong. In order to pursue their illegal careers, they had to become adept at various tactics of self-deception and denial, which together constituted a strategy of neutralization. When asked to describe their crimes, offenders would respond with various defenses, presented either singly or as a package. Researchers noted five main lines of defense:

Denial of responsibility ("It's not my fault")

Denial of injury ("They can afford it")

Denial of the victim ("They had it coming")

Condemnation of the condemners ("The police are bigger crooks than I am")

The appeal to higher loyalties ("The gang is my life")[3]

Some accounts add other variants of these techniques, including a *dehumanization of the victim* and a systematic *misrepresentation of consequences* (which emphasizes the benefits of the act and downplays the harm).

In different forms, such denial strategies have often surfaced when believers read scriptural accounts of mass murder. The crudest version is the appeal to higher loyalties, though in this case invoking not a gang but rather the Creator of the universe, from whom there is no appeal. That argument fails to satisfy many in modern times. Moreover, even those readers and interpreters who affect to be following this strategy in practice use the other defenses and denials on a regular basis. Usually subtly, and without comment, they add to or subtract from the scriptural story in ways that make it more acceptable to later tastes. They soften and civilize. In different ways, acts of brutality have to be humanized, either by adding to the original text reasons and motives for such behaviors, or by removing the victims altogether.[4]

Editing

THE CONQUEST TEXTS ARE clear about the acts they command: annihilation is to be total, no survivors will escape, and (at least in some accounts) the victims have done nothing to deserve their extermination. From an early date these interpretations bothered later generations, who like all readers through history approached the story not as it was but as they thought it should be. Even in the Old Testament, we see a kind of selective reading at work—for example, later passages justify the massacres by stressing the extreme evils of the Canaanites, so that they cease to be innocent victims. Whatever the remaining problems of the story, that at least makes God's decisions somewhat more comprehensible.[5]

One example of this civilizing process is the emphasis given to the story of Rahab, the only ordinary Canaanite in the conquest narrative who is named and given a face. Hers is a strange tale because it violates the rules of holy warfare that otherwise seem so implacable. Although Joshua's forces have an absolute obligation to exterminate everyone in Jericho, Rahab's willingness to help the Israelites allows her family to escape and join the Israelites. Despite the author's apparently inflexible belief in annihilation, the text still suggests that rules could be bent for a good Canaanite.[6]

Early rabbis, in the first centuries of the Common Era, softened the conquest story still further to make it conform to later Jewish ideas of propriety and civilized behavior, and to emerging concepts of just war. In one account, credited to the third-century writer Samuel b. Nahman, Joshua preceded the conquest of Canaan by issuing three *prostagma,* or proclamations, giving the native peoples three options: they could leave the country, make peace, or fight. According to this story, the Canaanites who fell at Jericho and elsewhere were thus the stubborn remnant who refused to listen to reason—but reason was, indeed, what they were offered.[7]

According to this retelling, some Canaanites made peace while still others fled, and the story of those exiles includes a devious twist. "What did the Girgashite do?" asks the rabbi. "He turned and went away from before [Israel]. And God gave him another land as beautiful as his own, namely Africa." The Phoenicians, who were kin to the Canaanites, developed the powerful colony at Carthage in North Africa, which flourished until the Romans annihilated it in 146 BCE. Canaanites indeed suffered genocide at the hands of a ruthless invader, but it was Romans, not Jews, who spilled the blood. In neutralization theory, this would be classified as the denial of responsibility. This revision of the Canaanite tale recalls the startling Talmudic reinterpretation of the Amalekite mythology, in which even Haman's descendants accommodated themselves to the Torah. In both cases, generous-minded scholars reconstructed divine commands according to their particular interpretation of what God should have ordered, rather than what the scripture happens to report.[8]

Phinehas's intervention offers another example of reinterpretation, of accepting the truth of a passage while smoothing its very rough edges. In the original story, Phinehas acts alone, stirred by zealous fury, and kills the offending couple. Later sources, both biblical and rabbinic, praised Phinehas without hesitation, but others were more restrained. One psalm recalled the zeal, while glossing over the violence: "Then stood up Phinehas, and executed judgment: and so the plague was stayed; and that was counted unto him for righteousness unto all generations for evermore." Some later rabbis read this to mean that Phinehas's noble deed was his prayer, not his act of violence.[9]

Other writers found Phinehas a major source of difficulty, because they knew all too well what might happen if every furious man thought that he was acting in the Lord's will. Jewish scholars stressed the fact that Phinehas "rose up from the midst of the congregation," suggesting that he was acting on communal authority. Presumably, they suggested, these authorities must have been discussing whether the culprits were liable to death for their misdeeds, so that Phinehas was not entirely a lone vigilante. Authors such as Philo and Josephus struggled to moderate Phinehas's actions by adding extra story elements: perhaps, among his other crimes, Phinehas's victim had also insulted Moses? Different Talmudic texts work still harder to make Phinehas's behavior look unacceptable, interpolating a hostile response by Moses and others to the killing, and suggesting traumatic effects on Phinehas himself.[10]

Spiritualizing

HISTORICALLY, ONE VERY COMMON response to the conquest tales has been to spiritualize them, to deny that actual violence was inflicted on real human beings. This at once represents a denial of injury and a denial of the victim—literally, since actual human beings were not victimized. For modern readers, whether Christians or Jews, such allegorical or spiritual interpretations can be puzzling or offputting, as they seem to reduce the historical account to mythological symbols. But as I will argue, these readings may not have been too far removed from the intent of the authors of the conquest passages, who thought of the Canaanites at least partly as symbols of a hostile paganism.

Jews, for instance, recognize a stern commandment to destroy Amalekites, but only a tiny minority contemplates such actions against actual peoples deemed to deserve this title. From the Talmud onward, mainstream Jewish thinkers have identified Amalek not as a race but as a set of evil desires or sinful impulses that separate us from God, and that must indeed be exterminated ruthlessly.[11] According to this understanding, God commanded war not against the race but against the *deed* of Amalek, a parallel to what Christians might understand as a sin against the Holy Spirit. For both Christians and Jews, the fight against that inner temptation is indeed perpetual: Amalek is always with us. One of the greatest spiritual teachers of Judaism was the eighteenth-century rabbi known as the Baal Shem Tov, who founded the Hasidic movement. He told his followers,

> Every time you experience a worry or doubt about how God is running the world—that's Amalek launching an attack against your soul. We must wipe Amalek out of our hearts whenever—and wherever—he attacks, so that we can serve God with complete joy.

The twentieth-century rabbi Menachem Schneerson, who attracted messianic hopes, agreed that "Amalek causes doubt and hesitation which cools the ardor of our divine service. Victory in our inner war with Amalek means devoting ourselves to God's service without reservations."[12]

Modern Orthodox Jews make Amalek a tempter figure similar to the Christian Devil. One website notes the psychological subtlety of the temptations, in words that recall C. S. Lewis's *Screwtape Letters*. Of course, writes a modern Orthodox believer, Amalek would not come right out and challenge the existence of God: anyone would see through that crude challenge. Instead, "Amalek might initially tell a person not to become excited about observing the *mitzvos* [commandments], or to believe in God in general, but not with absolute certainty. . . . [S]uch thoughts represent one of the biggest threats that an observant Jew might face."[13] Amalek has come a staggeringly long way from its historical origins as a tiny desert tribe around 1200 BCE.

Historically, Muslims have evolved very similar responses to their own violent texts, spiritualizing them and using familiar devices of allegory. One controversial hadith reports Muhammad returning from a battle and declaring, "We are finished with the lesser jihad; now we are starting the greater jihad." As he explained, warfare against an outer, physical adversary was one form of jihad, but that was only the lesser form. The true struggle—the greater jihad, *al-jihad al-akbar*—meant the fight against the evil desires and forces that prevented you controlling your mind and soul.[14]

Hard-line Islamist scholars have long challenged the authenticity of this hadith, but the basic idea has been immensely influential in Muslim history. This is a core doctrine of the Sufi schools, which have been central to the faith's intellectual and cultural development. The real war is against the *nafs,* the ego—what Bible readers might think of as the inner Amalekite, the Canaanite within. In the words of African Sufi leader Cheikh Ahmadou Bamba, "The warrior in the path of God is not he who takes his enemies' life but the one who combats his *nafs* to achieve spiritual perfection."[15]

Conquering Within

CHRISTIANS TOO HAVE SINCE earliest times read the Old Testament accounts through the lens of typology, so that ancient events prefigure or foreshadow the life of Jesus and the history of the early church. For some early Church Fathers, this search for Old Testament precedents, for "types" of later events in the Christian story, became so obsessive that every reference to wood prefigured the cross, every mention of water foreshadowed baptism.[16]

Such an approach defused potential concerns about acts of vio-

lence or bloodshed in the scripture, a matter of deep concern to
early Christians with their deep aversion to warfare and military
conflict. Just as the real, historical wood and water were transmuted
into theological symbols, so were the conquests and massacres, with
all their swords and spears. When St. Paul told his followers to "put
on the whole armor of God," he was saying nothing about worldly
weapons. As the popular English hymn proclaimed, Christian soldiers were marching not *to* war, but *as to* war. Once the conquest
story becomes a spiritual saga, then all the hostile and negative figures in that saga also acquire a symbolic character. As the names
became obsolete, Amalekites, Midianites, Canaanites, and others
all morphed easily into demonic figures, symbolic forms of the sins
and other temptations that Christians encountered en route to the
Promised Land. No actual Canaanites were harmed in the making
of this scripture.[17]

In this context, Christians could even accept the themes and institutions of *herem* warfare. St. Paul draws on this imagery, although
he visualizes it in purely cosmic terms. So does the book of Revelation, written around 95 CE. Revelation cannot be understood
except in the context of the traditions of biblical YHWH warfare,
from the trumpet blasts that assemble the holy warriors through the
annihilation of the demonic forces that rule a corrupted world. In
mystical mode, such a war was quite acceptable even to a religion
of peace and nonresistance. Who could deny that demons deserved
annihilation?[18]

Christian typology reached new heights in the early second
century, when a now-unknown Christian writer wrote what we
know as the Epistle of Barnabas. "Barnabas" (who probably wrote
in Egypt) has no doubt that the image of the cross is strongly present
in the Old Testament, especially in the account of the Israelite war
with Amalek. Moses prophesies to *Iesous*-Joshua what *Iesous*-Jesus
will someday do. Early Christian writers often used biblical texts
that differed from those we are familiar with, and they interpreted

them in distinctive ways. Barnabas read the Exodus text as prom-
ising that "in the last days, the Son of God will chop down the
entire house of Amalek at its roots." The destruction of Amalek is
now something foretold for the last days, a spiritual and apocalyptic
sign.[19]

Shadowing Mysteries

THROUGHOUT THE EARLY AND medieval Christian centuries an
amazing proportion of scholarly activity seems to have been devoted
to generating allegories that to a modern audience seem improbable
if not ludicrous. If we fail to understand this imagery, though, we
cut ourselves off absolutely from the early Christian worldview, to
say nothing of its cultural achievement: these types inspired a great
deal of Christian visual art. Only by understanding the love for allegory and typology can we understand how Christians neutralized
the savagery of the conquest.[20]

One pioneer of Christian Bible interpretation was the third-
century Egyptian thinker Origen, for whom a straightforward
historical reading of the Old Testament would have proved a real
challenge to faith. He was confronting Marcionites and Gnostics,
who charged that the Bible taught cruelty, and that the wars and
massacres could not be reconciled with the loving God revealed by
Christ. Origen was very sensitive to such charges, to the point of
agreeing that, if true, they gravely undermined Christian faith. But
that was a problem only if you read the stories literally, he said, and
no wise or educated person would do such a thing. Origen believed
that scripture should be read on three ascending levels. Lowest in
significance was the literal meaning of the text, and simple souls
might well consent to remain stuck there. But more advanced believers progressed to the moral interpretation, and ultimately to the
spiritual level of meaning.[21]

Once you accepted this approach, the book of Joshua ceased to be a stumbling block for Christian faith and actually became a prime source of inspiration. "This is therefore a work of highest compassion that the heretics accuse of cruelty." In a series of homilies devoted to expounding Joshua, Origen offers literally hundreds of allegories, analogies, and "figures," very few of which would come unbidden to a modern reader—proof, for Origen, that such readers must be very unspiritual. Joshua tells, for instance, how five enemy kings took refuge in caves, before the Israelites sought them out and killed them. Origen easily identifies these foes as sight, smell, hearing, taste, and touch, the senses through which sins can arise. In the past, these kings had held dominion in the cave of the human mind, but Joshua/Jesus defeated them and raised the spiritual banner.[22]

All the battles in the book of Joshua were, for Origen, wars waged against sin: "Within us are the Canaanites; within us are the Perizzites; here are the Jebusites." Take, for instance, the annihilation of the city of Ai. Yes, admitted Origen, Jews might become cruel and bloodthirsty when they read about Joshua's forces carrying out such massacres, but Christians know better. In fact, he said, the real meaning of the story of Ai lies within:

> Mysteries are truly shadowed in these words. . . . [W]e ought not to leave any of those demons deep within, whose dwelling place is chaos and who rule in the abyss, but to destroy them all. . . . Therefore, all holy persons kill the inhabitants of Ai: they both annihilate and do not release any of them. . . . Let us thrust Ai through with the edge of the sword, and let us extinguish all the inhabitants of chaos, all opposing powers. . . . Jesus came and struck down all the kings who possessed kingdoms of sin in us, and he ordered us to destroy all those kings and to leave none of them.[23]

When fighting demons, you don't take prisoners.

Although medieval Western readers had little access to Greek texts, they found their best guide to these allegorical approaches in Augustine. Like Origen before him, Augustine saw no problem in biblical accounts of massacre because they were not straightforward history. Every part of sacred scripture had to be understood in the context of the whole narrative, which culminated in Christ, and only in that context could we read any portion of the text. This solution certainly applied, for instance, to "the prophetic and symbolic character of the war with Amalek."[24]

Augustine rarely pressed any single interpretation of a given text: a reader might prefer one meaning or another. What mattered was reading the passage holistically, as part of the Bible's overall message, rather than as a simple record of past events. "Whatever the true interpretation may be, the pious student of the Scriptures will feel certain that in the command, in the action, and in the narrative there is a purpose and a symbolic meaning."[25] Augustine seemed to acknowledge no prescribed limit to the allegorical meanings that a "pious student" could derive from the text. Anything goes, in fact, in preference to the obvious literal meaning.

Hymning Massacre

SUCH ALLEGORICAL INTERPRETATIONS FLOURISHED through the Middle Ages and the Reformation, and indeed long afterward. The good news about such spiritual readings was that they limited the application of the text to real-world situations and conflicts. In 1637, the New England colony was engaged in a brutal war with the local Pequot Indians, whom the settlers naturally identified with Amalek. Writing to John Winthrop, radical Puritan Roger Williams protested the amount of "innocent blood" shed in the name of holy war. While Williams did not question that the colonists were a new Israel, he warned that the Amalek model should not be a basis for practical policy: "Many things may be spoken to prove the Lord's perpetual war with Amalek extraordinary and mystical." Other Bible passages contradicted such lessons, and these stories of mercy deserved more weight because they were clearly historical rather than "mystical."[26]

The potent tradition of allegory reached a mass audience through hymns and devotional texts. The spiritualized vision of the exodus and conquest gained a new popularity during the upsurge of hymn-writing during the eighteenth and nineteenth centuries. The faithful declared, "To Canaan's land I'm on my way, Where the soul of man never dies." The last obstacle en route to that cherished destination was the river Jordan, which symbolized death:

> On Jordan's stormy banks I stand,
> And cast a wishful eye
> To Canaan's fair and happy land,
> Where my possessions lie.

The native Canaanites who obstructed the route to Canaan obviously signified dark inner realities. Charles Wesley followed exactly in the rabbinic tradition when he identified Amalek as a driving force of sin rather than an objective reality. His hymn proclaimed,

> Jesus, we dare believe on Thee,
> Against this Amalek within,
> He soon extirpated shall be,
> The name, the last remains of sin.

The Wesleys were no less militant in their professed commitment to annihilate Canaanites.[27]

Later generations similarly spiritualized both the conquest and the destruction it entailed. In such a vision, defeated tribes survived only as symbols of moral evils, to be enumerated in grotesque detail. For a nineteenth-century preacher like Jonathan Bayley, "The Amorites are the lusts of the heart; the Hittites the more smooth and managing enemies of self-derived intelligence; the Canaanites, evils in general." Christians, accordingly, "must spiritually extirpate the Canaanite, the Hittite and the Amorite."[28]

Victorian Christians likewise transformed the tale of the annihilation of the people of Midian into an internal struggle against evil impulses. J. M. Neale's bizarre hymn was once widely sung and much loved:

> Christian, dost thou see them
> On the holy ground?
> How the troops of Midian
> Prowl and prowl around?
> Christian, up and smite them,
> Counting gain but loss;
> Smite them by the merit
> Of the Holy Cross.[29]

If Hitler's Holocaust had succeeded, presumably Christians in some future era would have recalled the prowling Jew as a menacing symbol of depravity. The idea could scarcely be considered offensive as it was not linked to any existing human reality. No one would survive to be offended.

In such allegorical accounts, our choice of language draws a sharp demarcation between the bloody events recorded and any disturbing modern parallels. Hymn-writers, like Bible commentators, steadfastly avoid using words that might draw attention to contemporary parallels. They deliberately choose archaic words that place the events in a distant dreamtime, a myth world. Israel is to *smite* and *slay* Midianites, not *massacre* or *murder* them. Even to suggest that a modern hymn might use a term such as "ethnic cleansing" or "genocide" in a biblical context is to underline the impossibility of truly acknowledging such moral complexity.

Censoring

ALTHOUGH PLENTY OF BOOKS still offer allegorical interpretations to scripture, most modern readers expect something over and above this. While they might use allegorical readings for devotional purposes, consumers also expect commentaries to offer critical and historical interpretations through which they can understand the "real" meaning of the text. However they might disagree about the uses of critical scholarship, both liberals and fundamentalists would today find Origen's approach to scripture alien and puzzling. The question "Did it happen like this?" clearly takes priority. But when we insist on reading the Old Testament as historical, we must somehow deal with the moral dilemmas of the violence, and many find a solution in wishing away the offending texts, through a kind of informal censorship.

Any text that endures for centuries necessarily alters to accommodate the changing tastes of readers. Modern observers mock the adaptation of classic stories to meet contemporary concerns about class, gender, or race, but this practice is long established. The famous fairy tales that we know today were originally far uglier, and the thought of exposing the young to these older and unimproved versions seems appalling. The seventeenth-century version of Little Red Riding Hood ends when the wolf devours the young girl. In earlier tales too, it is their cold-hearted mother, rather than an incoming stepmother, who throws Hansel and Gretel out of their home. Only in the nineteenth century did the Brothers Grimm turn these stories into something palatable and less, well, grim. Shakespeare was another early target for remodeling and moral correctness. In 1818, Thomas Bowdler issued his *Family Shakespeare,* "in which those words and expressions are omitted which cannot with propriety be read aloud in a family," hence the term "bowdlerize." Ironically, that word is itself a softening of an older term: earlier readers spoke of castrating a book.

The thought of castrating the Bible might be startling, but strictly orthodox believers are quite familiar with drastic forms of selection and editing. It is difficult to live in the United States without at some point seeing a Gideon New Testament—a free, mass-produced volume that is handed out prolifically. So common is the book that we may forget what a startling concept it is theologically, with its implication that the New Testament alone, severed from the Old, constitutes a working model of the Christian faith. Marcion would have nodded approvingly. In this instance, of course, the decision to circulate the New Testament alone has no theological agenda, but is rather a matter of economics and practicality. Once we take that step, though, it opens the way to offering the biblical text in a selective way that omits passages that might arouse concern or discomfort.

Biblical censorship has a long history, although different eras vary greatly in the biblical texts they find shocking or embarrassing. Often, too, the act of selection is justified in terms of impartial scholarship, although the thinkers and theologians responsible have fairly transparent agendas. Martin Luther, for example, wanted to expel several books from the Bible. He was prepared to "toss into the Elbe" the aggressively Jewish book of Esther; he also thought of denying full canonical status to the book of Revelation, which so easily lent itself to abuse by extremists.[30] In early national America, Thomas Jefferson tried to edit the Bible in the interests of his own distinctive form of liberal Christianity. On the grounds of restoring what he believed to have been its original form, Jefferson created a version of the Gospels that omitted all references to the supernatural, every word about miracles or the resurrection.[31]

Creators of still other Bibles have tried to withhold portions of the text from specific audiences. The fourth-century Christian Ulfilas translated the Bible into the language of the Gothic barbarians, but deliberately decided not to render the books of Samuel and Kings because his potential readers already had far too much firsthand experience of wars and assassinations. The Goths "were in more need of restraints to check their military passions than of spurs to urge them on to deeds of war." He saw no loss in omitting books that were "a mere narrative of military exploits." Although his decision seems quirky, Ulfilas was making an important statement about thinking through the consequences of making the scripture freely available. Among other things, his Gothic readers would not have been exposed to the story of Saul and the Amalekites, which has indeed provoked mayhem through the centuries.[32]

Later generations were more commonly concerned with sexual material. Once the Bible was widely available in vernacular languages, adolescents made it their business to hunt down every possible reference to breasts and harlots, while their teachers struggled to avoid acknowledging that the smutty passages were even there. While not actively denying the existence of the offending words, mainstream pastors and preachers pretended that they did not exist. The Song of Solomon has often given real difficulties, however much clergy tried to claim that it was a chaste allegory of the relationship between Christ and his church.

As sexual puritanism grew during the nineteenth century, the existence of the Bible's dirty bits proved a real embarrassment to Christians, while secularists mocked the scripture for a pervasive indecency that could harm the young. Apologist Reuben Torrey refuted such charges, saying that preachers would always exercise a de facto censorship over the text. For instance, he noted, "there are things in the first chapter of Romans that one cannot dwell upon in public address, and as a rule at least, one will omit two verses in the public reading of this chapter." Although he is too shy even to identify the offending passage, he is referring to verses

26 through 27, in which Paul condemns "vile affections"—namely, male homosexuality and even, doubly unspeakable in Torrey's day, lesbianism.[33] These verses were not censored, in the sense that some Protestant counterpart of the Vatican officially forbade printing or uttering them, but churchgoers never heard them. That is very much what has happened to the texts of conquest and massacre in modern Christian usage.

Textual Healing

WHILE MARCION HAD WANTED to remove the whole Old Testament from Christian use, most modern Christians acknowledge their indebtedness to the Hebrew Bible. But accepting the Old Testament does not suggest equal enthusiasm for every passage in that large collection, and over the past few decades many churches have in practice suppressed large portions of that work. They have done this by adopting a list of readings prescribed for use in their services that eliminate much of what is unpalatable.

Sometimes this is done informally, through a process of silent editing. One candidate for quiet elimination is the final verse of Psalm 137, about massacring the children of Babylon. The verse, doubly unfortunate because it comes at the end of a popular and impressive psalm, is often removed in practice. And not just in (most) churches and synagogues: when the pop music group Boney M had a worldwide hit with a version of the psalm in 1978 ("By the Rivers of Babylon"), the last verse also disappeared. Just as liable to be surreptitiously removed today from Christian use are the words that explain why Jesus's disciples were in hiding after the crucifixion: "for fear of the Jews."[34]

In modern times, churches have become more systematic in their reading practices, and in their purging of offending texts. Christians have always read Bible passages as an integral part of their services, and for this purpose they produce lectionaries, collections of texts appropriate for given days in the church year. These set readings draw from both Old and New Testaments, with the different elements chosen on the basis of some common theme or relationship, and usually some relationship to the day or season. Commonly, these texts provide the basis for the day's homily or sermon. In order to give congregations the widest exposure to scripture, readings are spread over a cycle of two or three years.[35]

Over such a span, believers easily work their way through the New Testament text, but the Old is much lengthier and more difficult to cope with. One solution is to read the whole text, however long the individual sections and however soporific the details may sound to modern ears ("Reaiah the son of Shobal begat Jahath; and Jahath begat Ahumai . . ."). Alternatively, one can select key passages from the whole; and that is what many churches do, with a special preference for texts that can easily be fitted into a Christian framework. An obvious example is the weighty promise in older translations of Isaiah that "a virgin shall conceive."[36]

From the 1960s onward, different denominations shared a common interest in liturgical reform. They cooperated to produce the *Revised Common Lectionary* (*RCL*), which first emerged in the late 1960s and which reached a final revised form in 1994. The work is a striking ecumenical achievement: it is used not just by mainstream Protestant denominations (Lutheran, Methodist, Episcopal, Presbyterian) but also by Roman Catholics, and by many smaller groupings. Moreover, the *RCL* is used not just in North America but across the English-speaking world.[37] Despite this wide acceptance, the *RCL* still stirs controversy in its treatment of the Old Testament. The lectionary follows Catholic usage in reading four Bible passages on a typical Sunday, with an Old Testament reading being followed by a psalm, then something from a New Testament Epistle, and then part of a Gospel. But because the Old Testament has to be read partially rather than in its entirety, the lectionary underplays or omits difficult portions. In consequence, the *RCL* has become a nonprovocative and anodyne canon-within-the-canon, which includes less than half the whole biblical text. Over half the Bible is now missing in liturgical action.

Assume that believers regularly attended a church that used the *Revised Common Lectionary*—in fact, that they never missed a single Sunday or special holy day. If they listened attentively to the readings, over the three-year cycle they would hear just a small and unrepresentative selection of the controversial books. (See Table 3: "Selected Old Testament Passages in the *Revised Common Lectionary.*")

TABLE 3
SELECTED OLD TESTAMENT PASSAGES IN
THE *REVISED COMMON LECTIONARY*

This table combines and consolidates readings for all three years of the liturgical cycle. The descriptions of the particular texts are in my words.

Exodus

1:8–2:10   Israel's captivity in Egypt

3:1–15   God's appearance to Moses

12   The Passover and the exodus from Egypt

14   Crossing the Red Sea

15:1b–13, 17–18, 20–21   The Song of Moses and Miriam

16:2–15   God giving manna in the wilderness

17:1–7   Moses drawing water from the rock

19:2–8a   God offering his covenant to Israel

20:1–20   The Ten Commandments

24:12–18   Moses receiving the law on the mountain

32:1–14   Israel turning from God to worship the Golden Calf

33:12–23   Moses approaching the glory of God (but being denied the full vision)

34:29–35   Moses's face shining after his encounter with God

Numbers

6:22–27   Aaron's blessing of Israel

11:4–6, 10–16, 24–30   Israel's demand for food in the wilderness

21:4–9   Moses raising the bronze serpent in the wilderness

Leviticus

19:1–2, 9–18   God proclaiming the moral laws for Israel

Deuteronomy

4:1–2, 6–9   God demanding obedience to his law

5:12–15   The Ten Commandments

6:1–9   The laws that Israel is to keep if it is to hold the land

8:7–18   God's promise of the land

11:18–21, 26–28   God's instructions regarding the commandments

18:15–20   God's promise to raise up a prophet

26:1–11   How Israelites should celebrate the first fruits of the land and recite the blessings of God

30:9–20   The command that Israelites must follow God to win long life and prosperity

34:1–12   The death of Moses

Joshua

3:7–17   Crossing the Jordan into the Promised Land

5:9–12   Eating the food of the Promised Land

24:1–3a, 14–25   A recounting of the history of Israel and a reminder of the need for faithful service to God

Judges

4:1–7   The story of Deborah

Ezra

  No readings

Nehemiah

  8:1–3, 5–6, 8–10   Ezra reading the law publicly

Esther

  7:1–6, 9–10; 9:20–22   The defeat and death of Haman

SOURCE: Consultation on Common Texts, *Revised Common Lectionary* (Nashville: Abingdon Press, 1992).

Actually, the process of cherry-picking is even more drastic than this table would suggest, as some of the readings are alternatives and thus might or might not be heard within a particular cycle. A year could pass without hearing a single verse from Joshua, say, or two years with nothing from Numbers or Leviticus.

Even within the favored books, the lectionary's compilers have made some draconian decisions about the material that is suitable or relevant. Texts have been chosen because they are felt to support the wider Christian message. Exodus is well represented as a saga of deliverance and redemption that prefigures the Christian salvation history. When Moses speaks with God on the mountain, that prepares the way for the Christian account of Christ's transfiguration, so that Exodus passage naturally had to appear in the *Lectionary.* Such a Christological focus explains the presence of the story about the bronze serpent that Moses raised for people to gaze upon and be healed. Christians have long seen that story as a foretaste of the crucifixion, and it is used thus in John's Gospel. Naturally, then, it also appears in the *Lectionary,* where it seems to be almost the only justification for the existence of the book of Numbers.[38]

Absent from the lectionary, though, are other potent sections of Numbers, including the tale of Phinehas, the destruction of King Sihon, and Moses's massacre of the Midianites. The copious selections from Exodus omit sensitive passages such as the prophecy of the expulsion of the native peoples and the order to suppress Canaanite religion. While the lectionary includes the Exodus account of Moses drawing water from the rock, it cuts the very next story, that of the struggle with Amalek.[39] Believers hear neither the warlike sections of Numbers and Deuteronomy, nor the segregationist passages of Ezra and Nehemiah. Preachers have no need to explain to their flocks such puzzling concepts as *herem,* or to discuss why Moses preserved from death only those Midianite women who remained untainted by sex.

Other hard books are treated just as gingerly. The two books of Samuel are well represented, because David prefigures Christ. Yet the struggle of Saul and the Amalekites does not feature, nor does the killing of Agag. This reads oddly, because the *Lectionary* does include the story that immediately follows that incident, when Samuel deserts Saul to find a new king and anoints David. Without the Amalekite incident, though, that story has no context or explanation.

Joshua features most prominently with a reading during Lent, which tells how the Israelites relied on manna for their food until they ate some of the produce from the land of Canaan, and thereupon the supplies of manna stopped. It would have been astounding if Christian tradition had not seen this story in eucharistic terms. Otherwise, the only readings from Joshua include the crossing of the Jordan and most of chapter 24, which summarizes the conquest. Listening to these texts, Christians are meant to see the Israelites entering Canaan as a foretaste of the church being redeemed from sin and death, crossing over the river into salvation.

So what is left out here? While all the passages that are included concern the conquest, conspicuously missing from them is the annihilation of the peoples of Canaan. That exclusion is not absolute, and Joshua 3 does include a promise to drive out the Canaanites—to drive out, not to exterminate. But the lectionary includes not a word from the heavily mined texts in chapters 6 through 11, the hard-core texts of massacre. Although the manna story leads immediately into the attack on Jericho, modern congregations get no taste of that event. As we see, the *RCL* offers the introductory verses of the final chapter, but then moves straight to verses 14 through 25, without alerting listeners to the transition. The omitted verses in question recount the conquest and destruction of the Amorites and the king of Moab, the fall of Jericho, and the removal of the seven peoples of Canaan. Leaving out that section, we imagine the rival peoples listed in this chapter as armed enemies in battle, not as civilian targets for genocide.

The largest religious institution in the United States, the Roman Catholic Church, specifies readings not just for every Sunday but for each and every weekday service, and for special feasts and solemnities. Yet even under those expanded conditions, any person who attended literally every possible service would hear only a highly selective view of the Old Testament. Any book that Christians can read with interest and enthusiasm is cited frequently—Catholics hear a very great deal from Isaiah—but Joshua is barely covered.

Modern preachers regularly proclaim the confrontational and challenging character of the Old Testament, by which they mean the social radicalism of Amos, or the withering critiques of war and injustice in prophets such as Isaiah and Jeremiah. Yet few indeed are the sermons that explore the injunction to leave nothing that breathes, or condemn those who fail to kill the last victim. Some churches presumably do preach on the conquest stories, on Phinehas and Joshua, on Ezra and Nehemiah, but they are definitely in a minority; and even those that do usually glide over the bloodier passages. Churches are prepared to hear harsh words, but they do so very selectively.

Of course, Christians are not forbidden to read the troubling texts on their own, either in a private context or in a common study group—although many such groups like to use the lectionary as a guide for scriptural reading, either using the texts for the coming Sunday or linking the study to a sermon. Ordinary readers are free to explore Joshua, Ezra, and Deuteronomy, but how many do?

STRATEGIES OF DENIAL AND selective reading undoubtedly work. Ordinary Christians and Jews simply do not know the genocidal passages, and one might say, the passing of such ideas from a religion is an excellent thing. But it does pose some real difficulties, as Christians in particular deceive themselves about the foundations of their faith, and of the scripture that they claim to follow. A bloodless Bible offers cheap Grace.

CHAPTER NINE

Historians and Prophets

My house shall be called a house of prayer for all peoples.

—ISAIAH 56:7

ALTHOUGH SOME CHRISTIANS MAY resort to rejecting whole sections of the Bible, such denial is unnecessary. However hard it may seem to accommodate the texts of terror, the task is not in fact impossible, and the results are entirely worthwhile. Ideally, such accommodation not only applies to reading and preaching the dark passages, but likewise illuminates many other parts of scripture that have become difficult or controversial over time.

History and Faith

THE FIRST ESSENTIAL STEP toward accommodation is understanding why the various books were written, and appreciating the core message that each is trying to teach. Above all, we have to know the form in which any story appears. The troubling Biblical accounts must be read as narrative, as story-telling, rather than as simple recorded observation.

The account of conquest and settlement in Deuteronomy-

Joshua is a *history*, a word that demands some explanation. In popular usage, if something is history it is a true account of events as they actually occurred: it's real. Scholars, though, use the word to suggest the literary form that an account takes, to distinguish it from a simple recounting of events, such as a set of annals or a chronicle (both forms of literature common in the ancient world). Our understanding of the conquest would be quite different if we had to rely on annals, which would give us a series of entries something like this:

In this year, Joshua took the city of Ai, and took great plunder.

In this year, Joshua marched toward the west.

In this year, Joshua killed five kings.

And so on, without comment or interpretation.

But the account in Deuteronomy-Joshua is not a chronicle or set of annals but a history. This does not necessarily mean that it is literally true as a record of events, but rather that we have a constructed narrative in which particular authors and editors have taken a story and framed it in ways that makes sense to them. It is a story with a point or theme, and one that is aimed at a particular audience. As the accounts have evolved over long periods, so have the themes stressed by successive editors. Sometimes, the need to speak to different audiences results in some weak links in the text, or even jarring contradictions.

As Baruch Halpern has argued, the Hebrew biblical writers were not just historians, but the *first* historians. They pioneered the writing of what we would come to call history, and that fact offers us both some good news and some bad news. On the good side, dealing with quite sophisticated historical narratives means that we have access to some wonderful ancient writing that offers superb and highly literary accounts of people and places. So potent are these stories that they are still inspiring our culture. (To take just one example, Leonard Cohen's song "Hallelujah," which builds on the story of King David, has been one of the most popular and influential pieces of music of the last thirty years.) But these histories are so powerful and so convincing that later generations run the risk of taking every word literally, as documented fact. Misunderstanding the authors' literary intent, readers wrench verses and stories out of their essential context.[1]

When we place the dark passages in the broader narrative and historical tradition, some startling lessons emerge. They no longer look like vestiges of a savage past that unaccountably survived within an increasingly sophisticated theological tradition; rather, we recognize that they emerged exactly as that complex tradition was reaching fruition. However much they seem to contradict the great Hebrew prophets, the dark passages were in fact intimately related to the teachings of these spiritual giants.

Both strands, the prophets and the histories, originally presented a common message addressed to roughly the same audiences. If we ask what Deuteronomy and Joshua are "really" about, their core theme is neither genocide nor warfare. Rather, the books represent the clearest declarations of two essential ideas in the Bible and in the Judeo-Christian worldview—namely, monotheism itself, and election or chosenness. They also rely absolutely on the idea that God intervenes directly in history, shaping and uprooting earthly states and social orders, an idea that is quite as fundamental to Judaism as it is to Christianity and Islam. Where these books differ from other, better-known sections of the Bible is not in their overall message, but in the vehicle they use to convey it.[2]

Faith in Progress

IF WE WERE TO read the Bible like a novel, starting from the beginning and moving forward, we would be tempted to see a process of moral and cultural development. In this view, a book like Joshua reflects a savage stage of society, which eventually gives place to the far more sophisticated worldview of Isaiah and the other prophets. The story begins with primitive bloodshed, but evolving moral consciousness means that such acts trouble later generations, who come to explain them away or reject them altogether.

The idea of God's progressive revelation to humanity is appealing. God may be the same yesterday, today, and forever, but human perceptions of Him have altered fundamentally through the millennia. At one stage in history, God seems to command things that are appropriate within a particular human society, but which cease to be so as humanity develops and progresses. Many evangelical Christians hold that God commanded different things in different historical eras, according to the kind of covenant then in force with his people. He had one covenant with Noah, for instance; another with Moses; while Christ's incarnation and death ushered in the final covenant under which we now live. From this point of view, believers living under later dispensations are not bound by the rules and principles of earlier eras. Liberal and progressive Christians (though coming from a very different standpoint) might agree, seeing an evolution of moral consciousness that ultimately allows believers to grow past the legalistic restraints of a Bible designed for a more primitive world.[3]

Perhaps God himself learns and evolves. One of popular culture's odder contributions to theology is the 1936 film *The Green Pastures*. Based on Marc Connelly's popular play, the film, with its stellar all-black cast, retells the stories of the Old Testament as imagined by children in a rural Southern Sunday school. Some characters are deliberately ludicrous, with their cotton-candy beards, while stereotypes run rampant: God is De Lawd. But the film's theme demands attention. As he deals with successive generations of humans, De Lawd becomes ever more disgusted with their evils and flaws, until he withdraws entirely from any contact with his creation. One day, though, God is shocked to hear of humans fighting bravely for right and justice. (Almost casually, the film offers images of tough, well-armed African American soldiers that are astonishing for this era of Hollywood history.) Still more amazing, these warriors are struggling in the name of a God they imagine, who is markedly superior to the temperamental and irascible De Lawd we have come to know. God himself has not told them to behave thus, and he can scarcely understand what they are doing. But these true Jews have moved far beyond the old judgmental God of wrath and vengeance. While they still respect Moses, they now follow great prophets like Hosea; and, through suffering, they have conceived of a pure deity of mercy. Not only have human beings risen morally, but so has God himself, who admits freely that he had fallen "way behind the times." He has learned from his creatures, and he comes to share in human sufferings through the self-giving of Jesus. People learn from God; God learns from people.[4]

Some thinkers have taken this idea of progress very seriously. In his book *The Evolution of God*, Robert Wright argues for just such a steady improvement over time in the message taught by the leading religions, seeing a consistent trend in the direction of universal tolerance and ethical consciousness. I would disagree somewhat with such a model: it is difficult to discern such an overall trend in any religion, and often the later commentators on scriptures are ethically far inferior to the texts they are discussing. But the evolutionary picture does offer a plausible shape for the Bible's narratives. At one extreme, a capricious and bloodthirsty tribal God appears in the conquest stories, set in the twelfth century BCE, while by the sixth century he has developed into the splendid universal God of mercy, justice, and love proclaimed by Isaiah and the other great prophets. Christians would then take the story up to the radical deity proclaimed by Jesus. To oversimplify to the point of parody, God in 1200 BCE was a reckless adolescent, but he matured significantly by 700, and by 500 he had achieved real wisdom and stability. By the first century CE, he was becoming a truly admirable character. God improved over time—or at least his followers learned to understand him better.[5]

If that pattern were indeed so clear-cut, it would solve some of the moral conundrums involved in accepting the most violent texts. Wright even suggests that such a model reflects not just changing human sensibilities, but possibly the work of a guiding consciousness raising humanity to new moral heights. "To the extent that 'God' grows, that is evidence—maybe not massive evidence, but some evidence—of higher purpose."[6]

Prophetic Faith

THE PROBLEM WITH SUCH an evolutionary approach is that the chronology just does not work. Although the most difficult texts, those in Deuteronomy and Joshua, describe events of the early Iron Age, they were written down much later—in fact, just at the time that the prophets were formulating their grand universal visions. In other words, the conquest passages, all the appalling tales of *herem* warfare, do not belong to the distant prehistory of the biblical story, but to its mainstream. They are not remote precursors of the prophetic era, but rather an integral part of that religious and literary process. The genocide tales are the indispensable other half of the story. That is why any attempt to purge or bowdlerize those texts, or to suppress them, inevitably distorts any faith that claims to be based on the Bible.

The critical period in our story runs from the eighth through the sixth centuries BCE, the heart of that transcontinental era of explosive cultural innovation that philosopher Karl Jaspers termed the Axial Age. In these years, Hebrew religion achieved awe-inspiring heights of insight and sophistication, culminating in the great prophets active between about 780 and 500 BCE. (See Table 4: "The

Hebrew Prophets.") This group included glorious figures such as Jeremiah, Ezekiel, Amos, and the two (possibly three) figures whose works are preserved under the name of Isaiah. Precise dating is impossible: Isaiah is not the only text in which scholars have detected multiple layers, composed at different eras, perhaps centuries apart.[7]

TABLE 4
THE HEBREW PROPHETS

All dates are approximate.

Date (BCE)	Prophets active
775	Amos
750	Hosea, Joel
725	First Isaiah, Micah
700	
675	
650	Nahum
625	Habakkuk
600	Jeremiah
575	Ezekiel
550	
525	Second Isaiah, First Zechariah
500	Malachi

The prophetic movement emerged at a deadly dangerous time for the Hebrew people, the period of near-terminal crisis that I described earlier. Shockingly, the northern kingdom of Israel was snuffed out in 721 BCE. That political disaster offered a traumatic shock to the remaining nation of Judah, especially as it coincided with a cultural transformation. The growth of the Assyrian Empire meant that states like Israel were now exposed to cultures and religions that would once have appeared inconceivably distant. Cosmopolitan influences inevitably made Hebrew thinkers question their familiar assumptions and raised the danger that local cultures would be overwhelmed. Israel both benefited and suffered from its pivotal geographical position, at the junction between the empires of Africa and Asia. As so often before and since, the Hebrew people had to choose between merging with these highly attractive other cultures, and fighting to remain distinct, preserving their particular religious faith.

The eighth-century crisis forced the Hebrew kings and the priestly elite to think agonizingly about their role in the wider world. Some rulers were happy to import foreign religious customs and practices, while others accepted a radical new monotheist vision, placing an absolute emphasis on God's exclusive covenant with this people. Prophets influenced kings like Hezekiah, and in turn derived inspiration from his example. The struggle over that vision raged throughout the seventh century, especially in the years leading up to the fall of Jerusalem in 586. Everything the prophets said, everything the historians wrote, has to be understood against this backdrop of crisis and imminent calamity. If the nation made a misstep, there could be twelve lost tribes, not just ten.[8]

The Burden of Election

WHILE THE PROPHETS EACH spoke with a distinct voice, some extraordinarily powerful themes emerged, ideas that would have an immense impact on later Judaism and Christianity. Paramount was the universalist idea of God as sovereign lord over the whole world and all its peoples, and not just over any one race or tribe. In the cultural crisis of the time, we can see this as a natural response to growing cosmopolitanism, and to the unprecedented exposure to the wider world. Following this God meant an absolute emphasis on practicing justice and ethical conduct in ways that were theoretically open to people of any race. What set the Hebrews apart was the uniquely weighty responsibility to fulfill those commands. Being a chosen people could look like a frightening burden.

Probably as early as the 770s, the book of Amos began with a series of withering denunciations of the neighboring pagan nations, as God threatened horrific vengeance. Hebrew listeners might have cheered what seemed like gung-ho nationalistic propaganda against any and all rivals, until the prophet issued an identical set of condemnations and threats against Judah and Israel themselves. As long as they trampled the poor and denied justice to the oppressed, the Hebrews were no better than any of their neighbors, and could expect to burn in the same fire. God declared, through Amos:

> You only have I known of all the families of
>   the earth:
> therefore I will punish you
> for all your iniquities.

"Therefore," not "But despite that." When the prophets invoked the ancient conquest of Canaan, it was never with the implication of "and soon our invincible legions shall pursue their manifest destiny in conquering neighboring lands." Rather, the message was, "and if we do not quickly recognize God's will, we will be next in line for removal." The linkage between land and law is explicit in Psalm 105:

> [God] gave them the lands of the heathen:
> and they inherited the labour of the people;
> That they might observe his statutes,
> and keep his laws.[9]

For the prophets, this ethical imperative meant downplaying the importance of ritual observance, unless it was combined with a passionate following of justice and mercy, above all to the poor. Micah denies that God would delight in the sacrifice of thousands of rams or bulls, or even of a firstborn son.[10] Amos's God furiously tells his people that "I hate, I despise your religious festivals; your assemblies are a stench to me. Even though you bring me burnt offerings and grain offerings, I will not accept them." That particular passage segues into one of the most celebrated phrases in American political rhetoric, in the words quoted by Martin Luther King Jr. Instead of false piety, says Amos, "let justice roll down like waters, and righteousness like an ever flowing stream." Religion without justice, without conscience, is worse than useless.[11]

Failure to follow God's law had catastrophic consequences. In the prophetic worldview, God often speaks the language of warfare and violence; but it is God, not human beings, who carries out these acts of destruction. Around 720, Isaiah declared that God would visit *herem* upon all other nations, giving them over to slaughter. In the age of Assyrian expansion, such a warning sounded all too plausible as a forecast of the political future. A later vision reported in Isaiah 63 offers one of the Bible's most shocking images—that of a God whose clothing drips with the blood of those he has massacred, like wine from a winepress. But if God is indeed a warrior, he chiefly contends against the Israel that betrays his commands, rather than against outside pagan foes.[12]

Warnings of catastrophe accumulated around 600, with the rise of a new generation of aggressive neighbors: if the Assyrians were gone, the Babylonians were no less dangerous. The prophet Jeremiah warns the people of Jerusalem not to trust blindly in the security of their temple, believing that it will somehow protect them and their city. Shiloh too, the sacred shrine of Israel, once had its special holy place, Jeremiah notes, and the Assyrians made short work of it. Jeremiah proclaims that an angry God will inflict *herem* upon Israel, and—in the splendidly threatening words of the King James translation—"make them an astonishment, and an hissing, and perpetual desolations." In Second Isaiah, God promises to "consign Jacob to destruction [*herem*], and Israel to scorn." The prophets imagined an ultimate day of wrath and judgment, which believers had to keep before their eyes. The idea would be fundamental to early Christianity, and to the later faith preached by Muhammad.[13]

The prophets were asking daring questions. Some even moved toward radical ideas of individual responsibility, which were startling at a time when guilt and sin were seen as a collective matter for the family and the clan. No, said the prophets, each individual must bear full responsibility for fulfilling God's covenant. Ezekiel quotes God as mocking the traditional idea that the child will suffer for the sins of his ancestors. Why, asks God, do you quote the proverb, "The fathers eat sour grapes, and the children's teeth are set on edge"? No, "Behold, all souls are mine; as the soul of the father, so also the soul of the son is mine: the soul that sinneth, it shall die." Applying this passage to the conquest texts creates intriguing results, not least in subverting the eternal enmity proclaimed against the Amalekites. In Ezekiel's vision, surely every individual Amalekite should be judged for his or her actions, and not for the treacherous behavior of remote ancestors.[14]

Dating the Deuteronomist(s)

It would be convenient to think that these prophetic statements, these bold visions of a purer Israel, were deliberately rejecting an older tribal savagery, which was best represented in the Deuteronomistic stories of the conquest. Joshua, in this view, would represent an old-fashioned kind of chauvinistic militarism, which radicals like Amos then subverted to the point of parody. Unfortunately for any effort at neat historical schemes, we can't simply consign the bloodiest passages to an ancient layer of scripture and assume that later generations grew out of their primitive tendencies.

Let's think back to the chronology described earlier. Recalling the stages at which the different portions of the Bible were written down, then Deuteronomy can be dated with fair confidence to the eighth and seventh centuries BCE, and the larger Deuteronomistic History to the sixth. In other words, the bloodiest passages of the Bible were written down in the very same years that the great prophets were preaching their messages of universalism and social justice. This was the time at which the book of Joshua was recording the conquest of Canaan, with a new emphasis on annihilation and genocide. Beyond merely describing the invasion, the history was embellishing this tale in ways that seem to us incomprehensibly malicious or sadistic. But by the time Joshua was written down in its canonical form, the greatest of the prophets were still active or recently dead. The conquest texts are products of the Axial Age.[15]

Read in this light, the distinctions between the prophetic and the historical texts fade rapidly, and "prophetic" values seem less distinctive. In the Hebrew tradition, in fact, the line separating history and prophecy all but disappears. The narrative historical books from Joshua through Kings are known as the Former Prophets (*Nevi'im Rishonim*), while explicitly prophetic books such as Isaiah are counted as the Later Prophets (*Nevi'im Aharonim*). The prophet Samuel is a central figure in the Deuteronomistic History, and of course Samuel actually kills Agag. In this act, it is Samuel the prophet, not Saul the king, who shows himself the true follower of *herem* warfare. The prophets Elijah and Elisha take up much of the space in the following historical books, which are conventionally known as 1 and 2 Kings. Ezekiel's bracing words about individual responsibility, about the father's guilt not descending to his kin, find echoes both in Deuteronomy itself and in 2 Kings.[16]

According to some theories, the overlap between the prophets and the historians might have been personal, not just ideological. Noting close parallels between the Deuteronomistic History and the prophet Jeremiah, some suggest that *the* Deuteronomist, the crucial final editor, might have been either Jeremiah himself or one of his close followers, possibly his scribe Baruch.[17]

Instead of being in conflict, the two approaches, prophetic and historical, were complementary. They were dual aspects of a single movement. The difference between the Deuteronomists and the prophets was one of avenue rather than destination, of genre rather than goal.

One God

THE DEUTERONOMISTS DEMANDED A radical separation between the people of Israel and their neighbors—more specifically, between the God of Israel and his rivals. Constantly before their eyes was the absolute need for complete monotheism, for purity in faith and worship, however significantly such a model broke with the authentic older traditions of the land. Just like the prophets whose words seem so magnificent today, they were also preaching an exalted vision of a God who ruled over all, and who was alone worthy of worship. The bitter words in Deuteronomy and Joshua were essential to later religious growth and evolution.[18]

According to this vision—whatever its basis in historical truth— the Israel that established itself in Canaan was a new creation, pledged to creating and maintaining a society absolutely pledged to God. A wholly new people lived in a land swept clean of older peoples, customs, and faiths. We often use the word "radical" without much sense of its origins, but radical is exactly the term for what is imagined here—namely, a change from the roots up. The new planting demanded an uprooting, an extirpation, of everything that had gone before. The more pressing the danger that the people might actually lose their land and identity, the more desperate the need to defend those things at all costs.[19]

Where the Deuteronomists differed from the prophets was in

presenting the implications of this view not in poetry and vision, but rather through a historical narrative, in which peoples such as the nations of Canaan served, in a way, the purpose of imaginary demons to be expelled. That meant telling a story, and at every possible stage heightening the degree of contrast and separation between Israel and those other nations or cultures. The fate of the Canaanites had to be painted in the darkest possible colors because the writers were sending an urgent, eleventh-hour warning to the Hebrew people, to turn back to God or else face annihilation. Israel had to kill its inner Canaanite. Perhaps the later commentators, Jewish and Christian, were not that misguided in seeing the massacres in allegorical terms.

To illustrate the message being offered to the Israelites, let me offer an imaginary historical parallel, a fable perhaps. Imagine an alternative America with a very different history, and with scanty knowledge of its actual past. This America possesses a potent national myth, which describes how the country was once occupied by a tyrannical race called the English, who had *absolutely no* connection with the later inhabitants of the land. We don't even know what language these evil creatures spoke. They were then overcome by the invading Americans, led by George Washington and Thomas Jefferson, who tried to exterminate every English man, woman, and child. However, enough of the English survived to leave a dark inheritance for the new nation. Whenever later Americans suffered tyranny or oppression, economic or religious exploitation, they blamed this on the sinister inheritance of the land's ancient occupants. Only by constantly struggling against the English past could Americans keep the country true to its founding principles. At some level, perhaps, the myth-makers might have known the flaws of this story, known that the rebellious Americans of 1776 drew overwhelmingly on a common English inheritance, political and racial, cultural and linguistic. But that critique scarcely mattered when the myth was so rhetorically valuable, and had become such a fundamental component of a sweeping reformist agenda.

Something like this process occurred in the biblical story. Only by declaring an absolute separation could the Deuteronomists lay the foundation for the religious reform they wanted to see: a total focus on the unity and absolute power of God. Only in a rigidly monotheistic society, they believed, could Israel accomplish the quest for justice that was its historical task.[20]

Through all the World

ONCE THE HISTORICAL FOUNDATION was laid, the prophets and biblical historians could explore the full implications of this absolute break with polytheism. For one thing, it meant a society quite different from the rigid hierarchies of neighboring nations, with their god-kings claiming to speak for Osiris or Asshur. Deuteronomy depicts a society without kings, and later books are deeply ambiguous about the virtues of monarchy. Just where did that foreign institution belong in "one nation, under God"? (And that question would have a lasting impact. As scholars such as Eric Nelson remind us, Deuteronomy provided a critical manifesto for the European Enlightenment, with its emphasis on the rights of the people, not of the monarch or traditional elites.)[21] As Israel sought a role in a world of competing empires, the prophets explored what it really meant to preach one God who ruled the whole world, Israel and the other nations. The Deuteronomistic vision gave a small nation the confidence to take on a whole world.

The new vision reached vaulting heights during the sixth century BCE. Israel's faith, its sense of its role and mission, had been severely tested during the sixty long years of exile in Babylon. It was especially in this century that prophets such as Jeremiah and Ezekiel placed a new stress on the importance of the land, and of the means by which the Israelites had won their inheritance. In 538, the new Persian king Cyrus allowed the Hebrew people to return to their land. That event called forth a celebration from the unknown prophet whom we know as Second Isaiah, whose words make up much of the second half of that book, and who proclaimed a startling new vision of God's role in history. For this prophet, Israel had its special mission, but God, ruler of all, fulfilled his purposes through whatever peoples he chose, and whether they knew it or not. The passages lauding Cyrus—obviously, not a Jew—contributed mightily to later beliefs about the messiah who was to come. Early and medieval Christians so venerated the book of Isaiah and quoted it so abundantly that it became to them effectively a fifth Gospel.[22]

Possibly at this point, other prophets too envisioned a universal reign of God, when all nations would come to Jerusalem's temple for guidance. As a passage now found in Micah promises, "the law shall go forth of Zion, and the word of the LORD from Jerusalem." (Although presented as the words of the eighth-century prophet Micah, the passage may have been written significantly later, perhaps in the sixth century.)[23] The vision is stunning; but it would not have been possible without the harsh monotheistic historical framework created by the Deuteronomist.

Christians who ignore or slight Deuteronomy are passing over a book in which Jesus and Paul found special treasures. But what could these treasures have been? Asking that question makes us think of the core ideas of Deuteronomy, not of the violent and extreme language in which they are sometimes phrased. The imagined war against outside peoples and customs symbolized a rejection of any and all things that distract or separate a people or an individual from God.

WE MIGHT ASK A provocative question: If the conquest texts in particular are so noxious, so evil, why not censor them from the Bible altogether, not just through discreet editing of the lectionary, but by a formal exclusion? This is after all what some critics demand that Muslims do with the warlike passages of the Qur'an. Just what would Jews and Christians lose from their faith? But without those texts, the rest of the Bible simply makes no sense. Without the conquest, without the covenant for the land, there is no Old Testament, and no Judaism. Without the Old Testament—all of it, including every part of Joshua and Deuteronomy—the New Testament becomes a tree without a trunk.

CHAPTER TEN

Preaching the Unpreachable

One must deal cleanly with the Scriptures.

—MARTIN LUTHER

AFTER A SCATHING DENUNCIATION of atrocities recounted in
Numbers and Deuteronomy, Mark Twain urged Christian preachers
to offer these texts to their congregations alongside the Beatitudes,
in order to give "an all-round view of Our Father in Heaven."[1]
Although his goal was to subvert religion, Twain's approach can be
applied rather differently. By all means, let congregations hear, perhaps for the first time, just what is written in the darker parts of the
Bible. More important, let them appreciate the different strategies
that Christians have employed through the centuries to deal with
these tales. The more honestly believers comprehend their faith, including its most unsettling components, the better they can engage
constructively with other religions, and with the enemies of all religions.

To that end, let us imagine a countercultural religious exercise. Let churches pledge themselves for a set period—say, several
months—to using the severest and most nightmarish texts for their
Bible study and preaching, the hardest of hard sayings. They should
read and preach on the texts of terror, to understand them and their

place in the larger pattern of scripture and of the faith as a whole. I use a Christian context for this suggestion, although similar theological issues emerge in Judaism, and some Jewish thinkers have offered impressive examples of what can be done in such matters: I think of Rabbi Lamm's struggle with the Amalekite text.[2]

It would be only too easy to assemble such a list of knotty texts. In fact, the main obstacle to the exercise would be the potential repetition. When we have wrestled with one passage in which God tells his followers to slaughter everything that breathes, how many other near-identical commands can we usefully discuss? But any of the conquest texts listed in Table 1 (see p. 36) would serve, as would (say) God's killing of the firstborn Egyptians, the command in Exodus that a witch should not be allowed to live, or the human sacrifice of Jephthah's daughter.[3]

Each reading in its way points to particular difficulties in the text, but each can be approached realistically. To take an example, what about the opening of Deuteronomy 7, which I cited at the beginning of this book as possibly the worst life-verse in the entire Bible? "You must destroy them totally. Make no treaty with them, and show them no mercy." Imagine that a modern-day cleric had to preach a sermon and had absolutely no alternative except to choose that radioactive text. What could she or he do?

Off-Limits

THE ISSUE OF DIVINE violence and injustice has surfaced in that vital bearer of American popular culture *The Simpsons,* where it is discussed by two of our society's best-known fictional Christians. In a 2010 episode entitled "The Greatest Story Ever D'ohed," Ned Flanders bemoans his failure to redeem Homer Simpson. However, urges Pastor Lovejoy, Ned should recall that God never gives up on anyone. When asked about Sodom and Gomorrah, Lovejoy explains that, far from giving up on those cities, God "lovingly destroyed them." If that phrase seems ludicrous, it does not fall too far short of some serious attempts to come to terms with the dark passages.

In approaching something like Deuteronomy 7, some options should be off-limits, or should at least be used with great caution. Each might carry some weight if argued carefully, but each in its way raises more questions than it answers, as many in fact as the idea of "lovingly destroying" a city. Christians should never seek to dismiss or underplay the Old Testament, or to try and consign the troubling texts to this supposedly more primitive tradition: "That's just the Old Testament!" And although it is difficult to imagine many people making such an argument today, no-one should use the concept of the afterlife to argue that God will ultimately make up the apparent injustices suffered by victims of massacre.[4]

Three more substantial approaches should be used very sparingly, if at all:

Don't Lightly Invoke An Incomprehensible Higher Wisdom

One tactic is to preach the text as it stands, and to explain that, however monstrous or unjust the words may seem to us, God nevertheless knows best. The ancient Israelites were only obeying orders, and we should follow their example. We could then read the text as a plea for absolute, unquestioning faith in God's will, a frank admission that his ways are far above ours: ours not to reason why. An argument might proceed like this: "God exercised his sovereign will, and it is not fitting for mere mortals to so much as query the decision. What God wills is by definition good and just, and only our flawed human perceptions prevent us understanding this." As John Calvin said, "As He, in whose hands are life and death, had justly doomed those nations to destruction, this puts an end to all discussion."[5]

But it really doesn't. It's true that strong theological traditions in many religions hold that God's ways are often incomprehensible to mere humans, who find it difficult to understand his will. Yet those same traditions also share a common abhorrence for the indiscriminate mass slaughter of whole populations. Such an act is not only a breach of a specific doctrine or divine command, but of most of them—indeed, of everything that believers live by.

Today, we commonly link Judaism, Christianity, and Islam together under the common label of the Abrahamic religions, named for the patriarch who was above all rewarded for his unquestioning faith. But such faith is problematic. Abraham's story also forces us to address the conflicting claims of religious demands and familiar ethical standards. The dilemma is familiar to modern theology, not least through the works of Søren Kierkegaard. In his influential *Fear and Trembling,* Kierkegaard examined an act that seemed morally appalling—namely, Abraham's willingness to kill his son on God's command. For Kierkegaard, Abraham's act was a glorious moment of absolute surrender to the divine will, whatever the violation of human ethics; it was a symbol of total commitment to God, making Abraham a "knight of faith." "Faith begins precisely there," Kierkegaard said, "where thinking leaves off."[6]

Kierkegaard was properly disturbed by the possible implications of his argument, and he would have been even more so had he extended his argument with a natural comparison, namely Saul's conflict with the Amalekites. Abraham obeyed an unacceptable command, but was miraculously saved from pursuing the order to its bloody conclusion. Saul, in contrast, refused to obey his command to kill an unarmed victim. Unlike Isaac, the victim died anyway, unsaved by divine intervention, and Saul's refusal doomed his kingship. Failure to complete an act of genocide meant that he could never rise to knightly rank among the heroes of faith. Would Kierkegaard, or any sane thinker, dared to pursue to its logical conclusion such a denigration of reason and morality?

Never Suggest that a People Deserves Ruin

Producing secular or political reasons why the Canaanites (or other groups) deserved annihilation leaves believers recycling genocidal statements that are discredited in the secular realm. Few modern thinkers could or should recycle the once familiar argument that we can summarize thus: "Although the extermination of a whole people would normally be wrong, the extremely evil and sinful nature of the peoples of Canaan justified this action in this particular instance. The victims fully earned their annihilation. We should be impressed that God restrained his just anger as long as he did." Scarcely more convincing is the argument that looks to the long-term historical good, the suggestion that native peoples had to be destroyed for God to accomplish his vast historical design. In this view, the slaughter of the Canaanites (and Midianites and Amalekites) had multiple long-term benefits for God's chosen people. Viewed in a long-term historical perspective, so the argument goes, things worked out well.[7]

Neither of these approaches is likely to command much sympathy today, partly because history and archaeology have given us a solid idea of the nature both of Canaanite society and of its supposed atrocities. Any religion involving child sacrifice is horrific, but the Canaanites were no worse than a thousand other societies that God did *not* damn to perdition. In terms of ethics and morality, the Western offshoot of Canaanite civilization that became Carthage behaved no worse than its Roman counterpart, which managed to retain a transcontinental empire for over a millennium.

Our own knowledge of recent history shows how easily such arguments for genocide might be applied in the modern world. Every oppressor believes that his enemies are uniquely vile or dangerous. Every tyrant knows that he is on the side of history, and that you can't make an omelet without breaking eggs. Every oppressor also knows the argument that justifies killing the children of the hated race: while those infants look harmless now, they will grow up to share the evils of their parents—nits make lice. As Matthew Tindal noted three hundred years ago, Israelite justifications for exterminating their foes read uncannily like those of later conquerors trying to justify their own acts of mass murder. If one race is destined to be chosen, are others chosen for elimination or expulsion? Or is their fate just irrelevant to the divine plan?

Don't Invalidate The Text As Part Of A Savage Antiquity

Nor should we treat the troubling text as pure archaeology, an obsolete relic of the harsh and primitive world in which Biblical books were written. Because society has moved on, one might think, modern listeners need pay no attention to the genocide verses except as an ugly fossil of ancient conflicts. To know the historical circumstances in which a text was written—so the argument goes—removes the need to respect that text in another, later context. From a cynical perspective, one might say that pronouncements in scriptures are eternally valid for just as long as believers think they should be.

If that is the case, though, it is not clear why any other passage of the Bible should carry the slightest authority, except insofar as it corresponds with the enlightened consensus of the modern world. That argument might seem attractive to a modern liberal audience troubled by biblical texts that appear hostile to women's authority in the churches, say, or to expressions of homosexuality. But we should not immediately assume the superiority of those enlightened assumptions, the idea of human history as an age-long struggle between antiquated scriptures and humane secular modernity. On occasion, what was at the time billed as the inevitable advance of progressive modernity has proved to be horribly flawed, while in retrospect certain traditional religious interpretations have emerged with far more credibility. It was not long ago that the overwhelming consensus of "progressive" thought included ideas that would appall a modern liberal, especially in the realm of eugenics and racial superiority. To argue that some texts and stories might legitimately be challenged or revoked does not mean that scripture has no substantial core of truth.

Just because a biblical passage outrages modern or progressive sentiments does not of itself invalidate that passage. Modern-day idealists and social activists happily cite the radical social doctrines of Jesus or the Old Testament prophets precisely because these texts constitute such a stark challenge to contemporary values. But as we have seen, the conquest texts are no more ancient or primitive than the much-esteemed prophets. If we propose that different parts of the Bible be accorded differing degrees of authority, then we have to spell out the criteria by which we are going to make those decisions.

Reading Clean

WITH THOSE CAVEATS IN mid, let us take Deuteronomy 7:1–2, and imagine that we came across that passage in the process of devotional reading, or in hearing or even preparing a sermon. How might we approach it? Obviously, what I am offering here is not intended as any kind of definitive reading, but rather a few personal impressions.

The first point would be to acknowledge freely that we respond to the words with shock: they are ugly; they are unacceptable. We need to hear and understand the notion of *herem* that appears in this passage, with all its awful implications, and to know that this was not just a standard manifestation of ancient warfare. It is quite legitimate to try to comprehend the historical background to this passage—when, for instance, it was written, under what circumstances, and whether it had any relationship to actual warfare or campaigns. But when we have done that, the words remain, and they are agonizing.

Approaching such a text, our hypothetical preacher could do worse than to follow the advice of Martin Luther, who had to deal with European contemporaries intoxicated by the scriptures they had discovered with such awe and excitement. The attitudes of these early modern Christians, in fact, closely resembled those of more recent first- and second-generation Christians in the emerging nations of Africa and Asia, still in the initial throes of an intense love affair with the Bible. Inspired by the scripture, some of Luther's extreme contemporaries wanted to import it wholesale into the modern world, using Old Testament legal codes to rule a Christian society.

Trying to calm his rivals, Luther urged that believers should be very careful in how they read scripture, and especially how they applied it in their own day. They should "read cleanly":

> From the very beginning, the Word has come to us in various ways. It is not enough simply to look and see whether this is God's word, whether God has said it; rather we must look and see to whom it has been spoken, whether it fits us. This makes all the difference between night and day. . . . The word in Scripture is of two kinds: the first does not pertain or apply to me, the other kind does.[8]

Not all words of the Bible apply to all readers. Passages addressed to David as king might be relevant to kings, but not to the rest of us, and we would be insane to pretend they do. More generally, for Luther, large sections of the Bible—especially the Hebrew law codes and rules of ritual purity—did not apply literally to Christians, who lived under the different arrangements prevailing under Christ. That did not mean that the Old Testament was repealed or obsolete, but people had to seek in it what was relevant to them. The medieval scholastics had a useful rule: *Quidquid recipitur ad modum recipientis recipitur,* or in English, roughly, "What people hear depends on who is doing the hearing." We see (and hear) things not as *they* are, but as *we* are.

The obvious question arising from Luther's comments is, "How do we know who God is speaking to?" Responding to the Deuteronomy passage, we might begin by asking just how human beings discern what they believe to be God's will, whether in their own lives or in the workings of history. We should think of the temptation to project human desires, human politics, and imagine them to be God's will, using that as an excuse for doing things that would be otherwise unacceptable. The text lends itself to rich interpretations for the nature and potential dangers of religious politics, for creating and imagining enemies so absolutely beyond the civilized pale that they have to be annihilated. Whether or not such a projection spawned this particular text, the warning about misreading divine intent is also useful.

Reading Whole

THROUGHOUT THE BIBLE, WE need to be very careful to consider particular words in the setting of the whole scripture—and not just the whole book of Deuteronomy, say, but the whole Bible itself. As in any literary work, individual verses and passages matter less for themselves than for the role they play in the composition of the whole work. In recent years, scholars have written a great deal about "narrative theology," emphasizing how we find truth in the stories of scripture, rather than in applying abstract propositions. We should also look at any given passage in the context of the *religion* as a whole, including its subsequent interpretation. It really matters how the passage has been used, and misused, and such textual abuse has befallen stories that on their surface seem quite harmless in contrast to the Conquest texts.

Imagine, for instance, that someone is preaching on one of the most notorious passages of Joshua, in which the great general reportedly trampled all the laws of science. According to the book's tenth chapter, Joshua was engaged in a fierce battle at Gibeon with his Amorite enemies, who threatened to escape under cover of darkness. In response to Joshua's fervent prayer, God prolonged the daylight in order to assure an Israelite victory. "So the sun stood still in the midst of heaven, and hasted not to go down about a whole day."[9] The story makes sense only in a pre-Copernican system of astronomy, one in which the sun circles the earth.

This is in scientific terms a close enough parallel to the moral dilemmas posed by scripture's genocide commands. It is utterly unacceptable, and has for many years been used to challenge fundamentalist concepts of scripture. Clarence Darrow used the Gibeon story to bludgeon William Jennings Bryan in the famous Scopes trial of 1925. In this instance, demonstrably, the biblical text is teaching an incorrect scientific view. But is it so irredeemably tainted that a modern reader or listener can derive nothing from it? Is it unreadable, or unpreachable? We return to Luther's criterion: What in the passage applies to me, to us? The point of the Gibeon story is not to offer a flawed lesson in astronomy, but rather to suggest other, quite fundamental themes that run through the book of Joshua and the Bible: that God chooses a people, and provides for them; and that God intervenes in history to achieve his ends, though our vocabulary may be too limited to assess why or how this happens. Skipping the Gibeon passage on astronomical grounds is like passing over Jesus's language about the lilies of the field because it falls short of botanical precision.

In Deuteronomy 7, the core message is again one of pure monotheism, under a God who is portrayed as exceedingly fearsome in order to remind the Hebrews of the very high stakes in winning and maintaining their chosenness. Following Luther's approach, we should begin by asking to whom those terror texts were directed, to whom they were relevant; and the answer is surely the Hebrews who first heard or read the text, and who were meant to learn what awaited them if they betrayed their covenant. Hearing Deuteronomy 7, those early listeners were not intended to stand on their guard against Amorites or Canaanites, but against themselves and their neighbors, who together made up a society pledged to God. For modern believers too, the text is not a message of hatred against any outsiders—still less a justification for violence or exclusion—but a call to absolute dedication.

Throughout Deuteronomy and Joshua, we find the critical theme of holiness, *kedushah*—the absolute holiness that characterizes God alone, and that separates his reality from any and all others. When the prophet Isaiah had his dazzling vision of God's heavenly court around 700 BCE, he saw the angels around the throne hymning "Holy [*Kadosh*], holy, holy, is the LORD of hosts: the whole earth is full of his glory." All the subsequent religious forms that grew from the Bible attempted in different ways to understand this holiness, this separateness, and to live according to its fierce principles.

For both the Deuteronomist and the prophets, this meant living as a holy and separate people in a holy land, and removing any vestiges of competing systems that might detract from that: you must be set apart! The Deuteronomist portrayed this idea in terms of sweeping military campaigns, a message that, misunderstood and vulgarized, has been read as authorizing racial supremacy and segregation. Read against the background of the prophets and the experience of history, though, those bloody verses teach a quite different theme: a holy people is judged not by its wars or victories, but by the nature of its life and its society, and above all by the role it plays for others, present and future. The passage is meant to teach righteousness, *tzedek,* a paramount biblical concept absolutely different from the derogatory term "self-righteousness," with which it is so often confused today.

Reading Deuteronomy 7 should make listeners explore the concept of "the holy," a concept that in modern contexts is all too often mired in images of spiritual arrogance and hypocrisy. What initially looks like an extreme manifestation of local tribal particularism is in fact the foundation for a global vision.

Reading from Below

MUCH OF THE BIBLE depends on two concepts: the theory of choosing or election, and the idea that God intervenes directly in human history. In each case, though, the Deuteronomic passage focuses on what we might call the dark side of those concepts. However much the Bible stresses that being chosen is above all a responsibility, it also means gaining advantages over others who are not chosen, raising questions about those forgotten others, the peoples driven from the land. And if God intervenes in the affairs of states, then sometimes, presumably, that means wars and conflicts, in which there must be losers as well as winners.

One nation's story of conquest and expansion means destruction and humiliation for others. From a Palestinian standpoint, Edward Said remarked that "there is no Israel without the conquest of Canaan and the expulsion or inferior status of Canaanites—then as now." Sometimes, the defeated retreat to fight another day, but at other times, says the Bible, they do not survive. According to Deuteronomy and Joshua, the defeated perished in the thousands, perhaps the hundreds of thousands. Any later reader has to think from the perspective of those defeated, the excluded, the *non*chosen. We have an obligation to read "from below"—that is, from the stance of outsiders.[10]

That basic recognition shapes a great deal of modern secular historical writing, particularly in the context of imperial expansion. It would be difficult today to tell the story of the nineteenth-century expansion of European powers or of the United States without taking account of the other side of the story, of the people who lost their lands and sovereignty. When the defeated people or their descendants survive, it is hard to forget the need to tell the story from both sides: the protests of survivors and their heirs help keep historians honest. But when history's losers have vanished even in name, and have left no accounts in their own words, a major effort of historical imagination is needed to reconstruct those voices— indeed, even to remember that their views ever mattered. W. H. Auden famously wrote that

> **History to the defeated**
> **May say Alas, but cannot help nor pardon.[11]**

In the case of vanished peoples like the Canaanites, history rarely even grunts a passing "Alas."

If secular historians recognize the need to acknowledge the victims as well as the conquerors, religious thinkers have at least as high an obligation to read narratives from both points of view. That is anything but a new insight for biblical scholarship, which for some decades has been transformed by the work of feminist readers. They have ransacked the biblical text to rediscover and reimagine the experience of those women characters who so often appear as victims or nameless marginal figures.[12]

But can we now apply the same insight to those defeated and subjected nations? Fortunately, to this end, we now live in a world where a large proportion of Christians live in lands that are only a generation or two removed from colonial or imperial rule, and have little difficulty in reading the story from the point of view of the suppressed and silenced. We can no longer resort just to allegorizing the defeated, seeing them as prowling demonic forces. They were real people, and we can make an imaginative effort to recapture their experience. Canaanites once had voices too.

When we read contextually, we are forced to consider older

passages in the light of later developments in the text, and in the religion. This is what the rabbis were doing when they rewrote the accounts of Joshua's wars to make them fit within the humanitarian laws of later Judaism. Whether or not the concept of "Show them no mercy" was tolerable at the time that Deuteronomy was written, it simply was *not* acceptable according to the worldview of later Jews, or Christians. That example forces us to think of what the core underlying values of those faiths are, how they have emerged, and how they must be used to reinterpret texts. We think about the mercy that is being denied here, and how and why granting such mercy came to be seen as a fundamental element of later faiths. Just why are we so shocked to read such accounts? What have we learned through the millennia, and how have we learned it?

Without those tales of slaughter and ethnic cleansing, later generations would not have developed the kind of religious consciousness that allowed them to look back in horror on earlier acts of bloodletting, whoever the victims might be. The moral dilemmas later believers face in dealing with the violent scriptures results precisely from the success of those same texts in achieving their cultural and religious goals.

Under the Table

INDIVIDUAL BIBLE PASSAGES OFTEN need to be interpreted in light of other texts. This is especially true of words as harsh and unyielding as those of Deuteronomy 7. At one point in the biblical record, the Canaanite people are supposedly to be annihilated; but in other biblical passages—in later stages of faith—perhaps they are not.

One of the oddest and most troubling passages in the Gospels tells of a Gentile woman who approaches Jesus, asking him to heal her young daughter. Jesus refuses, saying that his mission is first to the house of Israel: he must not take food from the children and throw it to dogs. She replies that his comment is fair, but that even the dogs are allowed to eat the scraps thrown under the banquet table. Amused by her wit, he provides the desired miracle, although the concession is exceptional. One interpretation of the passage is that it recalls a very early stage in the Jesus movement when the mission really was confined within the house of Israel, and Gentiles were unwelcome.[13]

But another interpretation is possible. The woman is from what we would now call Lebanon, and her race is given as Syro-Phoenician (in Mark) or, strikingly, Canaanite, *Chananaia,* in Matthew. The change of identification is odd, unless Matthew wants to stress how Jesus fits into the older biblical narrative. Matthew knows that Jesus claimed legal descent from King David and, before him, from his distant ancestor Rahab the Canaanite. In this miracle story, Jesus reaches out to the descendants of those peoples that the other *Iesous,* Joshua, was determined to kill. The story comes full circle, and the extermination order is repealed.

So perfectly does that story mesh with the Old Testament passages about the Canaanites that they would fit naturally side by side in a public reading of the sort found in Christian lectionaries. In fact, the more we explore the darkest Bible passages, the more they would benefit from being brought back into the wider story through public or liturgical readings. They should not be presented in isolation as frightening injunctions, but placed alongside the other passages that frame and expound their meaning, especially from the prophets. Not only can the dark passages be read, but they demand to be.

CHAPTER ELEVEN

Scripture Alone?

The letter kills, but the Spirit gives life.

—2 CORINTHIANS 3:6 (NIV)

A T THE BEGINNING OF this book, I described a situation that at first sight offers a direct linkage between scripture and real-world violence. The September 11 hijackers were apparently studying Qur'anic passages that urged war against infidels, and in their eyes, those texts justified the acts that followed. Islamist terrorists from groups such as al-Qaeda make generous use of the Qur'an in their statements and propaganda. Can we say, then, that the Qur'an inspires violence and hatred in the modern world? Yet as I have suggested, even asking such a question makes dubious assumptions about the nature of authority in religion, and particularly about the role of scripture.

The existence of a scripture in its own right inspires neither good nor evil among its followers. If the existence of bloody scriptural texts directly caused violence, then we would need to explain why the savage texts of the Old Testament have not inspired far more atrocities than they actually have. On occasion, both Christians and Jews have turned to Moses and Joshua to justify violence, but generally, in most eras and most societies, the vast majority of believers have not. As members of a society founded upon a Judeo-Christian tradition, we have not learned to take genocide and mass murder in their course as reflecting God's will. Most believers can and do live with outrageous scriptures without pursuing their implications, no matter how bloodily explicit their directions.

In an important book, John J. Collins asked, "Does the Bible justify violence?" The answer is simple: if the circumstances in which you live make you seek such justifications, then you will find them, and the same is true of the Qur'an. If you don't need them, you won't find them.[1]

Scripture and Experience

THE IDEA THAT A scripture represents the reliable genome of a whole religion is neither obvious nor universal. Many religions do believe that particular texts carry uniquely sacred status, however, and Protestant Christians see their canonized scripture as the vital source of belief and practice. Martin Luther famously declared that scripture alone, *sola scriptura,* was the yardstick of faith—although, as we have seen, he did not believe that every word of the Bible carried equal weight for latter-day believers.

But that Protestant inheritance has led later writers to assume that for other religions too the scripture must represent the authoritative core of belief. As the West encountered other faiths during the age of imperialism, scholars published anthologies of the world's sacred texts, which set the scriptures of all the great faiths alongside one another. Such efforts made the fundamental assumption that to know a scripture was to understand the religion—although often editors had to struggle to find texts that played the same role in particular faiths that the Bible did in Christianity or Judaism. It was only after encounters with Christians that Hindus decided that the Bhagavad Gita offered a succinct description of their own faith, a counterpart to the New Testaments so freely distributed by missionaries. When Robert Ballou published his *World Bible* in 1944, he claimed to offer "the gist of each of the world's eight most influential religious faiths, as revealed by their basic scriptures."[2]

But do scriptures, any scripture, contain the "gist" or kernel of any religion? One can make such an argument, and the compilers of such anthologies did. But they had a highly subjective view of what that gist might be, and what it "revealed." Most editors carefully selected and stressed passages that, in their opinion, showed the religions at their ethical and even mystical best, suggesting that members of all faiths could unite in these common goals, whatever their petty differences of ritual or custom. In practice, all the world's faiths seemed to become varieties of liberal Protestantism.[3]

However noble such an interpretation, it has little connection with the ordinary lived reality of any religious tradition, which is so thoroughly conditioned by its particular historical experience and cultural background. If we imagine an anthropologist from some very different society, even from another planet, trying to understand Christianity, how much could he know of the realities of that faith even by an exhaustive knowledge of the Bible? Imagine our alien anthropologist struggling to read every word of the Bible, to appreciate its key themes, and finally reaching the point at which he has absolute confidence in his ability to understand the nuances of Christianity (with the whole of Judaism thrown in as an academic bonus). He then tries to make sense of a Catholic mass in Chicago, or a pilgrimage in the Philippines, or a Quaker meeting in London, and falls into utter bafflement.

Our anthropologist learns that the practice of any given religion differs enormously around the globe, so that sometimes Christians in one country think and act more like their Muslim neighbors than like fellow Christians elsewhere in the world. He would increasingly learn the limitations of religious labels, and think instead in terms of forms of religious behavior that transcend the individual faith traditions. He might understand, for instance, the commonalities that linked Buddhist and Christian monks, no matter how radically different the scriptural foundations on which they operated. Or he might be impressed to see how closely the worship of Pentecostal Christians paralleled ecstatic practices in other traditions, including Sufi Islam.

The alien would be just as startled to study the diversity of Christian experience across time as well as space, to observe the very different beliefs held as utterly fundamental in various historical eras. However critical particular believers might think a given issue or cause, our anthropologist would often find one set of Christians believing something, while others believed something totally different; and he would not need to trouble himself with minor sects or splinter groups in order to find such variations. In one century, the vast majority of Christians were convinced that celibacy and world-denial were the highest virtues, while later adherents preached the supremacy of family values. In one era, most Christians espoused the notion of holy warfare just as wholly as their descendants rejected it. And in each period, mainstream believers rejected rival views as un-Christian or anti-Christian. In each case, believers claimed to be following the same scripture, however different the interpretations they reached. Particular texts and stories that resonated mightily in one age fell mute and forgotten in another. Whether contemplating the past or the present, finding any "gist" of Christianity would be ever more elusive, and so would the chance of locating such a thing in its scriptures.

This is not of course to say that scriptures do not shape a faith. Scriptural texts have an enormous influence in establishing guiding principles for a religion, and they also supply an arsenal of resources to which believers can turn anew in every generation. But believers can hold fast to the core ideas of a faith while ranging widely in terms of real-world practice and custom.

Violent Faith

THE RELATIONSHIP BETWEEN SCRIPTURE and behavior is particularly contorted in matters of violence and warfare. We talk about "religious violence," but when exactly can we say that a religion or a scriptural tradition directly caused an act of crime or terrorism?[4]

Sometimes, soldiers or militants explicitly draw inspiration from violent texts; on occasion, though, the linkage between word and deed is anything but obvious. In 2010, the U.S. government encountered a scandal when it was found that the sniper scopes its armed forces were using in Afghanistan and Iraq bore coded New Testament messages, so that (for instance) "JN8:12" referred to the Gospel of John, chapter 8, verse 12. This discovery was embarrassing in a conflict where the United States and its allies were striving to avoid any sense of engaging in a Christian holy war against Islam, and authorities promised to eliminate the texts in question. But what were these deadly words that a soldier was to invoke against the enemy he was about to slay? John 8:12 in fact seems innocuous, being the famous words "I am the light of the world. Whoever follows me will never walk in darkness, but will have the light of life." The other text used was 2 Corinthians 4:6, a similarly noncontroversial reference to Christ as the light shining in our hearts. Even the harshest critic of Christianity could hardly argue that such texts lent themselves naturally to sanctifying violence and war, although soldiers might have used them for spiritual sustenance. The lesson seems to be that, once a group or individual has decided that war is a holy and justified affair, they can seize on any available word or verse that consecrates the violence that is already taking place. Once someone has decided to do that, it scarcely matters what the text actually says.[5]

Also challenging assumptions about the relationship between scriptures and violence, it is all but impossible to separate religion as a causal factor distinct from ethnicity, class, or political status. In the modern world, Islam above all stands at the center of anxious debates about how ancient religions can adapt to modernity, with the Qur'an as a potent symbol of the clash of values. So can a religion overcome what appears to be the violence and primitivism of its scriptures, without compromising its integrity? Christians and Jews are the last people who should be asking such a question of others. But for the sake of argument, let us assume that the Qur'an does contain major difficulties that have to be dealt with: we think of the war passages that supply the most explicit justifications for understanding jihad as armed violence. Need these pose problems any more significant than those facing Christians and Jews?

Actually, Muslims, like other believers, have a long history of accommodating texts that have become troublesome or inconvenient. As with Jews and Christians, some Islamic scholars historicize the texts, making them relevant to a particular period in the time of Muhammad, but not applicable to later times. Others allegorize tales of battle and jihad. Islam, historically, is quite as diverse as Christianity, and has produced as wide a range of scriptural understandings.[6]

Muslims, in other words, have access to a range of resources very much like that of other religions when it comes to dealing with atrocious or violent scriptures. The difference is, of course, how they are presently applied. Muslims, overwhelmingly, live in states far poorer and weaker than those in the West, with far less developed educational institutions, and traditions of clerical power remain strong. Without democratic consent, public mechanisms of law enforcement lack widespread acceptance, and there is no counterweight to the very strong traditions of family and individual honor that shape behavior. In extreme cases, such concepts of honor have to be defended by violence, especially when facing threats to the strict sexual discipline demanded of the family's female members. Commonly, such societies come to believe that these traditional codes of honor are absolutely grounded in religious traditions, and they find convenient scriptural passages to justify their ways. We easily understand why, in the modern world, the religion of Islam so often takes the blame, unjustly, for keeping its followers mired in primitive values.[7]

If those political and social circumstances change, interpretations of fundamental scriptures will change likewise. By far the most important factor shaping such rereadings will be the substantial presence of Muslims in the West—in Europe and North America—where scholars can explore new interpretations free of traditional constraints. In coming decades, new interpretations of the Qur'an will have an impact quite as dramatic as new understandings of the Bible did to the Western world in the nineteenth century.

Islam and Violence

COMPLICATING ANY DISCUSSION OF religious violence is the widespread popular mythology surrounding the issue, the near-automatic Western assumption that violence and terrorism are rooted in Islam, and (often) Islam in terrorism and violence. Beyond doubt, religion is commonly used to justify violent acts, but Islam has no monopoly. Religion, moreover, does not necessarily incite adherents to acts more severe or extreme than deeds that claim no religious sanction. Any list of the bloodiest regimes in human history would begin with the militantly antireligious governments of the Soviet Union, Nazi Germany, Maoist China, and Communist Cambodia.

Nor is religious violence a simple category, synonymous with fanaticism or mindless savagery. On some occasions, religious motives have driven believers to massacre or oppress their rivals; at other times, religious-based violence has been defensible and even praiseworthy, as when faith inspired oppressed peoples to rise against foreign conquerors or tyrannical regimes. For a century after

1850, colonized peoples across Africa and Asia frequently defined their armed struggle against their European imperial masters as a Muslim jihad. Within the Christian tradition, few modern Westerners would criticize the religiously driven German activists whose interpretation of faith drove them to try to assassinate Adolf Hitler.[8]

The link between radical Islamist ideology and violence is neither as simple nor as obvious as it may appear today. Between the mid-1960s and the 1980s, Arab and Middle Eastern causes drove a wave of global terrorism very much like that later associated with al-Qaeda, making the "Arab terrorist" quite as familiar a demon stereotype as it is today. Then as now, Arab groups were associated with random massacres of Western civilians, with kidnapping and hostage-taking, and with attacks on airliners and transportation systems. The ultimate nightmare was that these extremists would obtain weapons of mass destruction.

The difference in that era was that those militant groups distanced themselves from any version of Islam. The most notorious terrorist chieftain of the era, Abu Nidal, was as celebrated a villain in the 1970s and 1980s as Osama bin Laden has been in more recent times; however, for the most part Abu Nidal served Iraq's secularist Ba'ath regime.[9] Like Abu Nidal himself, most Palestinian activists were secular socialist nationalists, and Christians often played a prominent role in the movement's leadership. Their leaders usually bore typical Arab Christian names, one celebrated example being George Habash, long-serving leader of one of the deadliest guerrilla groups.

These Middle Eastern movements had no notion of suicide terrorism, which is moreover unknown to the Islamic tradition. The first modern movement to use suicide attacks on a regular basis was Sri Lankan and mainly Hindu, with no Muslim connection whatever; and they adopted this method only as recently as the early 1980s. Only later did Middle Eastern and Islamist groups copy the tactic. In other cases too, hideous terrorist actions that we have come to associate so firmly with Islamic extremism have clearly non-Islamic roots. To quote Olivier Roy, one of the most respected European scholars of Islam and of Islamist terrorism, "The al-Qaeda video footage of the execution of foreign hostages in Iraq is a one to one re-enactment of the execution of Aldo Moro by the Red Brigades [in Italy in 1978], with the organization's banner and logo in the background, the hostage hand-cuffed and blind-folded, the mock trial with the reading of the sentence and the execution."[10]

This historical context matters for any discussion of the Qur'anic passages commonly cited as inspiring terrorism. If in fact reading passages such as the Qur'an's eighth and ninth suras drives faithful Muslims to commit acts of fanatical violence, then it is odd that so many believers escaped falling under those influences, and led thoroughly peaceful lives. If Islam incites or favors terrorism, we need to explain why Muslim terrorists should have been such latecomers on the historical scene. Why were they not the prophets and pioneers of terrorism, rather than the latecomers? Why, moreover, did they have to draw all their knowledge and tactics from fighters of other religions and of none—from Western anarchists and nihilists; from the Catholic IRA and Latin American urban guerrillas; from Communists and fascists; from Zionist Jews and Sri Lankan Hindus? To quote Olivier Roy again, "Al-Qaeda is not the expression of traditional Islam or even fundamentalist Islam; it is a new understanding of Islam, cloaked in western revolutionary ideology."[11]

However bloody texts may be, however explicit, their mere existence will not lead to actual violence unless and until particular circumstances arise. At that point, the texts can rise once again to the surface, to inspire and sacralize violence, to demonize opponents, and even to exalt the conflict to the level of cosmic war. But without those circumstances, without those particular conditions in state and society, the violence will not occur.

BY ALL MEANS, LET us explore the religious contexts underlying acts of violence, the significance of religious rhetoric and worldviews, and policymakers need to be alert to such considerations; but in most cases, the core scriptures of a faith do not account for such activities. If scripture passage X supposedly inspired terrorist group Y, then we need to explain why militants chose to draw on *that* scripture and not some radically contradictory text. No less important, we must understand why that same scripture has had no effect whatever in pushing millions of other believers toward comparably extreme acts.[12] Some of what we call "religious violence" may well be authentically religious in its character, but we must find its origins in places other than the basic texts of the faith.

ACKNOWLEDGMENTS

I WOULD LIKE TO THANK the colleagues and friends with whom I've discussed aspects of this project, or who have offered advice, including Nachman Ben-Yehuda, Christian Brady, Jonathan Brockopp, Baruch Halpern, Paul Harvey, Tommy Kidd, Gary Knoppers, Gregg Roeber, and Eric Seibert. None should be blamed for any errors in fact, faith, or doctrine that appear in these pages.

Thanks to Gareth Cook of the *Boston Globe*'s Ideas section, in which I first explored these concepts. Thanks also to my agent, Elyse Cheney, and to Roger Freet, my editor at HarperOne.

And, as always, thanks above all to my wife, Liz Jenkins.

NOTES

INTRODUCTION: MOTES AND BEAMS

1. "Full Text of Notes Found After Hijackings," *New York Times*, Sept. 29, 2001. There are several widely used English translations or versions of the Qur'an, the most popular being those of Marmaduke Pickthall, N. J. Dawood, Yusuf Ali, and Muhammad Asad. Except where otherwise stated, I have used the Pickthall translation, which is taken from Muhammad M. Pickthall, *The Meaning of the Glorious Qur'an,* 2nd edition (Beltsville, MD: Amana Publications, 1999). In the citations that follow, I indicate which translation I have used in particular verses. "Cast terror into the hearts" is from Qur'an 8:12 (Muhammad Asad, *The Message of the Qur'an* (Bitton, England: Book Foundation, 2003); "Then, when the sacred months" is from 9:5 (Pickthall); "O Prophet!" is from 9:73 (Pickthall). Reuven Firestone, *Jihad* (New York: Oxford Univ. Press, 1999); David Cook, *Understanding Jihad* (Berkeley: Univ. of California Press, 2005).

2. "Full Text of Notes Found After Hijackings." "Strike terror" is Qur'an 8:60, from N.J. Dawood, *The Koran, with a Parallel Arabic Text* (New York: Viking, 1990), adapted.

3. Qur'an 9:29.

4. "Those who make war" is Qur'an 5.33 (Dawood); "When you meet the unbelievers" is Qur'an 47.4 (Dawood). For bin Laden's statement, see http://www.pbs.org/newshour/terrorism/international/fatwa_1996 .html. The whole theme of jihad and Islamic attitudes of warfare and violence has spawned a large literature in recent years. See for instance Richard Bonney, *Jihad* (New York: Palgrave Macmillan, 2004); Andrew G. Bostom, *The Legacy of Jihad* (Amherst, NY: Prometheus Books, 2005); Mary R. Habeck, *Knowing the Enemy* (New Haven, CT: Yale Univ. Press, 2006); Laurent Murawiec, *The Mind of Jihad* (New York: Cambridge Univ. Press, 2008); Jarret M. Brachman, *Global Jihadism* (New York: Routledge, 2009).

5. Robert Spencer, *The Complete Infidel's Guide to the Koran* (Chicago: Regnery Press, 2009); David Marshall, *God, Muhammad and the Unbelievers* (Richmond, England: Curzon, 1999).

6. From many locations for the sentence beginning "All you need to see that Islam," see http://www.faithfreedom.org/Quran.htm. For Franklin Graham and Pat Robertson, see "Attacks on Muslims by Conservative Protestants," at http://www.religioustolerance.org/ reac_ter18b.htm; Paul M. Weyrich and William S. Lind, *Why Islam Is a Threat to America and the West* (Washington, DC: Free Congress Foundation, 2002). For critiques of Islam and the Qur'an, see for instance Robert Spencer, *Islam Unveiled* (San Francisco: Encounter Books, 2002); David Bukay, *From Muhammad to Bin Laden* (New Brunswick, NJ: Transaction, 2008); Brigitte Gabriel, *They Must Be Stopped* (New York: St. Martin's Press, 2008); Raymond Ibrahim, "Are Judaism and Christianity as Violent as Islam?" *Middle East Quarterly,* Summer 2009, 3–12; *Shariah: The Threat to America* (Washington, DC: Center for Security Policy, 2010), 71-72. For Islamic anti-Semitism, see Robert S. Wistrich, *A Lethal Obsession* (New York: Random House, 2010); Richard L. Rubenstein, *Jihad and Genocide* (Lanham, MD: Rowman & Littlefield, 2010).

7. The quotes are from Andrew C. McCarthy, "Bon Jovi Islam," *National Review,* June 17, 2010, at http://article.nationalreview.com/436543/bon-jovi-islam/andrew-c-mccarthy. Compare the lengthier treatment in Andrew C. McCarthy, *The Grand Jihad* (New York: Encounter, 2010).

8. Ibn Warraq, *Why I Am Not a Muslim* (Amherst, NY: Prometheus Books, 1995); Irshad Manji, *The Trouble with Islam* (New York: St. Martin's Press, 2004); Ayaan Hirsi Ali, *Infidel* (New York: Free Press, 2007); Wafa Sultan, *A God Who Hates* (New York: St. Martin's Press, 2009); Nonie Darwish, *Cruel and Usual Punishment* (Nashville, TN: Thomas Nelson, 2009); Mosab Hassan Yousef, *Son of Hamas* (Carol Stream, IL: SaltRiver, 2010), and see the interview with him at http://sheikyermami.com/2010/03/23/son-of-hamas-leader-mosab-hassan-yousef-calls-for-banning-the-koran/. For the Muslim defector group Former Muslims United, see http://formermuslimsunited.americancommunityexchange.org/. For Muslims Against Sharia, see http://www.reformislam.org/.

9. Andrew G. Bostom, "Why Islam's Jew-Hating Hadith Matter," *FrontPageMagazine.com,* Oct. 3, 2008, at *http://97.74.65.51/readArticle.aspx?ARTID=32563.*

10. "Act justly" is from Mic. 6:8; "Father, forgive them" is from Luke 23:34. As noted earlier, Bible translations are given in the King James Version except where otherwise specified.

11. John J. Collins, *Does the Bible Justify Violence?* (Minneapolis: Augsburg Fortress, 2004); Eric A. Seibert, *Disturbing Divine Behavior* (Minneapolis: Fortress Press, 2009). Compare Antony F. Campbell, *Making Sense of the Bible* (New York: Paulist Press, 2010); Dereck Daschke and Andrew Kille, eds., *A Cry Instead of Justice* (New York: T&T Clark, 2010); Paul Copan, *Is God a Moral Monster?* (Grand Rapids, Mich.: Baker, 2011).

12. Phyllis Trible, *Texts of Terror* (Augsburg Fortress, 1984). Trible's work inspired a number of later works, including Joy A. Schroeder, *Dinah's Lament* (Minneapolis: Fortress Press, 2007). Compare Susanne Scholz, *Sacred Witness* (Minneapolis: Fortress Press, 2010).

13. Athalya Brenner, "On the Rivers of Babylon (Psalm 137)," in

Jonneke Bekkenkamp and Yvonne Sherwood, eds., *Sanctified Aggression* (London: T&T Clark, 2003), 76–91.

14. Gerd Lüdemann, *The Unholy in Holy Scripture* (Louisville, KY: Westminster John Knox Press, 1997).

15. Judg. 16:30.

16. "I will make my arrows" is from Deut. 32:42. For the rules of warfare, see Deut. 20:16–18.

17. Josh. 8 and 10.

18. "Genocide means . . . acts committed with intent to destroy, in whole or in part, a national, ethnical, racial or religious group." Thomas W. Simon, *The Laws of Genocide* (Westport, CT: Praeger Security International, 2007); Ben Kiernan, *Blood and Soil* (New Haven, CT: Yale Univ. Press, 2007).

19. 1 Sam. 15; 1 Sam. 28:18 for the invocation of Samuel. According to one of the Bible's two conflicting accounts of Saul's death, an Amalekite was responsible. P. Kyle McCarter, *I Samuel* (Garden City, NY: Doubleday, 1980); David Toshio Tsumura, *The First Book of Samuel* (Grand Rapids, MI: Eerdmans, 2007).

20. Joel Kaminsky, *Yet I Loved Jacob* (Nashville, TN: Abingdon Press, 2007).

21. Num. 25:1–15.

22. Richard Kelly Hoskins, *Vigilantes of Christendom* (Lynchburg, VA: Virginia Publishing, 1990); Timothy K. Beal, "The White Supremacist Bible and the Phineas Priesthood," in Bekkenkamp and Sherwood, eds., *Sanctified Aggression,* 120–31; Mark Juergensmeyer, *Terror in the Mind of God,* 3rd ed. (Berkeley: Univ. of California Press, 2003).

23. A. Cohen, ed., "Ecclesiastes," in Harry Freedman and Maurice Simon, eds., *Midrash Rabbah,* 13 vols. in 10 (London: Soncino Press, 1939), vol. 8, 199.

24. James Turner Johnson, *Ideology, Reason, and the Limitation of War* (Princeton, NJ: Princeton Univ. Press, 1975); James Turner Johnson, *The Holy War Idea in Western and Islamic Traditions* (University Park: Pennsylvania State Univ. Press, 1997); R. Joseph Hoffmann, ed., *The Just War and Jihad* (Amherst, NY: Prometheus Books, 2006).

25. "Again and again" is from John McDonnell, *The Ulster Civil War of*

1641 and Its Consequences (Dublin, Ireland: M. H. Gill, 1879), 120–21. John Corrigan, "Amalek and the Religious Rhetoric of Extermination," in Chris Beneke and Christopher S. Grenda eds., *The First Prejudice* (Philadelphia: Univ. of Pennsylvania Press, 2010), 53-73.

26. For the centrality of the Exodus myth in Western culture, see Michael Walzer, *Exodus and Revolution* (New York: Basic Books, 1985). For Southwest Africa, see Isabel V. Hull, *Absolute Destruction* (Ithaca, NY: Cornell Univ. Press, 2005).

27. The linkage between monotheistic religions—all such religions—and violence has attracted much attention through the years. See for instance James G. Williams, *The Bible, Violence, and the Sacred* (San Francisco: HarperSanFrancisco, 1991); Regina M. Schwartz, *The Curse of Cain* (Chicago: Univ. of Chicago Press, 1997); Marc H. Ellis, *Unholy Alliance* (Minneapolis: Fortress Press, 1997); Peter Partner, *God of Battles* (Princeton, NJ: Princeton Univ. Press, 1998); Karen Armstrong, *The Battle for God* (New York: Random House, 2001). The terrorist attacks of September 2001 led scholars worldwide to a keen interest in the issue of religious-related violence and terrorism. From the many works that appeared in the following few years, see Oliver McTernan, *Violence in God's Name* (Maryknoll, NY: Orbis Books, 2003); Jack Nelson-Pallmeyer, *Is Religion Killing Us?* (Harrisburg, PA: Trinity Press International, 2003); J. Harold Ellens, ed., *The Destructive Power of Religion* (Westport, CT: Praeger, 2004); Leonard Weinberg and Ami Pedahzur, eds., *Religious Fundamentalism and Political Extremism* (London: Frank Cass, 2004); James F. Rinehart, *Apocalyptic Faith and Political Violence* (New York: Palgrave Macmillan, 2006); Bryan Rennie and Philip L. Tite, eds., *Religion, Terror and Violence* (New York: Routledge, 2008); Jack David Eller, *Cruel Creeds, Virtuous Violence* (Amherst, NY: Prometheus Books, 2010). For an evolutionary approach, see John Teehan, *In the Name of God* (Wiley-Blackwell, 2010).

28. For amnesia as a concomitant of social development, see Paul Connerton, *How Modernity Forgets* (New York: Cambridge Univ. Press, 2009).

29. "The Jews smote" is from Esther 9:5; "the fear of the Jews" is from

Esther 8:17; and "slew of their foes" is from Esther 9:16; "on the thirteenth day" is from Esther 9:17. Frederick W. Bush, "The Book of Esther," *Bulletin for Biblical Research* 8 (1998): 39–54; Linda Day, *Esther* (Nashville, TN: Abingdon Press, 2005).

30. Consultation on Common Texts, *Revised Common Lectionary* (Nashville, TN: Abingdon Press, 1992).

31. Paul Ricoeur, *Memory, History, Forgetting* (Chicago: Univ. of Chicago Press, 2004). For issues of biblical memory, see Ronald Hendel, *Remembering Abraham* (New York: Oxford Univ. Press, 2005).

32. Tony Judt, *Postwar* (New York: Penguin Press, 2005), 829. David Gross, *Lost Time* (Amherst: Univ. of Massachusetts, 2000); Gavriel D. Rosenfeld, "A Looming Crash or a Soft Landing?" *Journal of Modern History* 81 (2009): 122–58; Astrid Erll and Ansgar Nunning, eds., *A Companion to Cultural Memory Studies* (Berlin: De Gruyter, 2008); Pascal Boyer and James V. Wertsch, eds., *Memory in Mind and Culture* (New York: Cambridge Univ. Press, 2009). For the failure to remember every detail of an event as an intrinsic part of the process of recollection, see Michael F. Bernard-Donals, *Forgetful Memory* (Albany: State Univ. of New York Press, 2009). For deliberate cultural strategies to induce ignorance or forgetfulness, see Robert N. Proctor and Londa Schiebinger, eds., *Agnotology* (Palo Alto, CA: Stanford Univ. Press, 2008).

33. Kurt Danziger, *Marking the Mind* (New York: Cambridge Univ. Press, 2008); Sergio Della Sala, ed., *Forgetting* (New York: Psychology Press, 2010).

34. For the "virtue of forgetting," see Viktor Mayer-Schönberger, *Delete* (Princeton, NJ: Princeton Univ. Press, 2009). René Girard, "Violence in Biblical Narrative," *Philosophy and Literature* 23, no. 2 (1999): 387–92.

35. Elliott Horowitz, *Reckless Rites* (Princeton, NJ: Princeton Univ. Press, 2006). For "Think Amalek," see Jeffrey Goldberg, "Israel's Fears, Amalek's Arsenal," *New York Times,* May 17, 2009. For the Stuxnet worm and the Esther connection, see John Markoff and David E. Sanger, "In a Computer Worm, a Possible Biblical Clue," *New York Times,* September 29, 2010; Seymour M. Hersh, *The Samson Option* (New York: Random House, 1991).

36. Philip Jenkins, *The New Faces of Christianity* (New York: Oxford Univ. Press, 2006).

37. Dora Mbuwayesango, "Joshua," in Daniel Patte, J. Severino Croatto, Nicole Wilkinson Duran, Teresa Okure, and Archie Chi Chung Lee, eds., *Global Bible Commentary* (Nashville, TN: Abingdon Press, 2004), 64, 72; Robert Allan Warrior, "A Native American Perspective," in R. S. Sugirtharajah, ed., *Voices from the Margin* (Maryknoll, NY: Orbis, 1995), 277–87. For "Joshua Syndrome," see Mercedes Garcia Bachmann, "Deuteronomy," in Patte et al., eds., *Global Bible Commentary,* 58; Jong Sun Noh, "Joshua Syndrome and Emerging Threats to Life in the World," *CTC Bulletin* 20, no. 1 (2004), at http://www.cca.org.hk/resources/ctc/ctc04–01/ctc04–01c.htm.

38. Jione Havea, "Numbers," in Patte et al., eds., *Global Bible Commentary,* 49–50.

39. Sam Harris, *The End of Faith* (New York: W. W. Norton, 2004); Richard Dawkins, *The God Delusion* (Boston, MA: Houghton Mifflin, 2006); Christopher Hitchens, *God Is Not Great* (New York: Twelve, 2007). Dawkins is quoted from "Forgive Me, Spirit of Science," *New Statesman,* December 29, 2010, at http://www.newstatesman.com/religion/2010/12/king-james-bible-poetry-shall.

40. Matt. 8:26. Actually, this passage has itself been cleaned up in most translations. The original should better be read as "Why are you a bunch of cowards [*deiloi*]"?

41. Maarten J. J. Menken and Steve Moyise, eds., *Deuteronomy in the New Testament* (London; New York: T&T Clark, 2007).

CHAPTER ONE: EVERYTHING THAT BREATHES

1. Deut 7.1-2 (NIV); Deut 7.16 (NRSV). Moshe Weinfeld, *Deuteronomy 1–11* (New York: Doubleday, 1991), 357–83.

2. For the cannibalism story, see 2 Kings 6:24–33. John Day, *Molech* (Cambridge: Cambridge Univ. Press, 1989); Klaas Spronk, "The Daughter of Jephthah," in Jonneke Bekkenkamp and Yvonne Sherwood, eds., *Sanctified Aggression* (London: T&T Clark, 2003), 10–21.

3. Jonathan Kirsch, *The Harlot by the Side of the Road* (New York: Ballantine Books, 1997).

4. Moshe Weinfeld, *The Promise of the Land* (Berkeley: Univ. of California Press, 1993); Tremper Longman III and Daniel G. Reid, *God Is a Warrior* (Grand Rapids, MI: Zondervan, 1995).

5. Thomas B. Dozeman, *God at War* (New York: Oxford Univ. Press, 1996).

6. Num. 31:17–18 (NIV). Dennis T. Olson, *Numbers* (Louisville, KY: Westminster John Knox Press, 1996).

7. Exod. 17:14, 16. Terence E. Fretheim, *Exodus* (Louisville, KY: Westminster John Knox Press, 1991); Scott M. Langston, *Exodus Through the Centuries* (Oxford: Blackwell, 2006); Eric A. Seibert, *Disturbing Divine Behavior* (Minneapolis: Fortress Press, 2009), 169–82.

8. Deut. 2:33–34. For King Sihon, compare Baruch A. Levine, *Numbers 21–36* (New York: Doubleday, 2000).

9. Walter Brueggemann, *Divine Presence amid Violence* (Eugene, OR: Cascade, 2009).

10. Deut. 20:16-17 (my emphasis).

11. As in Deut. 20:16–17.

12. Gerd Lüdemann, *The Unholy in Holy Scripture* (Louisville, KY: Westminster John Knox Press, 1997) 36–54; John J. Collins, *Does the Bible Justify Violence?* (Minneapolis: Augsburg Fortress, 2004).

13. Gerhard von Rad, *Holy War in Ancient Israel* (Eugene, OR: Wipf & Stock, 2000 [1958]); Millard Lind, *Yahweh Is a Warrior* (Scottdale, PA: Herald Press, 1980); Philip D. Stern, *The Biblical Herem* (Atlanta: Scholars Press, 1991); Peter C. Craigie, *The Problem of War in the Old Testament* (Grand Rapids, MI: Eerdmans, 1978); Richard S. Hess, "War in the Hebrew Bible," in Richard S. Hess and Elmer A. Martens, eds., *War in the Bible and Terrorism in the Twenty-First Century* (Winona Lake, IN: Eisenbrauns, 2008), 19–32.

14. Louis H. Feldman, *"Remember Amalek!"* (Detroit, MI: Wayne State Univ. Press, 2004); Steven L. Jacobs, ed., *Confronting Genocide* (Lanham, MD: Lexington Books, 2009).

15. Josh. 7–8. For the book of Joshua, see Gordon Mitchell, *Together in the Land* (Sheffield, England: JSOT, 1993); A. Graeme Auld, "Joshua," in John H. Hayes, ed., *Hebrew Bible* (Nashville, TN: Abingdon, 2004), 71–81. Major commentaries on Joshua include J. Maxwell Miller and

Gene M. Tucker, eds., *The Book of Joshua* (New York: Cambridge Univ. Press, 1974); Marten H. Woudstra, *The Book of Joshua* (Grand Rapids, MI: Eerdmans, 1981); Robert G. Boling, *Joshua* (Garden City, NY: Doubleday, 1982); Richard S. Hess, *Joshua* (Downers Grove, IL: InterVarsity Press, 1996); Richard D. Nelson, *Joshua* (Louisville, KY: Westminster John Knox Press, 1997); J. Gordon McConville and Stephen N. Williams, *Joshua* (Grand Rapids, Mich.: W.B. Eerdmans, 2010).

16. Josh. 10:28–29 for Makkedah and Libnah; Josh. 10:40 for the rest. L. Daniel Hawk, "Conquest Reconfigured," in Brad E. Kelle and Frank Ritchel Ames, eds., *Writing and Reading War* (Leiden, Netherlands: Brill, 2008), 145–60.

17. Josh. 24:13.

18. But see John Lowden, *The Octateuchs* (University Park: Pennsylvania State Univ. Press, 1992).

19. Josh. 2:9.

20. Seibert, *Disturbing Divine Behavior*, 158–59; André Lemaire, "The Mesha Stele and the Omry Dynasty," in Lester L. Grabbe, ed., *Ahab Agonistes* (London: T&T Clark, 2007); Thomas L. Thompson, "Mesha and Questions of Historicity," *Scandinavian Journal of the Old Testament* 21, no. 2 (2007): 241–60.

21. For comparative studies of ancient warfare, see especially Lori L. Rowlett, *Joshua and the Rhetoric of Violence* (Sheffield, England: Sheffield Academic Press, 1996), and Feldman, *"Remember Amalek!"* For the Assyrians, see Steven W. Holloway, *Aššur Is King! Aššur Is King!* (Leiden, Netherlands: Brill, 2002). Michael G. Hasel, *Military Practice and Polemic* (Berrien Springs, MI: Andrews Univ. Press, 2005); C. L. Crouch, *War and Ethics in the Ancient Near East* (New York: Walter de Gruyter, 2009).

22. *Iliad* 6.55–60.

23. Robert Ferguson, *The Hammer and the Cross* (London: Allen Lane, 2009).

24. *The Histories of Polybius* (Loeb edition) 10.15, at http://penelope.uchi cago.edu/Thayer/E/Roman/Texts/Polybius/10*.html; J. E. Lendon, *Soldiers and Ghosts* (New Haven, CT: Yale Univ. Press, 2005).

25. For Mithridates, see Adrienne Mayor, *The Poison King* (Princeton, NJ: Princeton Univ. Press, 2009).

26. Lawrence H. Keeley, *War Before Civilization* (New York: Oxford Univ. Press, 1996); Steven LeBlanc and Katherine E. Register, *Constant Battles* (New York: St. Martin's Press, 2003); Elizabeth N. Arkush and Mark W. Allen, eds., *The Archaeology of Warfare* (Gainesville: Univ. Press of Florida, 2006).

27. For the Song of Deborah, see Judg. 5:30. Oded Lipschits and Joseph Blenkinsopp, eds., *Judah and the Judeans in the Neo-Babylonian Period* (Winona Lake, IN: Eisenbrauns, 2003).

28. J. Carter Johnson, "Deliver Us from Kony," *Christianity Today,* Jan. 2006, at http://www.christianitytoday.com/ct/2006/january/18.30.html; Matthew Green, *The Wizard of the Nile* (London: Portobello Books, 2008).

29. John Hagan and Wenona Rymond-Richmond, *Darfur and the Crime of Genocide* (New York: Cambridge Univ. Press, 2009).

30. Josh. 9 for the Gibeonites; Judg. 1:27–36 for the surviving ethnic groups. Marc Zvi Brettler, *The Book of Judges* (New York: Routledge, 2002); Carolyn Pressler, *Joshua, Judges, and Ruth* (Louisville, KY: Westminster John Knox Press, 2002); Victor H. Matthews, *Judges and Ruth* (New York: Cambridge Univ. Press, 2004); Susan Niditch, *Judges* (Louisville, KY: Westminster John Knox Press, 2008). For other biblical warrants for slavery, see Stephen R. Haynes, *Noah's Curse* (New York: Oxford Univ. Press, 2002).

31. Judg. 3:1–2.

32. Gen. 15:16.

33. "Hardened his spirit" is from Deut. 2:30; "For it was of the LORD" is from Josh. 11:20.

Chapter Two: Truth and History

1. Robert G. Boling, *Joshua* (Garden City, NY: Doubleday, 1982); Earl Kalland, Donald H. Madvig, Herbert M. Wolf, and F. B. Huey, *Deuteronomy, Joshua, Judges, Ruth, 1 and 2 Samuel,* vol. 3 in *The Expositor's Bible Commentary* (Grand Rapids, MI: Zondervan, 1992); Michaël N.

van der Meer, *Formation and Reformulation* (Leiden, Netherlands: Brill, 2004); for a thoughtful and wide-ranging perspective on Joshua, see Walter Brueggemann, *Divine Presence amid Violence* (Eugene, OR: Cascade Books, 2009); Jeremy M. Hutton, *The Transjordanian Palimpsest* (Berlin, Germany: Walter de Gruyter, 2009).

2. Alan J. Hauser and Duane F. Watson, eds., *A History of Biblical Interpretation,* vol. 1 (Grand Rapids, MI: Eerdmans, 2003).

3. John H. Hayes, ed., *Hebrew Bible* (Nashville, TN: Abingdon, 2004).

4. Thomas B. Dozeman and Konrad Schmid, eds., *A Farewell to the Yahwist?* (Atlanta: Society of Biblical Literature, 2006); Richard Elliott Friedman, *Who Wrote the Bible?* (Englewood Cliffs, NJ: Prentice Hall, 1987); Richard Elliott Friedman, *The Hidden Book in the Bible* (San Francisco: HarperSanFrancisco, 1998).

5. The finding of the Book of the Law is described in 2 Kings 22–23. For the background and context of Deuteronomy, see especially Moshe Weinfeld, *Deuteronomy 1–11* (New York: Doubleday, 1991). Compare Patrick D. Miller, *Deuteronomy* (Louisville, KY: John Knox Press, 1991); Walter Brueggemann, *Deuteronomy* (Nashville, TN: Abingdon Press, 2001); S. D. McBride, "Deuteronomy," in Hayes, ed., *Hebrew Bible,* 39–70.

6. Linda S. Schearing and Steven L. McKenzie, eds., *Those Elusive Deuteronomists* (Sheffield, England: Sheffield Academic Press, 1999); Antony F. Campbell and Mark A. O'Brien, *Unfolding the Deuteronomistic History* (Minneapolis: Fortress Press, 2000); Thomas Römer, ed., *The Future of the Deuteronomistic History* (Leuven, Belgium: Leuven Univ. Press, 2000); Albert de Pury, Thomas Römer, and Jean-Daniel Macchi, eds., *Israel Constructs Its History* (Sheffield, England: Sheffield Academic Press, 2000); Gary N. Knoppers and J. Gordon McConville, eds., *Reconsidering Israel and Judah* (Winona Lake, IN: Eisenbrauns, 2000); Jeffrey C. Geoghegan, *The Time, Place, and Purpose of the Deuteronomistic History* (Atlanta: Society of Biblical Literature, 2006); Thomas C. Römer, *The So-Called Deuteronomistic History* (London: T&T Clark 2006).

7. Volkmar Fritz and Philip R. Davies, eds., *The Origins of the Ancient Israelite States* (Sheffield, England: Sheffield Academic Press, 1996);

Keith W. Whitelam, *The Invention of Ancient Israel* (London: Routledge, 1996); Niels Peter Lemche, *The Israelites in History and Tradition* (London: SPCK, 1998); Philip R. Davies, *Scribes and Schools* (Louisville, KY: Westminster John Knox Press, 1998); Thomas L. Thompson, *Early History of the Israelite People* (Leiden, Netherlands: Brill, 2000).

8. Thomas Woolston, quoted in David M. Gunn, *Judges Through the Centuries* (Oxford, England: Wiley-Blackwell, 2005), 20. For evidence that the supposed genocide left many survivors, see 1 Kings 9:20–22. For early historical criticisms of these stories, see John William Colenso, *The Pentateuch and Book of Joshua Critically Examined,* 7 vols. (London: Longmans, Green, 1862–1879). Marc Zvi Brettler, *The Book of Judges* (New York: Routledge, 2002); Carolyn Pressler, *Joshua, Judges, and Ruth* (Louisville, KY: Westminster John Knox Press, 2002); Victor H. Matthews, *Judges and Ruth* (New York: Cambridge Univ. Press, 2004); Susan Niditch, *Judges* (Louisville, KY: Westminster John Knox Press, 2008).

9. Eric A. Seibert, *Disturbing Divine Behavior* (Minneapolis: Fortress Press, 2009), 99–108.

10. Neil Asher Silberman and David Small, eds., *The Archaeology of Israel* (Sheffield, England: Sheffield Academic Press, 1997); Robert D. Miller II, *Chieftains of the Highland Clans* (Grand Rapids, MI: Eerdmans, 2005).

11. Steven A. Leblanc, *Prehistoric Warfare in the American Southwest* (Salt Lake City: Univ. of Utah Press, 1999); Christy G. Turner and Jacqueline A. Turner, *Man Corn* (Salt Lake City: Univ. of Utah Press, 1999); Glen E. Rice and Steven A. LeBlanc, eds., *Deadly Landscapes* (Salt Lake City: Univ. of Utah Press, 2001).

12. William G. Dever, *Who Were the Early Israelites, and Where Did They Come From?* (Grand Rapids, MI: Eerdmans, 2003), 29–74.

13. "Supports almost *nothing*" is from Dever, *Who Were the Early Israelites?,* 71, italics in original; William G. Dever, *What Did the Biblical Writers Know, and When Did They Know It?* (Grand Rapids, MI: Eerdmans, 2001).

14. Amy Dockser Marcus, *The View from Nebo* (Boston, MA: Little

Brown, 2000); Seymour Gitin, J. Edward Wright, and J. P. Dessel, eds., *Confronting the Past* (Winona Lake, IN: Eisenbrauns, 2006).

15. Robert Drews, *The End of the Bronze Age* (Princeton, NJ: Princeton Univ. Press, 1993); Lester L. Grabbe, ed., *Israel in Transition,* vol. 1 (New York: T&T Clark, 2008).

16. Eliezer D. Oren, ed., *The Sea Peoples and Their World* (Philadelphia: University Museum, Univ. of Pennsylvania, 2000); Oliver Dickinson, *The Aegean from Bronze Age to Iron Age* (New York: Routledge, 2006); Marc Van De Mieroop, *The Eastern Mediterranean in the Age of Ramesses II* (Oxford: Blackwell, 2007); Assaf Yasur-Landau, *The Philistines and Aegean Migration at the End of the Late Bronze Age* (Cambridge: Cambridge Univ. Press, 2010).

17. Baruch Halpern, *The Emergence of Israel in Canaan* (Chico, Calif.: Scholars Press, 1983); Israel Finkelstein, *The Archaeology of the Israelite Settlement* (Jerusalem: Israel Exploration Society, 1988); Jonathan N. Tubb, *Canaanites* (London: British Museum Press, 1998); Israel Finkelstein and Neil Asher Silberman, *The Bible Unearthed* (New York: Free Press, 2001); K. L. Noll, *Canaan and Israel in Antiquity* (New York: Sheffield Academic Press, 2001); Jonathan M. Golden, *Ancient Canaan and Israel* (Santa Barbara, Calif.: ABC-Clio, 2004); Israel Finkelstein and Amihai Mazar, *The Quest for the Historical Israel,* ed. Brian B. Schmidt (Leiden, Netherlands: Brill, 2007); Richard S. Hess, Gerald A. Klingbeil, and Paul J. Ray Jr., eds., *Critical Issues in Early Israelite History* (Winona Lake, IN: Eisenbrauns, 2008).

18. "Some were born Israelites" is from Dever, *Who Were the Early Israelites?,* 182; Ann E. Killebrew, *Biblical Peoples and Ethnicity* (Atlanta: Society of Biblical Literature, 2005). For the theory that Israel originated in a mass slave uprising in Egypt, see Norman K. Gottwald, *The Tribes of Yahweh* (Sheffield, England: Sheffield Academic Press, 1999, 20th anniversary edition); Avi Faust, *Israel's Ethnogenesis* (Oakville, CT: Equinox, 2006).

19. Compare James C. Scott, *The Art of Not Being Governed* (New Haven, CT: Yale Univ. Press, 2009).

20. Marcus, *The View from Nebo;* Dever, *Who Were the Early Israelites?;*

Yehezkel Kaufmann, *The Biblical Account of the Conquest of Canaan,* 2nd ed. (Jerusalem: Magnes Press, Hebrew Univ., 1985); Hershel Shanks, William G. Dever, Baruch Halpern, and P. Kyle McCarter, *The Rise of Ancient Israel* (Washington, DC: Biblical Archaeological Society, 1992); Dever, *What Did the Biblical Writers Know?,* 108–25. For the evidence of language, see Seth L. Sanders, *The Invention of Hebrew* (Urbana: Univ. of Illinois Press, 2009); "Earliest Known Hebrew Text In Proto-Canaanite Script Discovered In Area Where David Slew Goliath," *Science Daily,* Nov. 3, 2008, at http://www.science daily.com/releases/2008/11/081103091035.htm. Isaiah 19:18 describes Hebrew as a "language of Canaan."

21. Johannes C. De Moor, *The Rise of Yahwism,* 2nd ed. (Leuven, Belgium: Uitgeverij Peeters, 1997); John Day, *Yahweh and the Gods and Goddesses of Canaan* (Sheffield, England: Sheffield Academic Press, 2000).

22. Judith M. Hadley, *The Cult of Asherah in Ancient Israel and Judah* (New York: Cambridge Univ. Press, 2000); Beth Alpert Nakhai, *Archaeology and the Religions of Canaan and Israel* (Boston, MA: American Schools of Oriental Research, 2001); William G. Dever, *Did God Have a Wife?* (Grand Rapids, MI: Eerdmans, 2005); Baruch Halpern, *From Gods to God* (Tübingen, Germany: Mohr Siebeck, 2009), 57–131; Francesca Stavrakopoulou and John Barton, eds., *Religious Diversity in Ancient Israel and Judah* (New York: Continuum, 2010).

23. Halpern, *From Gods to God;* Baruch Halpern, *David's Secret Demons* (Grand Rapids, MI: Eerdmans, 2001); Kari Latvus, *God, Anger and Ideology* (Sheffield, England: Sheffield Academic Press, 1998).

24. Lester L. Grabbe, ed., *Like a Bird in a Cage* (London: Sheffield Academic Press, 2003); Cynthia R. Chapman, *The Gendered Language of Warfare in the Israelite-Assyrian Encounter* (Winona Lake, IN: Eisenbrauns, 2004); Paul S. Evans, *The Invasion of Sennacherib in the Book of Kings* (Leiden, Netherlands: Brill, 2009).

25. Halpern, *From Gods to God,* 57–131; Weinfeld, *Deuteronomy 1–11,* notes parallels between Deuteronomy and contemporary Assyrian royal language.

26. Jack Miles, *God: A Biography* (New York: Alfred A Knopf, 1995), 117–18, 154–59.

27. "The Lord your God will deliver" is from Deut. 7:23 (NIV); for the tale of the hornets, see Exod. 23:27–29; Deut. 7:19–23; Josh. 24:12. Norman C. Habel, *The Land Is Mine* (Minneapolis: Fortress Press, 1995); Weinfeld, *The Promise of the Land,* 85–87.

28. Gen. 15:16.

29. Deut. 9:4.

30. Lev. 18:24–25 (NIV). Brueggemann, *Divine Presence amid Violence.*

31. Deut. 32: "Cleanse the land" is from v. 43 (NRSV); "terror" is from v. 25.

32. Thomas R. Neufeld, *Put on the Armour of God* (Sheffield, England: Sheffield Academic Press, 1997); Mic. 4:13.

33. Moshe Weinfeld, *The Promise of the Land,* 91; Megan Bishop Moore, "Fighting in Writing," in Brad E. Kelle and Frank Ritchel Ames, eds., *Writing and Reading War* (Leiden, Netherlands: Brill, 2008), 57–66; Michael G. Hasel, "Assyrian Military Practices and Deuteronomy's Laws of Warfare," in Kelle and Ritchel Ames, eds., *Writing and Reading War,* 67–81.

34. Deut. 13: 6–16 (NIV).

35. "He put down the idolatrous priests" is from 2 Kings 23:12; "[He] slew all the priests of the high places" is from 2 Kings 23:20; "And like unto him" is from 2 Kings 23:25.

36. Dennis T. Olson, *Numbers* (Louisville, KY: John Knox Press, 1996), 152–56; Baruch A. Levine, *Numbers 21–36* (New York: Doubleday, 2000), 277–303.

37. For Ezra and Nehemiah, see Charles Fensham, *The Books of Ezra and Nehemiah* (Grand Rapids, MI: Eerdmans, 1983); H. G. M. Williamson, *Ezra-Nehemiah,* vol. 16 in *Word Biblical Commentary* (Nashville, TN: Thomas Nelson, 1985); Matthew Levering, *Ezra and Nehemiah* (Brazos Press, 2007); Mark J. Boda and Paul L. Redditt, *Unity and Disunity in Ezra-Nehemiah* (Sheffield, England: Sheffield Phoenix Press, 2008); Joseph Blenkinsopp, *Judaism, The First Phase* (Grand Rapids, MI: Eerdmans, 2009).

38. Ezra 9:1–2.

39. Neh. 13:30 (NRSV). Rainer Albertz and Bob Becking, eds., *Yahwism After the Exile* (Assen, Netherlands: Royal Van Gorcum, 2003); Gary

N. Knoppers, Lester L. Grabbe, and Deirdre N. Fulton, eds., *Exile and Restoration Revisited* (London: T&T Clark, 2009).

CHAPTER THREE: WORDS OF THE SWORD

1. Throughout this chapter, I have used Jane Dammen McAuliffe, ed., *Encyclopaedia of the Qur'an,* 5 vols. (Leiden, Netherlands: Brill, 2001–2005); Jane Dammen McAuliffe, ed., *The Cambridge Companion to the Qur'an* (New York: Cambridge Univ. Press, 2006); Andrew Rippin, ed., *The Blackwell Companion to the Qur'an* (Malden, MA: Blackwell, 2006). See also Brian A. Brown, *Noah's Other Son* (New York: Continuum, 2007). For the commentary tradition, see Feras Hamza and Sajjad Rizvi, eds., *An Anthology of Qur'anic Commentaries* (New York: Oxford Univ. Press, 2008), vol. 1.

2. See for instance Robert Wright, "The Meaning of the Koran," *New York Times*, September 14, 2010, at http://opinionator.blogs.nytimes.com/2010/09/14/the-meaning-of-the-koran/. Obviously, I disagree with a number of recent studies of Islam and violence, including such works as Robert Spencer, *Islam Unveiled* (San Francisco: Encounter Books, 2002); and Richard L. Rubenstein, *Jihad and Genocide* (Lanham, MD: Rowman & Littlefield, 2010).

3. Jack Nelson-Pallmeyer, *Is Religion Killing Us?* (Harrisburg, PA: Trinity Press International, 2003); J. Harold Ellens, ed., *The Destructive Power of Religion* (Westport, CT: Praeger, 2004); R. Joseph Hoffmann, ed., *The Just War and Jihad* (Amherst, NY: Prometheus Books, 2006); Gabriel Said Reynolds, ed., *The Qur'an in Its Historical Context* (New York: Routledge, 2008). For violence in other faith traditions, see for instance Michael K. Jerryson and Mark Juergensmeyer, eds., *Buddhist Warfare* (New York: Oxford Univ. Press, 2010).

4. David Marshall, *God, Muhammad and the Unbelievers* (Richmond, England: Curzon, 1999).

5. The film *Fitna* can be found online, for instance at http://www.break.com/usercontent/2009/2/Fitna-Documentary-about-Islam–660675.html.

6. Richard Bonney, *Jihad* (New York: Palgrave Macmillan, 2004);

David Cook, *Understanding Jihad* (Berkeley: Univ. of California Press, 2005); R. Joseph Hoffmann, ed., *The Just War and Jihad* (Amherst, NY: Prometheus Books, 2006).

7. Again, this passage is very widely quoted in anti-Muslim websites: see for instance http://muhammadsquran.blogspot.com/2009/03/at-taubah-95-verse-of-sword.html.

8. Qur'an 47:4 (Dawood).

9. Qur'an 17:16.

10. Matt. 13:37–42.

11. Michael Cook, *The Koran: A Very Short Introduction* (New York: Oxford Univ. Press, 2000), 33–36; Abdullah Saeed, *Interpreting the Qur'ān* (New York: Routledge, 2006).

12. Matt. 5:18.

13. Had they not been removed, the Satanic Verses would have followed Qur'an 53:19–20. "God renders null and void" is from Qur'an 22:52.

14. Andrew Rippin, *The Qur'an and Its Interpretative Tradition* (Burlington VT: Ashgate/Variorum, 2001).

15. Mohamed A. Mahmoud, *Quest for Divinity* (Syracuse, NY: Syracuse Univ. Press, 2007); Nasr Abu Zaid, *Rethinking the Qur'an* (Utrecht, Netherlands: Humanistics Univ. Press, 2004); Nasr Abu Zaid with Esther R. Nelson, *Voice of an Exile* (New York: Praeger, 2004); Hussein Abdul-Raof, *Schools of Qur'anic Exegesis* (New York: Routledge, 2010).

16. For the reformist tradition, see for instance Charles Kurzman, *Modernist Islam, 1840–1940* (New York: Oxford Univ. Press, 2002); Michaelle Browers and Charles Kurzman, eds., *An Islamic Reformation?* (Lanham, MD: Lexington Books, 2004); Suha Taji-Farouki, ed., *Modern Muslim Intellectuals and the Qur'an* (New York: Oxford Univ. Press, 2004); Massimo Campanini, *The Qur'an* (New York: Routledge, 2010).

17. Andrew G. Bostom, *The Legacy of Islamic Antisemitism,* reprint ed. (Amherst, NY: Prometheus Books, 2008).

18. Compare Spencer, *Islam Unveiled;* Robert Spencer, ed., *The Myth of Islamic Tolerance* (Amherst, NY: Prometheus Books, 2005). Martin Gilbert, *In Ishmael's House* (New Haven, CT: Yale Univ. Press, 2010), offers a scholarly account of the Jewish experience in Arab lands.

19. *Sahih Bukhari,* book 041, no. 6985. See for instance http://www.muslim access.com/sunnah/hadeeth/muslim/041.html.

20. "The Covenant of the Islamic Resistance Movement," 1988, at http://avalon.law.yale.edu/20th_century/hamas.asp.

21. For Muhammad's relations with the Jews of Medina, see Michael Lecker, "Glimpses of Muhammad's Medinan Decade," in Jonathan E. Brockopp, ed., *The Cambridge Companion to Muhammad* (Cambridge: Cambridge Univ. Press, 2010), 61–79. For the 523 massacres, see Irfan Shahîd, *The Martyrs of Najrân* (Brussels, Belgium: Société des Bollandistes, 1971); compare Gérard Garitte, ed., *La Prise de Jérusalem par les Perses en 614* (Louvain, Belgium: Secrétariat du CorpusSCO, 1960).

22. Qur'an 5:82.

23. Ibn Warraq, *What the Koran Really Says* (Amherst, NY: Prometheus Books, 2002) and Ibn Warraq, *Which Koran?* (Prometheus Books, 2009); Reynolds, ed., *The Qur'an in Its Historical Context;* Philip Jenkins, *The Lost History of Christianity* (San Francisco: HarperOne, 2008); Fred M. Donner, *Muhammad and the Believers* (Cambridge, MA: Belknap Press, 2010).

24. Qur'an 2:61–62.

25. Qur'an 3:112.

26. Qur'an 4:54–55.

27. Qur'an 2:61–66; Cook, *The Koran,* 97–100. Compare Qur'an 7:163–66, where Sabbath-breaking likewise provokes the transformation.

28. John 8:44; Luke 11:50 (NIV).

29. Allegedly Qur'an 4:55.

30. Allegedly Qur'an 33:26.

31. Allegedly Qur'an 2:96.

32. Allegedly Qur'an 59:14.

33. Qur'an 2:256. Thomas Sizgorich, *Violence and Belief in Late Antiquity* (Philadelphia: Univ. of Pennsylvania Press, 2009).

CHAPTER FOUR: SONS OF JOSHUA

1. Ps. 78:55 (NIV).

2. Ps. 105:44 (NIV).

3. Ps. 136:18–21

4. Neh. 9:22–24 (NIV).

5. Charles Kannengiesser, ed., *Handbook of Patristic Exegesis* (Leiden, Netherlands: Brill, 2006); Steve Moyise, *Evoking Scripture* (London: T&T Clark, 2008).

6. Alois Grillmeier, *From the Apostolic Age to Chalcedon*, vol. 1 in *Christ in the Christian Tradition*, rev. ed., trans. John Bowden (Louisville, KY: Westminster John Knox, 1975); Raymond E. Brown, *An Introduction to New Testament Christology* (Mahwah, NJ: Paulist Press, 1994); Richard N. Longenecker, *Biblical Exegesis in the Apostolic Period*, 2nd ed. (Grand Rapids, MI: Eerdmans, 1999); John J. O'Keefe and R. R. Reno, *Sanctified Vision* (Baltimore: Johns Hopkins Univ. Press, 2005); J. Levison and P. Pope-Levison, "Christology," in William A. Dyrness and Veli-Matti Kärkkäinen, eds., *Global Dictionary of Theology* (Downers Grove, IL: InterVarsity Press, 2008), 167–86.

7. Maarten J. J. Menken and Steve Moyise, eds., *Deuteronomy in the New Testament* (London; New York: T&T Clark, 2007).

8. From many patristic texts, see Michael Slusser, ed., *Dialogue with Trypho* by St. Justin Martyr (Washington, DC: Catholic Univ. of America Press, 2003).

9. Robert C. Hill, ed., *The Questions on the Octateuch by Theodoret of Cyrus*, 2 vols. (Washington, DC: Catholic Univ. of America Press, 2007), vol. 2, 262–63.

10. "Overthrew seven nations in Canaan" is from Acts 13:19 (NIV); Stephen is quoted at Acts 7:45 (NIV). For Rahab in the New Testament, see Heb. 11:30–32; James 2:24–26.

11. Hill, ed., *Questions on the Octateuch*, vol. 1, 223, for Amalek; vol. 2, 285, for "There are those."

12. Eric A. Seibert, *Disturbing Divine Behavior* (Minneapolis: Fortress Press, 2009), 71–77, terms these two arguments "Divine Immunity" and "Just Cause," respectively.

13. Rom. 9:21–23. For a typical use of this argument, see Irenaeus, "Against Heresies," chap. xxix, at http://www.ccel.org/ccel/schaff/anf01.ix.vi.xxx.html. The image of the divine potter is derived from

Jeremiah 18, although significantly that passage does not portray God as wholly arbitrary or capricious: God judges and destroys nations according to the sins they commit.

14. Roland Teske, ed., *Answer to Faustus, a Manichaean* (Hyde Park, NY: New City Press, 2007).

15. Augustine, "Contra Faustum," book xxii, at http://www.newadvent .org/fathers/140622.htm.

16. Augustine, "Contra Faustum," book xxii, at http://www.newadvent .org/fathers/140622.htm.

17. John Calvin, *Commentaries on the Book of Joshua,* trans. Henry Beveridge, at http://www.ccel.org/ccel/calvin/calcom07.html.

18. Calvin, *Commentaries,* at http://www.ccel.org/ccel/calvin/calcom07 .ix.ii.html. Ronald Goetz, "Joshua, Calvin, and Genocide," *Theology Today* 32, no. 3 (1975), at http://theologytoday.ptsem.edu/oct1975/ v32-3-article5.htm.

19. Calvin, *Commentaries,* at http://www.ccel.org/ccel/calvin/calcom07 .xiii.iii.html.

20. Calvin, *Commentaries,* at http://www.ccel.org/ccel/calvin/calcom07 .xiii.iii.html.

21. Calvin, *Commentaries,* at http://www.ccel.org/ccel/calvin/calcom07 .ix.ii.html.

22. "Matthew Henry's Concise Commentary on the Bible," at http:// mhc.biblecommenter.com/joshua/8.htm. Compare Stephen J. Stein, "Jonathan Edwards and the Cultures of Biblical Violence," in Harry S. Stout, Kenneth P. Minkema, Caleb J. D. Maskell, eds., *Jonathan Edwards at 300* (Lanham, MD: Univ. Press of America, 2005), 54–64.

23. For nineteenth-century debates, see Timothy Larsen, *Contested Christianity* (Waco, TX: Baylor Univ. Press, 2004).

24. R. L. Dugdale, *The Jukes,* rep. ed. (New York: Arno Press, 1970); Henry Herbert Goddard, *The Kallikak Family* (New York: Arno Press, 1973 [1912]); Nathaniel Deutsch, *Inventing America's "Worst" Family* (Berkeley: Univ. of California Press, 2009). For the eugenics movement, see Elof Axel Carlson, *The Unfit* (Cold Spring Harbor, NY: Cold Spring Harbor Laboratory Press, 2001); Edwin Black, *War Against the Weak* (London: Four Walls Eight Windows, 2003).

25. Christine Rosen, *Preaching Eugenics* (New York: Oxford Univ. Press, 2004).

26. Jonathan Bayley, *From Egypt to Canaan* (London: George P. Alvey, 1867), 93. Seibert, *Disturbing Divine Behavior,* 77–80, calls this the "Greater Good" argument.

27. John W. Haley, *An Examination of the Alleged Discrepancies of the Bible* (Andover, MA: Warren F. Draper, 1876), 95; emphasis added.

28. Reuben Archer Torrey, *Difficulties and Alleged Errors and Contradictions in the Bible* (New York: Fleming H. Revell, 1907 [1900]), 47–52.

29. Torrey, *Difficulties,* 47.

30. All quotes are from Torrey, *Difficulties,* 48–49.

31. This and the preceding quote are from Torrey, *Difficulties,* 49–50.

32. Thomas W. Davis, *Shifting Sands* (New York: Oxford Univ. Press, 2004); Burke O. Long, *Planting and Reaping Albright* (University Park: Pennsylvania State Univ. Press, 1997).

33. William Foxwell Albright, *From the Stone Age to Christianity,* 2nd ed. (Garden City, NY: Doubleday, 1957 [1940]), 280–81; Michael Prior, *Zionism and the State of Israel* (London: Routledge, 1999), 169–70; Keith W. Whitelam, *The Invention of Ancient Israel* (London: Routledge, 1996).

34. Michael Prior, ed., *Western Scholarship and the History of Palestine* (London: Melisende, 1998).

35. Albright, *From the Stone Age to Christianity,* 281.

36. For "Ai Spy," see L. Daniel Hawk, *Joshua* (Collegeville, MN: Liturgical Press, 2000), 107–35. Other books treat the "war crimes" issues very seriously: see for instance Jerome Creach, *Joshua* (Louisville, KY: Westminster John Knox Press, 2003). For evangelical debates over the moral issues, see Paul Copan, "Is Yahweh a Moral Monster?" *Philosophia Christi* 10, no. 1 (2008): 7–37; Wesley Morriston, "Did God Command Genocide?" *Philosophia Christi* 11, no. 1 (2009): 7–26; Randal Rauser, "Let Nothing That Breathes Remain Alive," *Philosophia Christi* 11, no. 1 (2009): 27–41; Paul Copan, "Yahweh Wars and the Canaanites," *Philosophia Christi* 11, no. 1 (2009): 73–91.

37. Paul Copan, "Yahweh Wars and the Canaanites," at http://epsociety. org/library/articles.asp?pid=63&ap=2. Paul Copan, *Is God a Moral Monster?* (Grand Rapids, Mich.: Baker, 2011), 158-97.

38. C. S. Cowles, Eugene H. Merrill, Daniel L. Gard, and Tremper Longman III, *Show Them No Mercy* (Grand Rapids, MI: Zondervan, 2003), 31.

39. Cowles et al., *Show Them No Mercy*, 93. For Eugene H. Merrill, see his *Deuteronomy* (Nashville, TN: Broadman & Holman, 1994).

40. "Squatters on the land" is from Eugene H. Merrill, *Deuteronomy* (Nashville, TN: Broadman & Holman, 1994), 176–80, compare 286–87; "the pedagogical value" is from Cowles et al., *Show Them No Mercy*, 87.

41. Daniel L. Gard in Cowles et al., *Show Them No Mercy*, 55.

42. "Joshua and the Conquest of Canaan," at http://www.bible-history .com/old-testament/joshua-promised-land.html.

43. Ralph F. Wilson, "Why the Slaughter of Jericho?" at http://www.jesus walk.com/joshua/herem.htm.

44. "God's Command to Exterminate the Canaanites," at http://reformed baptistfellowship.wordpress.com/2007/05/21/god%E2%80%99s-command-to-exterminate-the-canaanites-a-biblical-apology/.

45. James F. Williams, "How Can a Just God Order the Slaughter of Men, Women and Children?" at http://www.probe.org/site/c.fd KEIMNsEoG/b.4220297/k.6E2/How_Can_a_Just_God_Order_ the_Slaughter_of_Men_Women_and_Children.htm.

Chapter Five: Warrant for Genocide

1. C. S. Cowles, Eugene H. Merrill, Daniel L. Gard, and Tremper Longman III, *Show Them No Mercy* (Grand Rapids, MI: Zondervan, 2003), 94. My chapter title, "Warrant for Genocide," is taken from Norman Cohn's distinguished book on the roots of anti-Semitism.

2. "It is our duty" is from Elliott Horowitz, *Reckless Rites* (Princeton, NJ: Princeton Univ. Press, 2006), 120–21; Ralph Niger, quoted in Andrew Holt, "Feminine Sexuality and the Crusades," in Albrecht Classen, ed., *Sexuality in the Middle Ages and Early Modern Times* (New York: Walter de Gruyter, 2008), 449–70. For the medieval image of Moses as war-leader, see Meyer Schapiro, *Words and Pictures* (The Hague, Netherlands: Mouton, 1973), 20–22.

3. James Turner Johnson, *Ideology, Reason, and the Limitation of War* (Princeton, NJ: Princeton Univ. Press, 1975); James Turner Johnson, *The Holy War Idea in Western and Islamic Traditions* (University Park: Pennsylvania State Univ. Press, 1997).

4. R. Joseph Hoffmann, ed., *The Just War and Jihad* (Amherst, NY: Prometheus Books, 2006).

5. For the Taborites, see Wolfgang Menzel, *The History of Germany from the Earliest Period to 1842* (London: George Bell, 1908), 167; Martin Luther, "How Christians Should Regard Moses," in Timothy F. Lull, ed., *Martin Luther's Basic Theological Writings*, 2nd ed. (Minneapolis: Augsburg Fortress, 2005), 124–32.

6. Timothy George, "War and Peace in the Puritan Tradition," *Church History* 53, no. 4 (1984): 492–503.

7. John Knox, *A Vindication of the Doctrine That the Sacrifice of the Mass Is Idolatry* (1550) at http://www.swrb.ab.ca/newslett/actualNLs/vindi cat.htm. For his call for a new Phinehas, see Franklin L. Ford, *Political Murder* (Cambridge, MA: Harvard Univ. Press, 1985), 154.

8. Thomas Harding, ed., *The Decades of Henry Bullinger* (New York: Cambridge Univ. Press, 1849), 376–77 for "upon men which are incurable," 380 for "the laws of war." Johnson, *Ideology, Reason, and the Limitation of War*, 110–17.

9. Quoted in Johnson, *Ideology, Reason, and the Limitation of War*, 118–33: the quote about the soldier is from 122.

10. Quoted in Johnson, *Ideology, Reason, and the Limitation of War*, 128.

11. Michael Braddick, *God's Fury, England's Fire* (London: Penguin, 2009).

12. John Morrill, "The Faith of Oliver Cromwell," Honeyman Lecture, Tyndale College, Toronto, Canada, 10 Mar. 2009, accessible through http://alumni.tyndale.ca/. For discussions of Phinehas's motivation, see Martin Dzelzainis, "Incendiaries of the State," in Thomas Corns, ed., *The Royal Image* (Cambridge: Cambridge Univ. Press, 1999), 74–95.

13. Quoted in Kerby A. Miller, Arnold Schrier, Bruce D. Boling, and David N. Doyle, eds., *Irish Immigrants in the Land of Canaan* (New York: Oxford Univ. Press, 2003), 5.

14. John McDonnell, *The Ulster Civil War of 1641 and Its Consequences*

(Dublin, Ireland: M. H. Gill, 1879), 120–22; "the curses which befell" is from Timothy Gorringe, *God's Just Vengeance* (New York: Cambridge Univ. Press, 1996), 27.

15. Anthony D. Smith, *Chosen Peoples* (New York: Oxford Univ. Press, 2003), 142. A. R. Fausset, *A Critical and Expository Commentary on the Book of Judges* (London: James Nisbet, 1885), 26.

16. Matthew Tindal, *Christianity as Old as the Creation* (New York: Garland, 1978 [1730]), 263–64.

17. Quoted in Alfred A. Cave, "Canaanites in a Promised Land," *American Indian Quarterly* 12, no. 4 (1988): 286; compare Michael Prior, *The Bible and Colonialism* (Sheffield, England: Sheffield Academic Press, 1997). For the role of the Bible in shaping early modern definitions of race, see Colin Kidd, *The Forging of Races* (Cambridge: Cambridge Univ. Press, 2006).

18. John Winthrop, "A Modell of Christian Charity" (1630), at http://www.academicamerican.com/colonial/docs/winthrop.htm. Conrad Cherry, ed., *God's New Israel,* rev. ed. (Chapel Hill: Univ. of North Carolina Press, 1998), 30–60. For the mythology of the exodus and the Promised Land, see Michael Walzer, *Exodus and Revolution* (New York: Basic Books, 1985). John Corrigan, "Amalek and the Religious Rhetoric of Extermination," in Chris Beneke and Christopher S. Grenda, eds., *The First Prejudice* (Philadelphia: University of Pennsylvania Press, 2010), 53–73.

19. Cotton Mather, *Magnalia Christi Americana,* 2 vols. (Hartford, CT: S. Andrus and son, 1853–1855), vol. 1, 553. Corrigan, "Amalek and the Religious Rhetoric of Extermination"; John Corrigan and Lynn S. Neal, eds., *Religious Intolerance in America* (Chapel Hill: Univ. of North Carolina Press, 2010).

20. Michael Wigglesworth, "God's Controversy with New England," accessible through http://digitalcommons.unl.edu/etas/36/.

21. Increase Mather, "A Brief History of the War with the Indians in New England," at http://digitalcommons.unl.edu/libraryscience/31/. "This day Amalek prevailed over Israel" is from "Diary by Increase Mather," at http://www.archive.org/stream/matherdiary00mathrich/matherdiary00mathrich_djvu.txt.

22. Cotton Mather, *Magnalia Christi Americana,* vol. 2, 552–80, for the Indian wars, and vol. 1, 118–31, for "Nehemias Americanus"; "while you are in the field" is from Susan Niditch, *War in the Hebrew Bible* (New York: Oxford Univ. Press, 1993), 3–4, quoting Mather's 1689 sermon "Souldiers Counselled and Comforted." Elliott Horowitz, *Reckless Rites,* 121.

23. Roland H. Bainton, *Christian Attitudes Toward War and Peace* (Nashville, TN: Abingdon, 1960); Henry Gibbs, *The Right Method of Safety* (Boston, MA: 1704); Theodore Roosevelt, *The Winning of the West* (New York: Putnam, 1906), vol. 3, 14. John Corrigan's "Amalek and the Religious Rhetoric of Extermination" offers a number of similar American examples from the eighteenth and nineteenth centuries. Compare Chris Mato Nunpa, "A Sweet-Smelling Sacrifice," in Steven L. Jacobs, ed., *Confronting Genocide* (Lanham, MD: Lexington Books, 2009).

24. Benjamin Franklin, *Autobiography,* at http://books.eserver.org/non fiction/franklin/bf6.html.

25. Cherry, ed., *God's New Israel,* 61–112. For Jefferson's second inaugural address, see http://www.bartleby.com/124/pres17.html.

26. For the figure of Moses in American mythology, see Bruce Feiler, *America's Prophet* (New York: William Morrow, 2009). For the violent metaphors that pervaded American religious discourse in this era, see Jeffrey Williams, *Religion and Violence in Early American Methodism* (Bloomington, IN: Indiana Univ. Press, 2010).

27. For the *Times,* see Christopher Herbert, *War of No Pity* (Princeton, NJ: Princeton Univ. Press, 2007), 107; Brian Stanley, "Christian Responses to the Indian Mutiny of 1857," in W. J. Sheils, ed., *The Church and War* (Oxford: Blackwell, 1983), 277–89.

28. Edward Curtis, "The Blessing of Jael," *The Old Testament Student,* 4 (1884): 12–18.

29. Donald Harman Akenson, *God's Peoples* (Ithaca, NY: Cornell Univ. Press, 1992), 66–69.

30. Anthony D. Smith, *Chosen Peoples* (New York: Oxford Univ. Press, 2003).

31. Lev. 20:2–7; Exod. 34:13.

32. The Hormah passage is from Judg. 1:17. Ludwig A. Rosenthal, "Einiges über die Agada in der Mechilta," in George Alexander Kohut, ed., *Semitic Studies in Memory of Rev. Dr. Alexander-Kohut* (Berlin: S. Calvary, 1897), 463–84; Franz Meffert, *Israel und der alte Orient* (Mönchengladbach, Germany: Volksvereins-Verlag, 1921).

33. For Engels and "Ausrottung," see http://www.mlwerke.de/me/me16/me16_459.htm.

34. David Olusoga and Casper W. Erichsen, *The Kaiser's Holocaust* (London: Faber & Faber, 2010); Isabel V. Hull, *Absolute Destruction* (Ithaca, NY: Cornell Univ. Press, 2005); Carl-J. Hellberg, *Mission, Colonialism and Liberation* (Windhoek, Namibia: New Namibia Books, 1997); Jan-Bart Gewald, "The Great General of the Kaiser," *Botswana Notes and Records* 26 (1994): 67–76.

35. Cathie Carmichael, *Genocide Before the Holocaust* (New Haven, CT: Yale Univ. Press, 2009); Volker M. Langbehn, ed., *German Colonialism, Visual Culture, and Modern Memory* (New York: Routledge, 2010); Shelley Baranowski, *Nazi Empire* (New York: Cambridge Univ. Press, 2010).

36. Dickson Adeyanju, "Pastor Bakare and His Burden of Prophecies," at http://www.nigerdeltacongress.com/particles/pastor_bakare_and_his_burden_of.htm.

37. David F. Dawes, "Rwanda's Genocide," at http://www.canadianchristianity.com/cgi-bin/bc.cgi?bc/bccn/0601/intrwanda.

CHAPTER SIX: AMALEKITE NIGHTMARES

1. 2 Macc. 12:13–16. Lawrence H. Schiffman and Joel B. Wolowelsky, eds., *War and Peace in the Jewish Tradition* (New York: KTAV, 2007); Frank Ritchel Ames, "The Meaning of War," in Brad E. Kelle and Frank Ritchel Ames, eds., *Writing and Reading War* (Leiden, Netherlands: Brill, 2008), 19–32. For the complex nuances of Jewish attitudes towards war and violence through the centuries, see Robert Eisen, *The Peace and Violence of Judaism* (New York: Oxford Univ. Press, 2011).

2. Michael Wise, Martin Abegg, Jr., and Edward Cook, *The Dead Sea*

Scrolls (San Francisco: HarperSanFrancisco, 1996), 151, 150–72; Geza Vermes, ed., *The Complete Dead Sea Scrolls in English* (New York: Allen Lane/Penguin Press, 1997), 161–89; Jean Duhaime, *The War Texts* (London: T&T Clark, 2004).

3. Tremper Longman III and Daniel G. Reid, *God Is a Warrior* (Grand Rapids, MI: Zondervan, 1995).

4. Gérard Garitte, ed., *La Prise de Jérusalem par les Perses en 614* (Louvain, Belgium: Secrétariat du CorpusSCO, 1960); Seth Schwartz, *Imperialism and Jewish Society, 200 B.C.E. to 640 C.E.* (Princeton, NJ: Princeton Univ. Press, 2001); Elliott Horowitz, *Reckless Rites* (Princeton, NJ: Princeton Univ. Press, 2006), 228–41; Leo Duprée Sandgren, *Vines Intertwined* (Grand Rapids, Mich.: Baker Academic, 2010).

5. Ecclus. 45:28; 1 Macc. 2:26. Mark Andrew Brighton, *The Sicarii in Josephus's Judean War* (Leiden, Netherlands: Brill, 2009).

6. "Phinehas," *Jewish Encyclopedia,* at http://www.jewishencyclopedia.com/view.jsp?artid=282&letter=P; "Zealots," *Jewish Encyclopedia,* at http://www.jewishencyclopedia.com/view.jsp?artid=49&letter=Z. For the apocalyptic vision of Phinehas, see James Hastings, ed., *A Dictionary of the Bible* (New York: Scribner, 1900), 854. For commentaries on the Phinehas passage, see Judah J. Slotki, ed., "Numbers," in Harry Freedman and Maurice Simon, eds., *Midrash Rabbah,* 13 vols. in 10 (London: Soncino Press, 1939), vol. 6, 827–52: "If a man sheds the blood" is at 829–30.

7. Shalom Carmy, "The Origin of Nations and the Shadow of Violence," in Schiffman and Wolowelsky, eds., *War and Peace in the Jewish Tradition,* 163–200; Alastair G. Hunter, "(De)Nominating Amalek," in Jonneke Bekkenkamp and Yvonne Sherwood, eds., *Sanctified Aggression* (London: T&T Clark, 2003), 92–108.

8. Exod. 17:14–15. Louis H. Feldman, *"Remember Amalek!"* (Detroit, MI: Wayne State Univ. Press, 2004).

9. Norman Lamm, "Amalek and the Seven Nations," in Schiffman and Wolowelsky, eds., *War and Peace in the Jewish Tradition,* 201–38.

10. Jon D. Levenson, *Esther* (Louisville, KY: Westminster John Knox Press, 1997); Michael V. Fox, *Character and Ideology in the Book of Esther,* 2nd ed. (Grand Rapids, MI: Eerdmans, 2001); Carol M.

Bechtel, *Esther* (Louisville, KY: John Knox Press, 2002); Sidnie White Crawford and Leonard J. Greenspoon, eds., *The Book of Esther in Modern Research* (London: T&T Clark International, 2003).

11. Maurice Simon, ed., "Esther," in Freedman and Simon, eds., *Midrash Rabbah,* vol. 9, 92ff: "My ancestor Agag" is at 96. Elaine Rose Glickman, *Haman and the Jews* (Northvale, NJ: Jason Aronson, 1999); Jo Carruthers, *Esther Through the Centuries* (Oxford: Blackwell, 2008). For the synagogue reading, see Eveline van Staalduine-Sulman, *The Targum of Samuel* (Leiden, Netherlands: Brill, 2002), 320.

12. Esther 9:16. See Horowitz, *Reckless Rites.*

13. J. Rabbinowitz, ed., "Deuteronomy," in Freedman and Simon, eds., *Midrash Rabbah,* vol. 7, 111. Charlotte E. Fonrobert and Martin S. Jaffee, eds., *The Cambridge Companion to the Talmud and Rabbinic Literature* (New York: Cambridge Univ. Press, 2007).

14. For the Mekhilta quote, see Moshe Sokolow, "What Is This Bleeting of Sheep in My Ears?" in Schiffman and Wolowelsky, eds., *War and Peace in the Jewish Tradition,* 149; Avi Sagi, "The Punishment of Amalek in Jewish Tradition," *Harvard Theological Review* 87, no. 3 (1994): 323–46. For Maimonides, see Hunter, "(De)Nominating Amalek," 103; Horowitz, *Reckless Rites,* 129–34.

15. Eliav Shochetman, "He Who Is Compassionate to the Cruel Will Ultimately Become Cruel to the Compassionate," at http://www.acpr .org.il/ENGLISH-NATIV/06-issue/shochetman–6.htm; A.Cohen, ed., "Ecclesiastes," in Freedman and Simon, eds., *Midrash Rabbah,* vol. 8, 199.

16. Feldman, *"Remember Amalek!"* 77–78. For the Kaiser's visit, David Golinkin, "Are Jews Still Commanded to Blot Out the Memory of Amalek?" at http://www.schechter.edu/insightIsrael.aspx?ID=27.

17. For the Eichmann case, see "Amalek," athttp://www.statemaster .com/encyclopedia/Amalek.

18. "Letters of Rav Kook," at http://www.orot.com/letter11.html.

19. Henry Leroy Finch, *Simone Weil and the Intellect of Grace* (New York: Continuum, 1999), 106–7; see also Michael Prior, *The Bible and Colonialism* (Sheffield, England: Sheffield Academic Press, 1997), 152–73.

20. David Hirst, *The Gun and the Olive Branch,* 3rd ed. (New York: Nation Books, 2003).

21. Nachman Ben-Yehuda, *Theocratic Democracy* (New York: Oxford Univ. Press, 2010); Eric Kaufmann, *Shall the Religious Inherit the Earth?* (London: Profile Books, 2010).

22. Stephen Spector, *Evangelicals and Israel* (New York: Oxford Univ. Press, 2008).

23. Idith Zertal and Akiva Eldar, *Lords of the Land* (New York: Nation Books, 2007); Nur Masalha, *The Bible and Zionism* (London: Zed Books, 2007), 149–54; Ami Pedahzur and Arie Perliger, *Jewish Terrorism in Israel* (New York: Columbia Univ. Press, 2009).

24. Nur Masalha, "Reading the Bible with the Eyes of the Canaanites," *Holy Land Studies* 8 (2009): 55–108. Fred Halliday, *Islam and the Myth of Confrontation* (London: I. B. Tauris, 2003); Basem L. Ra'ad, *Hidden Histories* (London: Pluto Press, 2010).

25. Pedahzur and Perliger, *Jewish Terrorism in Israel;* Masalha, "Reading the Bible with the Eyes of the Canaanites."

26. See http://www.memri.org/content/en/main.htm.

27. For Ben-Gurion, see "Ben-Gurion on the Threat from Amalek," at http://jeffreygoldberg.theatlantic.com/archives/2009/05/ben_gurion_on_amalek.php.

28. Soloveitchik is quoted in Shochetman, "He Who Is Compassionate"; Dina Porat, "Amalek's Accomplices," *Journal of Contemporary History* 27 (1992): 695–729; Gershon Greenberg, "Ultra-Orthodox Jewish Thought About the Holocaust Since World War II," in Steven T. Katz, ed., *The Impact of the Holocaust on Jewish Theology* (New York: New York Univ. Press, 2005), 132–60; Eran Kaplan, *The Jewish Radical Right* (Madison: Univ. of Wisconsin Press, 2005).

29. "The Palestinians are Amalek" and "the Amalek and the Hitler" are from Horowitz, *Reckless Rites,* 1–3; Moshe Greenberg, "On the Political Use of the Bible in Modern Israel," in David P. Wright, David Noel Freedman, and Avi Hurvitz, eds., *Pomegranates and Golden Bells* (Winona Lake, IN: Eisenbrauns, 1995), 461–72.

30. For Reimer, see Shmuly Yanklowitz, "Genocide in the Torah," at

http://www.myjewishlearning.com/beliefs/Issues/War_and_Peace/Combat_and_Conflict/Types_of_War/Genocide.shtml.

31. For Yisrael Hess, see Nur Masalha, *The Bible and Zionism* (London: Zed Books, 2007), 150.

32. Masalha, *The Bible and Zionism*.

33. Shochetman, "He Who Is Compassionate."

34. Kobi Nahshoni, "Rabbi Eliyahu: Life of One Yeshiva Boy Worth More Than 1,000 Arabs," at http://www.ynet.co.il/english/articles/0,7340,L–3527410,00.html; Mois Navon, "Remember Amalek," at http://www.aish.com/print/?contentID=48967261&section=/h/pur/t; Yisrael Rosen is quoted from Nadav Shragai, "An Amalek in Our Times?" *Haaretz*, Mar. 26, 2008, at http://www.haaretz.co.il/hasen/spages/968452.html.

35. Amos Harel, "IDF Rabbinate Publication During Gaza War: We Will Show No Mercy on the Cruel," *Haaretz*, Jan. 26, 2009, at http://www.haaretz.com/hasen/spages/1058758.html. "I will pursue my enemies" is from Ps. 18:37–38.

36. Horowitz, *Reckless Rites;* Relly Sa'ar, "Poraz 'Repulsed' by Cases of Jews Spitting on Christians," *Haaretz*, Oct. 12, 2004, at http://www.haaretz.com/hasen/pages/ShArt.jhtml?itemNo=487887; John L. Allen Jr., "Jews Move to Halt Spitting at Christians in Jerusalem," *National Catholic Reporter*, Jan. 5, 2010, at http://ncronline.org/blogs/ncr-today/jews-move-halt-spitting-christians-jerusalem.

37. Horowitz, *Reckless Rites*.

38. Norman Lamm, "Amalek and the Seven Nations."

39. Vered Vinitzky-Seroussi, *Yitzhak Rabin's Assassination and the Dilemmas of Commemoration* (Albany: SUNY Press, 2009); Ehud Sprinzak, *Brother Against Brother* (New York: Free Press, 1999). "Rabbi Mordechai Eliyahu," obituary, *The Independent,* July 16, 2010.

40. Ben-Yehuda, "Theocratic Democracy," 279–80; Noah J. Efron, *Real Jews* (New York: Basic Books, 2003). "Rav Kook explained" is from "Pinchas: Zealotry for the Sake of Heaven," at http://www.ravkooktorah.org/PINHAS58.htm.

41. "Reform Jews Say Israel Chief Rabbi's Sermon Advocates Their

Death," July 9, 1996, quoted at http://www.catholicculture.org/news/features/index.cfm?recnum=856.

42. Chanan "My Pink Shirt and the Haredim," Nov. 11, 2006, at http://www.blogsofzion.com/index.php?s=romeima.

43. Jeffrey Goldberg, "Protect Sharon from the Right," *New York Times,* Aug. 5, 2004.

44. Yael Meyer, "Shas Rabbi Ovadia Yosef Issues Call for Destruction of Education Minister Sarid," Mar. 19, 2000, at http://web.archive.org/web/20020926052905/http://www.irac.org/article_e.asp?artid=248. More recently, Rabbi Yosef opined that Gentiles have no reason to exist except to serve Jews: Natasha Mozgovaya, "ADL Slams Shas Spiritual Leader For Saying Non-Jews 'Were Born To Serve Jews,'" *Haaretz,* October 10, 2010, at http://www.haaretz.com/jewish-world/adl-slams-shas-spiritual-leader-for-saying-non-jews-were-born-to-serve-jews-1.320235.

45. Jeffrey Goldberg, "The Point of No Return," *Atlantic,* September 2010.

CHAPTER SEVEN: JUDGING GOD

1. Milne is quoted from Carlin Romano, "Are Sacred Texts Sacred?" *Chronicle of Higher Education,* Sept. 21, 2007. For the role of scripture in inciting "misotheism," see Bernard Schweizer, *Hating God* (New York: Oxford Univ. Press, 2010).

2. Martin Buber, *Meetings,* 3rd ed. (London: Routledge, 2002), 62–64.

3. Yuri Stoyanov, *The Other God* (New Haven, CT: Yale Univ. Press, 2000).

4. Antti Marjanen and Petri Luomanen, eds., *A Companion to Second-Century Christian 'Heretics'* (Leiden, Netherlands: Brill, 2005); Karen L. King, *What Is Gnosticism?* (Cambridge, MA: Belknap Press of Harvard Univ. Press, 2005).

5. George Lucas has explained that the name Darth Vader is meant to suggest "Dark Father," supposedly in Dutch, but that translation really does not work. Bentley Layton, *The Gnostic Scriptures* (Garden City, NY: Doubleday, 1987); James M. Robinson, *The Nag Hammadi*

Library in English, 4th rev. ed. (Leiden, Netherlands: Brill, 1996); Gerard P. Luttikhuizen, *Gnostic Revisions of Genesis Stories and Early Jesus Traditions* (Leiden, Netherlands: Brill, 2006); Birger A. Pearson, *Ancient Gnosticism* (Minneapolis: Fortress Press, 2007).

6. Saturninus is from Irenaeus, "Against Heresies," chap. xxiv, at http://www.ccel.org/ccel/schaff/anf01.ix.ii.xxv.html.

7. Cerdo is quoted from Philip R. Amidon, ed., *The Panarion of St. Epiphanius, Bishop of Salamis* (New York: Oxford Univ. Press, 1990), 143; 133 for the Cainites. See also Alexander Roberts and James Donaldson, eds., *The Apostolic Fathers: Justin Martyr, Irenaeus,* in *Ante-Nicene Fathers* (New York: Scribner, 1926), vol. 1, 352; 358 for the Cainites. Frank Williams, trans., *The Panarion of Epiphanius of Salamis,* 2 vols. (Leiden, Netherlands: Brill, 1987–1994), vol. 1, 241–48 (Ophites), 248–54 (Cainites), and 255–62 (Sethians).

8. Roberts and Donaldson, eds., *The Apostolic Fathers,* vol. 1, 352–53; Williams, trans., *The Panarion of Epiphanius of Salamis,* vol. 1, 272–337; Robert Smith Wilson, *Marcion* (London: Clarke, 1933); E. C. Blackman, *Marcion and His Influence* (New York: AMS Press, 1978 [1948]); Eric A. Seibert, *Disturbing Divine Behavior* (Minneapolis: Fortress Press, 2009), 54–68.

9. "The author of evils" is from Irenaeus, "Against Heresies," xxvii, at http://www.ccel.org/ccel/schaff/anf01.ix.ii.xxviii.html; Tertullian, "Against Marcion," at http://www.newadvent.org/fathers/03121.htm and http://www.newadvent.org/fathers/03122.htm.

10. For God's hardening the heart, see Irenaeus, "Against Heresies," xxix, at http://www.ccel.org/ccel/schaff/anf01.ix.vi.xxx.html; for "Cain, and those like him," see xxvii, http://www.ccel.org/ccel/schaff/anf01.ix.ii.xxviii.html.

11. Williams, trans., *The Panarion of Epiphanius of Salamis,* vol. 2, 219–308: "Some good God of the Law!" is from 302.

12. Williams, trans., *The Panarion of Epiphanius of Salamis,* vol. 2, 227; Roland Teske, ed., *Answer to Faustus, a Manichaean* (Hyde Park, NY: New City Press, 2007).

13. Samuel N. C. Lieu, *Manichaeism in the Later Roman Empire and Medieval China* (Tübingen, Germany: Mohr, 1992).

14. Elaine H. Pagels, *The Gnostic Gospels* (New York: Random House, 1979).

15. For the modern search for a dejudaized Jesus, see the accounts in Philip Jenkins, *Hidden Gospels* (New York: Oxford Univ. Press, 2000); Susannah Heschel, *The Aryan Jesus* (Princeton, NJ: Princeton Univ. Press, 2008).

16. Stewart J. Brown and Timothy Tackett, eds., *Enlightenment, Reawakening and Revolution 1660–1815* (New York: Cambridge Univ. Press, 2006); David Sorkin, *The Religious Enlightenment* (Princeton, NJ: Princeton Univ. Press, 2008).

17. Christoph A. Stumpf, *The Grotian Theology of International Law* (Berlin: Walter de Gruyter, 2006); David Armstrong, ed., *Routledge Handbook of International Law* (New York: Routledge, 2009).

18. S. J. Barnett, *Idol Temples and Crafty Priests* (New York: St. Martin's Press, 1999).

19. John Toland, *Christianity Not Mysterious* (London: 1702), 37; W. Neil, "The Criticism and Theological Use of the Bible 1700–1950," in Stanley F. Greenslade, ed., *The Cambridge History of the Bible* (Cambridge: Cambridge Univ. Press, 1975), vol. 3, 240–54; James A. Herrick, *The Radical Rhetoric of the English Deists* (Columbia: Univ. of South Carolina Press, 1997).

20. Stephen Lalor, *Matthew Tindal, Freethinker* (New York: Continuum, 2006).

21. "That though the literal sense" is from Matthew Tindal, *Christianity as Old as the Creation* (New York: Garland, 1978 [1730]), 262; "The holier men in the Old Testament" is from 264–65; "'Tis no doubt the interest" is from 270–71.

22. Tindal, *Christianity as Old as the Creation,* 274–75.

23. Tindal, *Christianity as Old as the Creation,* 273; Justin Champion, *Republican Learning* (Manchester, England: Manchester Univ. Press, 2003).

24. For Tindal and "the pursuit of happiness" see Lalor, *Matthew Tindal,* 5. Charles H. Talbert, ed., *Reimarus: Fragments* (Chico, CA: Scholars Press, 1985; reprint of 1970 edition from Fortress Press). For early European debates over biblical authority, see Paul S. Spalding, *Seize*

the Book, Jail the Author (West Lafayette, IN: Purdue Univ. Press, 1998).

25. Thomas Paine, *The Age of Reason* (New York: Wright & Owen, 1831), part 1, sect. 4.

26. Paine, *The Age of Reason,* part 2, sect. 6.

27. Quoted in James Smith, *The Christian's Defence* (Cincinnati, OH: J. A. James, 1843), 296.

28. Voltaire, "Des Moeurs des Juifs," *Oeuvres Complètes de Voltaire: Philosophie* (Paris: Armand-Abree, 1830), vol. 2, 21–22.

29. Mark Twain, *Letters from the Earth,* ed. Bernard DeVoto (New York: Perennial, 1974), 54–55; Howard G. Baetzhold and Joseph B. McCullough, eds., *The Bible According to Mark Twain* (New York: Touchstone Books, 1996); Seibert, *Disturbing Divine Behavior,* 40–43.

CHAPTER EIGHT: COMING TO TERMS

1. Georges R. Tamarin, *The Israeli Dilemma* (Rotterdam, Netherlands: Rotterdam Univ. Press, 1973).

2. Leon Festinger, Henry W. Riecken, and Stanley Schacter, *When Prophecy Fails* (Minneapolis: Univ. of Minnesota Press, 1956); Joel Cooper, *Cognitive Dissonance* (Thousand Oaks, CA: Sage, 2007); Carol Tavris, *Mistakes Were Made (But Not By Me)* (New York: Harcourt, 2007).

3. David Matza, *Delinquency and Drift* (New Brunswick, NJ: Transaction, 1990); Franklyn W. Dunford and Phillip R. Kunz, "The Neutralization of Religious Dissonance," *Review of Religious Research* 15, no. 1 (1973): 2–9.

4. For different strategies of reading the unacceptable texts, see Eric A. Seibert, *Disturbing Divine Behavior* (Minneapolis: Fortress Press, 2009), 209–42. Robert Eisen, *The Peace and Violence of Judaism* (New York: Oxford Univ. Press, 2011).

5. Lesleigh Cushing Stahlberg, *Sustaining Fictions* (New York: T&T Clark, 2008).

6. Jerome Creach, *Joshua* (Louisville, KY: Westminster John Knox Press, 2003), 42.

7. J. Rabbinowitz, ed., "Deuteronomy," in Harry Freedman and Maurice Simon, eds., *Midrash Rabbah,* 13 vols. in 10 (London: Soncino Press, 1939), vol. 7, 116.

8. Serge Lancel, *Carthage* (Cambridge, MA: Blackwell, 1994). "The descendants of Haman studied Torah in Benai Berak. The Holy One, blessed be He, purposed to lead the descendants of that wicked man too under the Wings of the *Shechinah*," Babylonian Talmud, Sanhedrin 96b, at http://www.come-and-hear.com/sanhedrin/sanhedrin_96 .html#96b_18.

9. Ps. 106:29–31.

10. Louis H. Feldman, *"Remember Amalek!"* (Detroit, MI: Wayne State Univ. Press, 2004). The brutal story of Jephthah offers a similar example of reinterpretation. In the original account (Judges 11:29–40), Jephthah presumably sacrifices his daughter after making a rash vow to God. Later rabbis strove mightily to avoid this interpretation, suggesting that rather than being killed, she was merely sworn to a life of perpetual virginity. See Joshua Berman, "Medieval Monasticism and the Evolution of Jewish Interpretation of the Story of Jephthah's Daughter," *Jewish Quarterly Review* 95.2 (2005): 228–56.

11. Moshe Sokolow, "What Is This Bleeting of Sheep in My Ears?" in Lawrence H. Schiffman and Joel B. Wolowelsky, eds., *War and Peace in the Jewish Tradition* (New York: KTAV, 2007), 133–62.

12. The Baal Shem Tov is quoted for instance in "The Song That Transformed Amalek," at http://www.decoupageforthesoul.com/rebbe saysadar5763.htm; Rabbi Schneerson is quoted from http://www.chabad .org/library/article_cdo/aid/150871/jewish/Amalek-The-Perpetual-Enemy-of-the-Jewish-People.htm.

13. "Remember What Amalek Did to You," at http://www.chabad.org/ parshah/article_cdo/aid/704644/jewish/Remember-What-Amalek-Did-to-You.htm.

14. G. F. Haddad, "Documentation of Greater Jihad Hadith," at http:// www.livingislam.org/n/dgjh_e.html.

15. Cheikh Anta Mbacké Babou, *Fighting the Greater Jihad* (Athens: Ohio Univ. Press, 2007); Annabel Keeler, *Sufi Hermeneutics* (New York: Oxford Univ. Press, 2006).

16. Michael Slusser, ed., *Dialogue with Trypho,* by St. Justin Martyr (Washington, DC: Catholic Univ. of America Press, 2003).

17. Thomas R. Neufeld, *Put on the Armour of God* (Sheffield, England: Sheffield Academic Press, 1997); A. Graeme Auld, *Joshua Retold* (Edinburgh: T&T Clark, 1998), 129–39.

18. Shelly Matthews and E. Leigh Gibson, eds., *Violence in the New Testament* (London: T&T Clark, 2005).

19. "The Epistle of Barnabas," in Bart Ehrman, ed., *Apostolic Fathers,* 2 vols. (Cambridge, MA: Harvard Univ. Press, 2003), vol. 2, 59.

20. Joseph T. Lienhard with Ronnie J. Rombs, eds., *Exodus, Leviticus, Numbers, Deuteronomy* (Downers Grove, IL: InterVarsity Press, 2001); John R. Franke, ed., *Joshua, Judges, Ruth, 1–2 Samuel* (Downers Grove, IL: InterVarsity Press, 2005).

21. Seibert, *Disturbing Divine Behavior,* 61–64; Elizabeth Dively Lauro, *The Soul and Spirit of Scripture Within Origen's Exegesis* (Leiden, Netherlands: Brill, 2005); Elizabeth Dively Lauro, ed., *Origen: Homilies on Judges* (Washington, DC: Catholic Univ. of America Press, 2010).

22. Cynthia White, ed., *Origen: Homilies on Joshua* (Washington, DC: Catholic Univ. of America Press, 2002), 125 for "This is therefore a work"; the story of the five kings is at 118–19.

23. White, ed., *Origen: Homilies on Joshua,* 34 for "Within us are the Canaanites"; 92–93 for "Mysteries are truly shadowed"; compare 145.

24. Augustine, "Reply to Faustus," xxii, at http://www.ccel.org/ccel/schaff/npnf104.iv.ix.xxiv.html.

25. Augustine, "Reply to Faustus," xxii, at http://www.ccel.org/ccel/schaff/npnf104.iv.ix.xxiv.html.

26. John Russell Bartlett, ed., *The Letters of Roger Williams 1632–1682* (Providence, RI: Narragansett Club, 1874), 10.

27. G. Osborn, ed., *The Poetical Works of John and Charles Wesley* (London: Wesleyan-Methodist Conference Centre, 1870), vol. 9, 125–26. Jeffrey Williams, *Religion and Violence in Early American Methodism* (Bloomington: Indiana Univ. Press, 2010).

28. Jonathan Bayley, *From Egypt to Canaan* (London: George P. Alvey, 1867), 93–94.

29. Available at http://cyberhymnal.org/htm/c/h/chridost.htm.

30. The sayings are widely quoted, but see for instance Patrick F. O'Hare, *The Facts About Luther* (New York: Frederick Pustet, 1916), 207–8.

31. Thomas Jefferson, *The Jefferson Bible* (Boston, MA: Beacon Press, 1989).

32. E. A. Thompson, *The Visigoths in the Time of Ulfila* (Oxford: Clarendon Press, 1966).

33. Reuben Archer Torrey, *Difficulties and Alleged Errors and Contradictions in the Bible* (New York: Revell, 1907), 62–63, citing Rom. 26–27.

34. For Ps. 137, see Susan Gillingham, *Psalms Through the Centuries* (Oxford: Blackwell, 2008); "for fear of the Jews" is from John 20:19.

35. Frank C. Senn, *Christian Liturgy* (Minneapolis: Augsburg Fortress, 1997).

36. Isa. 7:14.

37. Consultation on Common Texts, *Revised Common Lectionary* (Nashville, TN: Abingdon Press, 1992); Roger E. Van Harn, ed., *The Lectionary Commentary,* 3 vols. (Grand Rapids, MI: Eerdmans, 2001); David Lyon Bartlett and Barbara Brown Taylor, *Feasting on the Word* (Louisville, KY: Westminster John Knox Press, 2008); Roger E. Van Harn and Brent A. Strawn, eds., *Psalms for Preaching and Worship* (Grand Rapids, MI: Eerdmans, 2009).

38. Num. 21:6–9; John 3:14–15.

39. Exod. 17.

Chapter Nine: Historians and Prophets

1. Baruch Halpern, *The First Historians* (San Francisco: Harper & Row, 1988).

2. Joel Kaminsky, *Yet I Loved Jacob* (Nashville, TN: Abingdon Press, 2007).

3. Timothy Larsen and Daniel J. Treier, eds., *The Cambridge Companion to Evangelical Theology* (Cambridge: Cambridge Univ. Press, 2007); Ben Witherington III, *The Problem with Evangelical Theology* (Waco, TX: Baylor Univ. Press, 2005).

4. Thomas Cripps, ed., *The Green Pastures* (Madison: Univ. of Wisconsin Press, 1979).

5. Robert Wright, *The Evolution of God* (Boston, MA: Little, Brown, 2009); Jack Miles, *God: A Biography* (New York: Knopf, 1995).

6. Wright, *The Evolution of God*, 214.

7. Philip J. King, *Amos, Hosea, Micah* (Philadelphia: Westminster Press, 1988); Richard E. Rubenstein, *Thus Saith the Lord* (New York: Harcourt, 2006).

8. Diana V. Edelman and Ehud Ben Zvi, eds., *The Production of Prophecy* (Oakville, CT: Equinox, 2010); Oded Lipschits and Joseph Blenkinsopp, eds., *Judah and the Judeans in the Neo-Babylonian Period* (Winona Lake, IN: Eisenbrauns, 2003); Stephen L. Cook, *The Social Roots of Biblical Yahwism* (Leiden, Netherlands: Brill, 2004).

9. Amos 3:2; Psalm 105: 44-45. Francis I. Andersen and David Noel Freedman, *Amos* (New Haven, CT: Yale Univ. Press, 2007); Göran Eidevall, *Prophecy and Propaganda* (Winona Lake, IN: Eisenbrauns, 2009); Tchadvar S. Hadjiev, *The Composition and Redaction of the Book of Amos* (New York: De Gruyter, 2009).

10. Mic. 6:8. Francis I. Andersen and David Noel Freedman, *Micah* (New Haven, CT: Yale Univ. Press, 2006); compare Andersen and Freedman, *Hosea*.

11. Amos 5:21–24.

12. For *herem* against the nations, see Isa. 34:1–5; the image of God dripping with blood is from Isa. 63:1–4. Corrine Carvalho, "The Beauty of the Bloody God," in Julia M. O'Brien and Chris Franke, eds., *The Aesthetics of Violence in the Prophets* (New York: T&T Clark, 2010); Matthijs J. de Jong, *Isaiah Among the Ancient Near Eastern Prophets* (Leiden, Netherlands: Brill, 2007).

13. Jeremiah's warning not to trust in the temple is found in Jeremiah 7:1-7; for threats of *herem* against Israel, see Jeremiah 25:8-11; for *herem* against Jacob, see Isaiah 43:28 (NIV).

14. Ezek. 18:1–4. Bernard M. Levinson, *Legal Revision and Religious Renewal in Ancient Israel* (New York: Cambridge Univ. Press, 2008).

15. Antony F. Campbell and Mark A. O'Brien, *Unfolding the Deuteronomistic History* (Minneapolis: Fortress Press, 2000); Jeffrey C. Geoghegan, *The Time, Place, and Purpose of the Deuteronomistic History* (Atlanta: Society of Biblical Literature, 2006); Thomas C. Römer, *The So-Called Deuteronomistic History* (London: T&T Clark, 2006).

16. For Samuel, see Roy L. Heller, *Power, Politics, and Prophecy* (New

York: T&T Clark, 2006). For concepts of individual responsibility, see Deut. 24:16. Levinson, *Legal Revision and Religious Renewal in Ancient Israel.*

17. Richard Elliott Friedman, *Who Wrote the Bible?* (Englewood Cliffs, NJ: Prentice Hall, 1987).

18. Baruch Halpern, *From Gods to God* (Tübingen, Germany: Mohr Siebeck, 2009).

19. Kaminsky, *Yet I Loved Jacob.*

20. Thomas C. Römer, ed., *The Future of the Deuteronomistic History* (Leuven, Belgium: Leuven Univ. Press, 2000); Albert de Pury, Thomas Römer, and Jean-Daniel Macchi, eds., *Israel Constructs Its History* (Sheffield, England: Sheffield Academic Press, 2000).

21. Eric Nelson, *The Hebrew Republic* (Cambridge, MA: Harvard Univ. Press, 2010); compare Joshua A. Berman, *Created Equal* (New York: Oxford Univ. Press, 2008).

22. Lipschits and Blenkinsopp, eds., *Judah and the Judeans in the Neo-Babylonian Period;* John F. A. Sawyer, *The Fifth Gospel* (New York: Cambridge Univ. Press, 1996).

23. Mic. 4:2; compare Isa. 2:3.

CHAPTER TEN: PREACHING THE UNPREACHABLE

1. Mark Twain, *Letters from the Earth,* ed. Bernard DeVoto (New York: Perennial, 1974), 56. Howard G. Baetzhold and Joseph B. McCullough, eds., *The Bible According to Mark Twain* (New York: Touchstone Books, 1996).

2. Norman Lamm, "Amalek and the Seven Nations," in Lawrence H. Schiffman and Joel B. Wolowelsky, eds., *War and Peace in the Jewish Tradition* (New York: KTAV, 2007), 201–38. Robert Eisen, *The Peace and Violence of Judaism* (New York: Oxford Univ. Press, 2011).

3. For killing witches, see Exod. 22:18; William J. Webb, *Slaves, Women and Homosexuals* (Downers Grove, IL: InterVarsity Press, 2001); Klaas Spronk, "The Daughter of Jephthah," in Jonneke Bekkenkamp and Yvonne Sherwood, eds., *Sanctified Aggression* (London: T&T Clark, 2003), 10–21.

4. Eric A. Seibert, *Disturbing Divine Behavior* (Minneapolis: Fortress Press, 2009), 220–33.

5. John Calvin, quoted in C. S. Cowles, Eugene H. Merrill, Daniel L. Gard, and Tremper Longman III, *Show Them No Mercy* (Grand Rapids, MI: Zondervan, 2003), 17.

6. Søren Kierkegaard, *Fear and Trembling*, ed. Stephen Evans and Sylvia Walsh (New York: Cambridge Univ. Press, 2006), 12-20; Bruce Chilton, *Abraham's Curse* (New York: Doubleday, 2008).

7. For the "greater good" argument, see Seibert, *Disturbing Divine Behavior*.

8. Martin Luther, "How Christians Should Regard Moses," in Timothy F. Lull, ed., *Martin Luther's Basic Theological Writings*, 2nd ed. (Minneapolis: Augsburg Fortress Press, 2005), 124–32.

9. Josh. 10:12–13.

10. Edward W. Said, "Michael Walzer's *Exodus and Revolution*," in Edward W. Said and Christopher Hitchens, eds., *Blaming the Victims* (London: Verso, 2001), 161–78; William D. Hart, *Edward Said and the Religious Effects of Culture* (New York: Cambridge Univ. Press, 2000); Walter Brueggemann, *Texts Under Negotiation* (Minneapolis: Augsburg Fortress 1993); Walter Brueggemann, *The Book That Breathes New Life* (Minneapolis: Fortress Press, 2005); Cheryl Anderson, *Ancient Laws and Contemporary Controversies* (New York: Oxford Univ. Press, 2009).

11. W. H. Auden, "Spain 1937."

12. From a vast literature, see for instance Phyllis Trible, *Texts of Terror* (Philadelphia: Fortress Press, 1984); Elisabeth Schüssler-Fiorenza, *In Memory of Her* (New York: Crossroad, 1984); Elisabeth Schüssler-Fiorenza, *But She Said* (Boston, MA: Beacon Press, 1992); A. K. M. Adam, ed., *Postmodern Interpretations of the Bible* (St. Louis, MO: Chalice Press, 2001); Susan Frank Parsons, ed., *The Cambridge Companion to Feminist Theology* (New York: Cambridge Univ. Press, 2002); Jacqueline E. Lapsley, *Whispering the Word* (Louisville, KY: Westminster John Knox Press, 2005); Susanne Scholz, *Introducing the Women's Hebrew Bible* (New York: T&T Clark, 2007); Amy-Jill Levine and Maria Mayo Robbins, eds., *A Feminist Companion to Patristic Literature* (New York: T&T Clark, 2008).

13. Mark 7:25–30/Matt. 15:21–28: the two passages are closely related, but they have some significant variations. Walter C. Kaiser, Peter H. Davids, Frederick Fyvie Bruce, and Manfred T. Brauch, *Hard Sayings of the Bible* (Downers Grove, IL: InterVarsity Press, 1996), 424–25.

CHAPTER ELEVEN: SCRIPTURE ALONE?

1. John J. Collins, *Does the Bible Justify Violence?* (Minneapolis: Augsburg Fortress, 2004).

2. Robert O. Ballou, *World Bible* (New York: Viking, 1944), 13. Compare Robert Ernest Hume, *Treasure-House of the Living Religions* (New York: Scribner, 1933); Robert O. Ballou, Friedrich Spiegelberg, and Horace L. Friess, eds., *The Bible of the World* (New York: Viking, 1939); Lewis Browne, ed., *The World's Great Scriptures* (New York: Macmillan, 1946).

3. For the substantial differences separating faiths, see Stephen Prothero, *God Is Not One* (San Francisco: HarperOne, 2010).

4. For the concept of religious violence, see Mark Juergensmeyer, *Terror in the Mind of God,* 3rd ed. (Berkeley: Univ. of California Press, 2003); Mark Juergensmeyer, *Global Rebellion* (Berkeley: Univ. of California Press, 2008); Charles Selengut, *Sacred Fury* (Lanham, MD: Rowman & Littlefield, 2008).

5. For the sniper scopes affair, see Joseph Rhee, Tahman Bradley, and Brian Ross, "U.S. Military Weapons Inscribed with Secret 'Jesus' Bible Codes," *ABC News,* Jan. 18, 2010, at http://abcnews.go.com/Blotter/us-military-weapons-inscribed-secret-jesus-bible-codes/story?id=9575794.

6. G. R. Hawting and Abdul-Kader A. Shareef, eds., *Approaches to the Qur'an* (New York: Routledge, 1993); Suha Taji-Farouki, ed., *Modern Muslim Intellectuals and the Qur'an* (New York: Oxford Univ. Press, 2004); Michaelle Browers and Charles Kurzman, eds., *An Islamic Reformation?* (Lanham, MD: Lexington Books, 2004); Walter H. Wagner, *Opening the Qur'an* (South Bend, IN: Univ. of Notre Dame Press, 2008).

7. Joseph M. Skelly, ed., *Political Islam from Muhammad to Ahmadinejad* (Santa Barbara, CA: Praeger Security International, 2010).

8. Søren Dosenrode, ed., *Christianity and Resistance in the Twentieth Century* (Leiden, Netherlands: Brill, 2009).

9. Patrick Seale, *Abu Nidal* (New York: Random House, 1992).

10. "When Religion and Culture Part Ways," interview with Olivier Roy by Eren Gvercin, June 5, 2010, at http://www.signandsight.com/features/2025.html.

11. "When Religion and Culture Part Ways." Compare Graham E. Fuller, *A World Without Islam* (New York: Little, Brown and Company, 2010).

12. William T. Cavanaugh, *The Myth of Religious Violence* (New York: Oxford Univ. Press, 2009).

INDEX